The International Library of Ethics, Law and Technology

Volume 26

Technologies are developing faster and their impact is bigger than ever before. Synergies emerge between formerly independent technologies that trigger accelerated and unpredicted effects. Alongside these technological advances new ethical ideas and powerful moral ideologies have appeared which force us to consider the application of these emerging technologies. In attempting to navigate utopian and dystopian visions of the future, it becomes clear that technological progress and its moral quandaries call for new policies and legislative responses. Against this backdrop, this book series from Springer provides a forum for interdisciplinary discussion and normative analysis of emerging technologies that are likely to have a significant impact on the environment, society and/or humanity. These will include, but be no means limited to nanotechnology, neurotechnology, information technology, biotechnology, weapons and security technology, energy technology, and space-based technologies.

Nicholas Kluge Corrêa

Normative Ethics, Artificial Intelligence, and Value Alignment

From Normative Theory to Engineering Practices

Springer

Nicholas Kluge Corrêa
Institut Für Philosophie
Institut für Informatik
Universität Bonn
Bonn, Nordrhein-Westfalen, Germany

ISSN 1875-0044 ISSN 1875-0036 (electronic)
The International Library of Ethics, Law and Technology
ISBN 978-3-032-22149-0 ISBN 978-3-032-22150-6 (eBook)
https://doi.org/10.1007/978-3-032-22150-6

This Springer imprint is published by the registered company Springer Nature Switzerland AG
The registered company address is: Gewerbestrasse 11, 6330 Cham, Switzerland

I dedicate this book to my family and friends.
Thank you for believing in me. I love you all.

Foreword

The emergence of artificial intelligence (AI) as a defining technology of the twenty-first century has reignited a set of perennial philosophical questions about knowledge, agency, and normativity. What does it mean for a machine to make a decision? Can an artificial system participate in the moral domain, or even threaten it? How do we ensure that our technologies reflect, rather than undermine, our ethical commitments?

Nicholas Kluge Corrêa's *Normative Ethics, Artificial Intelligence, and Value Alignment* offers one of the most comprehensive and rigorous attempts to address these questions to date. It stands at the crossroads of philosophy and engineering, refusing the comforting illusion that these domains can be neatly separated.

The author's dual training as philosopher and machine learning engineer enables him to weave a unique bridge between conceptual analysis and technical implementation—between normative theory and code. In doing so, he achieves what few scholars in either field have managed: a genuinely interdisciplinary account of value alignment that does not merely translate philosophical principles into technical parameters, but redefines what it means for AI to be *normatively situated* in human life. He thus combines the necessary technical expertise with a deep understanding of the philosophical challenges in this impressive and path-breaking book.

Philosophy has long engaged with the problem of normativity: how can human agents discern, justify, and act upon the right course of action? Kluge extends this inquiry to nonhuman agents, asking how artificial systems can—or should—be guided by values that we can collectively recognize as binding. Rather than treating AI ethics as a catalogue of principles or "best practices," he proposes a dynamic framework of *normative mediation* that connects moral reasoning with the design and training of AI systems.

At the heart of this proposal lies *Dynamic Normativity*—a concept that constitutes the book's principal innovation. Dynamic Normativity rejects static notions of value alignment, in which ethical criteria are externally imposed on AI systems, and instead conceives alignment as an evolving process of adaptation between human agents and their technological counterparts. In doing so, Kluge rides the most recent wave of AI ethics, one that goes beyond the idea of external regulation or control and begins to implement ethics in the very constitution of the system.

On this view, ethical AI is not a product but an ongoing negotiation between multiple normative orders—social, political, epistemic, and technical. This insight alone marks a decisive advance beyond the current landscape of AI ethics, which too often oscillates between moral idealism and technical reductionism.

The structure of the book itself mirrors this philosophical movement. It begins with a meta-ethical and metaphysical grounding of AI, interrogating what it means for an artifact to act intelligently or autonomously. From there, it proceeds to analyze the mechanisms of learning, inference, and preference modeling that underlie machine cognition. These analyses are not purely descriptive: they reveal how each computational layer encodes specific normative assumptions—about efficiency, coherence, or rationality-that must be critically examined.

By systematically connecting ethical reasoning to machine learning architectures, Kluge performs a conceptual translation rarely attempted in the field. The result is not a simple ethics "add-on" to technology, but a new mode of thinking about AI development as *a normative enterprise in itself.* He reminds us that every algorithm embodies a view of the world—a structure of relevance, attention, and exclusion—that shapes the horizon of possible actions. Thus, the task of alignment cannot be outsourced to engineering alone; it must be philosophically grounded from the outset.

One of the most compelling aspects of Kluge's project is methodological. While many studies call for interdisciplinarity, few enact it as convincingly as this one. Each chapter stages a dialogue between distinct modes of inquiry: descriptive ethics and technical design, metaphysical reflection and empirical analysis, philosophical argument and data visualization. His *Worldwide AI Ethics* (WAIE) dataset, for instance, represents a remarkable contribution in its own right—a transparent and reproducible meta-analysis of global AI guidelines that exposes the normative blind spots of the current discourse.

By transforming ethical guidelines into machine-readable data, Kluge literalizes the connection between philosophical reflection and computational practice. He demonstrates that the study of normativity can itself become an experimental science, without losing its conceptual depth. This synthesis, in my view, is not merely timely but foundational for the future of both philosophy and AI research.

The innovation of *Normative Ethics, Artificial Intelligence, and Value Alignment* lies in its refusal to accept the false dichotomy between humanistic and technical rationality. Kluge shows that the moral and epistemic challenges of AI are not new—they are extensions of philosophical questions about autonomy, interpretation, and responsibility—but that their contemporary expression requires a new conceptual apparatus. Dynamic Normativity provides precisely that: a framework capable of capturing the fluid, distributed, and feedback-driven nature of human–machine interaction.

Equally important is the book's critical stance toward the hegemony of Euro-American ethical discourse in AI. By exposing the geographical and institutional biases of existing guidelines, Kluge calls for a pluralistic ethics that recognizes the global diversity of moral vocabularies. In this sense, his work is not only a contribution to AI ethics but also to a renewed cosmopolitanism of reason: an attempt to articulate a shared normative grammar in a technologically mediated world.

For readers in philosophy, this book reopens the question of normativity in an age when human judgment is increasingly entangled with algorithmic processes. For engineers, it offers a roadmap for embedding ethical reflection within design itself, rather than treating it as an afterthought. For policymakers and ethicists, it provides empirical clarity about the global moral landscape of AI, showing both where consensus exists and where critical reflection must continue.

In sum, *Normative Ethics, Artificial Intelligence, and Value Alignment* exemplifies what I take to be the true vocation of philosophy today: to illuminate the conceptual foundations of our technological civilization and to ensure that our innovations remain in dialogue with our humanity. Nicholas Kluge Corréa's work invites us to think—not only about how to build better machines, but also about how to build a more reflective and responsible world.

Bonn and Porto

Prof. Dr. Markus Gabriel — Chair for
Epistemology, Modern, and Contemporary
Philosophy at the University of Bonn, Bonn,
Germany
October 2025

Preface

The beginning is the most important part of the work.

—Plato, The Republic

I began writing this book in early 2021 as my doctoral dissertation. Since then, the field has undergone significant shifts, particularly between 2022 and 2024. ChatGPT launched and reached 100 million users in just two months. The Future of Life Institute called for a moratorium on large-scale training runs[1] for systems more powerful than GPT-4. The European Union passed the AI Act.[2] Meanwhile, artificial intelligence (AI) systems have rapidly expanded their range of capabilities, from generating photorealistic images,[3] to writing code,[4] creating video,[5], and even solving long-standing scientific puzzles like protein folding and biomolecular interaction prediction.[6]

Unlike philosophy's steady and slow currents, AI research jets forward rapidly. Consequently, many technical facets explored in this book are poised to become outdated as the field evolves. Yet, I aspire (perhaps very naively) for this book's philosophical underpinnings to endure longer. Therefore, I urge the reader to consider this work within the context of its creation. A great deal has transpired over the past four years. Research on alignment has firmly established itself in the mainstream. Unlike the bygone era of 2015–2020, when the subjects we will soon delve into were restricted to blog posts, unpublished manuscripts, and word-of-mouth lore, alignment has transcended mere academic curiosity. Nowadays, alignment research (to a great extent) has evolved into a driving force behind the development of products and services that are eagerly pursued by the market. What

1 🔗 futureoflife.org/open-letter/pause-giant-ai-experiments

2 🔗 artificialintelligenceact.eu

3 🔗 openai.com/index/dall-e-3

4 🔗 github.com/features/copilot

5 🔗 openai.com/index/sora

6 🔗 deepmind.google/technologies/alphafold

was once a set of revolutionary and experimental ideas is now a procedure accessible to anyone with minimal technical understanding.

Mea culpa aside, in this work, we (the reader and I) will explore issues of ethics and normativity within the context of artificial intelligence, taking an applied stance toward one of the most significant challenges of the field. This approach will come from two angles: the humanistic, grounded in philosophy and the lived realities of human values, and the technical, rooted in machine learning, algorithm design, and the practical implementation of value alignment mechanisms in real-world systems.

In this work, I'll strive for interdisciplinary development by taking both a humanistic (philosophical) and technical (engineering-based) approach. However, the reader must decide how well such a goal has been approximated. As a philosopher, I will seek to develop foundations for this work, drawing inspiration from various areas of philosophy that support our entire knowledge tree, such as Metaphysics and Metaethics. As a machine learning (ML) engineer, I aim to implement the ideas presented in this work to bridge the gap between theory and practice.

Both approaches are complementary and essential to dealing with the problems we face. Both engineers and philosophers can (perhaps) agree that unaligned AI systems are undesirable and that an unaligned AI community is ill-equipped to solve its issues. However, to address these problems, we first need to understand what we mean when discussing AI, what we want to avoid, and where we wish to go. In the end, answering these questions, or simply attempting to do so, can help make AI research a more *"humane"* discipline. A goal that, by itself, should be enough.

Now, what can you expect as you go through the chapters of this book?

- In Chap. 1, I present an overview of AI Ethics as an active research field, focusing on how the normative discourse around AI has taken shape. This foundational section offers a descriptive and critical analysis of the current landscape, serving as an accessible entry point for readers new to the subject.
- In Chap. 2, we venture into the territory of unknown risks tied to Artificial General Intelligence (AGI). Given the growing attention to AI's potential as an existential risk, I bring these long-term concerns into focus and introduce the reader to the core ideas shaping this line of reasoning.
- In Chap. 3, I define, both technically and philosophically, what I mean by *alignment* as a problem. We will explore the limitations of current AI development paradigms and consider how philosophy might help untangle this puzzle. The chapter concludes with a set of necessary and sufficient conditions that guide the rest of the book. Using this set of conditions as our guide when dealing with alignment is what I call Dynamic Normativity—a normative foundation for building aligned AI systems.
- In Chap. 4, I lay out the metaphysical and metaethical foundations of my proposal. Since *"AI"* is a contested term, we will give it, in this chapter, a more precise definition. For those interested in the philosophical foundations of this field (aka, Philosophy of AI), this is the chapter for you. At the same time, this

chapter helps foreground the assumptions and biases that shape the practical turn of this book.

- While Chap. 4 defends the necessity and coherence of the conditions underlying Dynamic Normativity, the final three Chaps. 5, 6, and 7 offer a minimal set of strategies and methodologies for tackling the value alignment problem, arguing that if a particular set of requirements are met, we can say that a minimal level of alignment has been achieved. Regarding the practical implementations, think of these as field notes, documentation of experiments, and extensions of alignment approaches I explored between 2021 and 2023 (back when dinosaurs still roamed the Earth). Still, I believe some of these artifacts might still be useful.

At various points in this book, the reader will be directed to external materials, such as dashboards, code repositories, demos, and other resources (🔗), which should make the reading of this book more dynamic and practical. In essence, this work sought to create tools and instructions so that other researchers could practically approach alignment research (and other ethical issues involving AI). While the book alone should be able to stand on its own regarding its narrative and intellectual constructions, there is much to gain if one is willing to open a browser and explore the additional content.

Now, let us begin.

Bonn, Germany
May 2025

Nicholas Kluge Corrêa

Acknowledgments This work is based on the inaugural dissertation delivered by the author to the Institute of Philosophy at the University of Bonn (Germany) and the Graduate Program in Philosophy at the Pontifical Catholic University of Rio Grande do Sul (Brazil) in partial fulfillment of the requirements for the cotutelle degree of Doctor of Philosophy. This research was funded by both the Programa de Excelência Acadêmica (PROEX) of the Coordenação de Aperfeiçoamento de Pessoal de Nível Superior (CAPES) and the Deutscher Akademischer Austauschdienst (DAAD). During the editing of this book, the author was also funded by the Ministerium für Wirtschaft, Industrie, Klimaschutz und Energie des Landes Nordrhein-Westfalen (Ministry for Economic Affairs, Industry, Climate Action and Energy of the State of North Rhine- Westphalia), as part of the KI.NRW-flagship project Zertifizierte KI. The author is also thankful for all the support given by RAIES (Rede de Inteligência Artificial ética e Segura) and FAPERGS (Fundação de Amparo à Pesquisa do Estado do Rio Grande do Sul), which supported financially several of the research outputs mentioned in this book.

Competing Interests The author has no competing interests to declare that are relevant to the content of this manuscript.

Contents

Part I

Every inquiry begins with a question, even if the question itself is not yet fully formed. The first part of this book is an attempt to give shape to the question that animates the rest: *What does it mean to align artificial intelligence with human values—and why is this so difficult?* Before we can propose solutions, build frameworks, or write a single line of training code, we need to understand the terrain. And the terrain, as we shall see, is anything but flat.

We begin where most contemporary discussions of AI responsibility begin—with ethics. Not the grand, centuries-old enterprise of moral philosophy in the abstract, but the concrete, often messy phenomenon of AI ethics as it has materialized in the last decade: a proliferation of guidelines, principles, and declarations drafted by governments, corporations, and international bodies alike. These documents aim to steer technological progress toward human values. But do they succeed? Do they even agree with one another? The opening chapter takes a critical look at this landscape through the lens of a comprehensive meta-analysis, exposing not only the recurring themes but also the silences—the *blank spots*—that haunt the normative conversation around AI. This examination matters because alignment, as a research agenda, inherits both the ambitions and the blind spots of the ethical discourse that surrounds it.

From this broad normative overview, we narrow our focus to a concern that has migrated from the margins of science fiction to the center of serious academic debate: the prospect of artificial general intelligence and the existential risks it may bring. The second chapter traces the intellectual lineage of these anxieties, from early philosophical thought experiments and speculative fiction to the contemporary formalization of what is now called the *control problem*. Far from indulging in dystopian speculation, the aim here is to show how these ideas—once dismissed as fringe—have become foundational to safety-oriented AI research. Understanding where these concerns came from, and why they resurfaced with such urgency, is essential to appreciating the stakes of alignment work.

Yet, alignment cannot remain a purely philosophical or speculative notion if it is to matter in practice. It must confront the realities of how modern AI systems actually learn. The third chapter performs this grounding by situating the alignment problem squarely within the paradigm of gradient-based learning—the computational backbone of nearly all contemporary machine learning. Here, alignment is reframed not as an abstract philosophical puzzle but as a concrete technical limitation: one that arises from the gap between what we want a system to learn and what the learning process itself can guarantee. The distinction between *outer alignment* (specifying the right objective) and *inner alignment* (ensuring the system faithfully pursues it) emerges as a central organizing principle, one that demands both philosophical clarity and methodological rigor.

Finally, with the conceptual and technical landscape surveyed, the fourth chapter steps back to lay the philosophical foundations upon which the rest of this work is built. Every framework rests on assumptions—about the nature of intelligence, the structure of normativity, the possibility of encoding values into computational systems, and more. Rather than accepting these assumptions implicitly, this chapter makes them explicit, articulating the metaphysical and metaethical commitments that underpin the proposed framework of *Dynamic Normativity*. What does it mean for a system to behave normatively? What kind of intelligence are we dealing with, and what kind are we building? These are the sort of questions that, if left unasked, will quietly undermine any subsequent theoretical or empirical effort.

Taken together, these four chapters trace a deliberate arc: from the current state of AI ethics and its limitations, through the existential dimensions of the alignment challenge, into the technical reality of how learning systems work, and finally down to the philosophical bedrock on which any serious alignment framework must stand. The aim is not to resolve these questions prematurely but to ensure we are asking them with the precision and honesty they deserve. Only then can we move forward—toward the methods, experiments, and interventions that make up the second half of this book.

Chapter 1
Worldwide AI Ethics, Principles, and Blank Spots

Once men turned their thinking over to machines in the hope that this would set them free. But that only permitted other men with machines to enslave them.

—Frank Herbert, Dune

Abstract This chapter offers a critical entry point into the normative dimensions of AI development by examining a specific manifestation of contemporary AI ethics: the proliferation of ethical guidelines. While the question *"What should I do?"* is timeless, the rapid technological evolution of recent decades has amplified the urgency of addressing the moral consequences of our creations. Today, as artificial intelligence becomes increasingly embedded in our social, political, and personal spheres, the dissonance between technological progress and ethical clarity remains stark. Rather than attempting an exhaustive overview of AI ethics, this chapter narrows its scope to analyze the field's dominant response: drafting and disseminating AI guidelines. Through the lens of the *Worldwide AI Ethics* (WAIE) meta-analysis, we explore the normative content of these documents, identifying common themes, patterns, and contradictions. While these guidelines represent a well-intentioned attempt to steer technological development toward human values, they often fall short of philosophical coherence or practical impact. The chapter outlines future challenges and opportunities for AI ethics, emphasizing the need for a more grounded, critical, and actionable normative framework.

Keywords AI ethics · Ethical guidelines · Normative frameworks · Meta-analysis

N. Kluge Corrêa, *Normative Ethics, Artificial Intelligence, and Value Alignment*, The International Library of Ethics, Law and Technology 26,
https://doi.org/10.1007/978-3-032-22150-6_1

1.1 Introduction

Since immemorial times, humankind has been dealing with the *"what should I do?"* question. And at every step of the progress ladder, from fire to people walking on the moon, the normative uncertainty that moves us to question our actions and deeds has not gone away. These questions are usually tied to what we can do and undo. What we can build and what we can destroy. Hence, as technological advancements continue to shape our world and as we witness our lives becoming increasingly entangled in this process, for many (if not all), it remains uncertain whether this progress will ultimately align with our fundamental values and ideals (whatever these may be). In short, we cannot escape the normative conundrum, even though precisely defining what the *"good life"* is will (perhaps) be forever out of our reach.

However, there is much merit involved in grappling with these questions. In the context of technology and AI, we find a variety of disciplines, including sociology (Rosa and William 2009), literature (Davis 1992), and philosophy (Feenberg 2012), that relentlessly try to understand how our moral landscape is affected, and affects, the byproducts of our need to build and reshape the universe as *we* see fit.

Reviewing this entire field is too grand a feat for this book. However, this chapter will aim to present a descriptive analysis of a particular type of AI ethics discourse. More specifically, the part that has evolved into what we call *"AI Guidelines"*, i.e., a type of document that has been prevalent in the literature for a significant portion of the last decade. We can understand these guidelines as a distilled and concentrated version of the normativity emerging from the minds of those engaged in AI Ethics. Through this analysis, I aim to promote a critique of our current landscape while also presenting avenues for future work that I believe hold more promise.

More specifically, in Sect. 1.2, we will explore a detailed analysis of the current state of AI ethics, drawing from an extensive literature review of the field entitled Worldwide AI Ethics (WAIE) (Corrêa et al. 2023), which at the moment of this writing, remains as the largest meta-analysis of the field. In Sect. 1.3, we will review the limitations of WAIE while presenting a critique of the field, exposing some of its current deficits and contradictions. Lastly, in Sect. 1.4, we will narrow our focus to the academic paradoxes associated with the principle-practice gap in AI ethics, while also proposing directions for future work and research in line with our vision of what AI ethics *should be.*

At first sight, one might ask why it is necessary to begin with a survey of principles and guidelines when the larger concern of this book is the so-called "alignment problem." The reason is twofold. First, principles have become the most visible and widely recognized articulation of society's normative expectations for AI. While highly abstract debates in philosophy and technical AI safety may seem remote to many readers, the principialist framework offers a common vocabulary that bridges experts and the public. In this sense, guidelines provide us with an accessible entry point into the broader value-alignment discussion: they are the closest thing we currently have to a publicly negotiated *"baseline"* of what values should guide AI.

Second, and more importantly, these documents allow us to see alignment not only as a technical challenge of mapping preferences into machines, but as a normative challenge of determining which preferences and principles deserve to be privileged in the first place. When companies, governments, and civil society organizations publish guidelines, they implicitly or explicitly stake claims about what values should guide their alignment. Hence, these guidelines reveal the contours of our shared normative imagination, highlighting areas where consensus is strong and identifying points where ambiguity or outright contradiction persists.

In this light, Chap. 1 is designed not as a digression but as a necessary prelude. By mapping the field of AI principles and guidelines, we lay the groundwork for later chapters, especially when questions regarding *constitutions* and the *aggregation of preferences* arise.

1.2 Introducing Worldwide AI Ethics

Since around 2012, there has been a significant surge in both AI research and industry applications. This surge can be attributed to several factors. Firstly, the breakthrough success of deep learning (DL) has revitalized progress in areas where previous paradigms had reached a state of stagnation. Secondly, advancements in hardware and our ability to perform computations at scale have played a pivotal role. Additionally, the availability of vast amounts of data has provided fertile ground for further advancements based on the learning paradigm. Furthermore, the exponential increase in investments, fueled by extensive media hype, is the cherry on top. All these factors combined have helped the field of AI to massively extend the capabilities of intelligent autonomous systems and expand the scope of what can be achieved through intelligent automation (Krizhevsky et al. 2012; Schmidhuber 2015; Goodfellow et al. 2016; Chollet 2021; Prince 2023).

For example, if we look at the submission history on ArXiv[1] from 2009 to 2021 (Fig. 1.1),[2] we notice that since 2018, publications relating to computer science have been the most frequently submitted type of content.

Furthermore, within the scope of Computer Science, the most frequently submitted sub-categories for papers are *"Computer Vision and Pattern Recognition"*, *"Machine Learning"*, and *"Computation and Language"*, i.e., areas where the learning paradigm[3] has established itself as the *de facto* mode of operation (Fig. 1.2).

---

[1] ArXiv (pronounced *"archive"*) is a free, open-access repository for scientific research papers.

[2] arxiv.org/about/reports/2021_usage

[3] With learning paradigm, we are referring to a fundamental approach to AI development, which involves designing algorithms or systems that can improve their performance or behavior based on data or experiences. *"De facto mode of operation"* implies that within the mentioned fields, the predominant way of tackling problems or advancing research is through the learning paradigm.

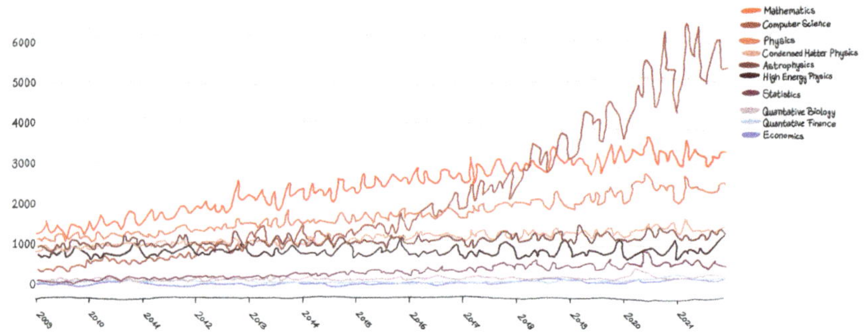

Fig. 1.1 ArXiv submissions history (2009–2021)

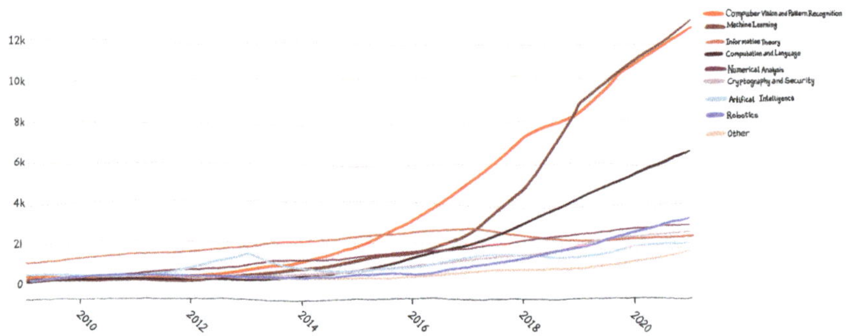

Fig. 1.2 ArXiv submissions history in computer science

This exponential increase in research output is highly correlated with the amount of money invested in the field (Zhang et al. 2021, 2022; Maslej et al. 2023). While these advancements have brought numerous benefits in terms of expanding AI capabilities, they also introduce risks and side effects that raise several ethical concerns, including risks to privacy, the potential for increased surveillance, the environmental impact of the industry, and the amplification of prejudices that disproportionately harm vulnerable groups. Consequently, the expansion of the AI industry has given rise to a *"boom"* in AI Ethics—a period marked by an unprecedented demand for regulation, normative guidance, and general activity in this field (Corrêa et al. 2023).

One of the central questions surrounding this boom is what ethical premises should guide the development of AI technologies. However, is there agreement on those premises and how they are defined? Given the ever-growing lists of normative declarations published, it is easy to get lost in this normative discourse, especially if you just stumbled into AI ethics. For example, imagine you are a policymaker tasked with writing a report that will inform a legislative effort to create regulations for AI technologies. Where do you start? What can you use to base your assertions? Meanwhile, even if you are an expert, organizing this varied normative discourse into a searchable database can supercharge your work. Fortunately, this is precisely what WAIE is: a tool that allows people to explore the field of AI ethics and its discourse.

In short, WAIE draws inspiration from the previous works of past meta-analysts and meticulously surveys a wide array of available ethical guidelines related to AI development, presenting an extensive analysis of 200 documents as its source, including governance policies of private companies, declarations from academic institutions, governmental and non-governmental recommendations, and other guidelines published by many different stakeholders. Ultimately, WAIE aimed to explore whether a consensus exists regarding the normative discourse presented in ethical guidelines surrounding the development of AI. In other words, what are the resonances and conflicts when we say *"AI should ..."*.

Remember when we discussed external materials related to this book? WAIE is one of them. Hence, I recommend the reader check the WAIE dashboard[4] for a dive into AI ethics discourse. You can also find a very satisfying visualization of the WAIE dataset in its embedding analysis.[5] And for the avid data scientists, check WAIE's code repository[6] to see how the analysis came to be.

WAIE has a foundational character in this work, as much of what I will discuss for the rest of this book will make more sense if we all have a common ground to stand on. At the same time, the principles and normativity extracted from WAIE will, again and again, be called in later chapters on the basis that values x, y, and z appear to be something most of us can agree to be of value.

In the next section, we will step back and examine the work of past explorers, which will enable us to compare WAIE with past studies.

1.2.1 Jobin, Hagendorff, and Fjeld

Ana Jobin, Thilo Hagendorff, and Jessica Fjeld led the past explorations that I would like to present in this brief session.

The first study to promote a systemic meta-analysis of published AI ethical guidelines was that of Jobin et al. (2019). In it, these authors sought to investigate whether a global agreement on emerging questions related to AI ethics and governance would arise. The research identified 84 documents containing ethical guidelines for intelligent autonomous systems, utilizing the *Preferred Reporting Items for Systematic Reviews and Meta-Analyses* (PRISMA) framework (Liberati et al. 2009). At the time, some of them were the most mentioned guidelines in the literature, like the Organization for Economic Co-operation and Development Recommendation of the Council on Artificial Intelligence (Yeung 2020), the High-Level Expert Group on AI Ethics Guidelines for Trustworthy AI (AI HLEG 2019),

4 nkluge-correa.github.io/worldwide_AI-ethics/dashboard.html

5 nkluge-correa.github.io/worldwide_AI-ethics/embeddings.html

6 github.com/Nkluge-correa/worldwide_AI-ethics

the University of Montreal Declaration for responsible development of artificial intelligence (University of Montréal 2018), the Villani Mission's French National Strategy for AI (Lexcellent 2019), among many others. One of the main findings in Jobin et al. work was uncovering the most common ethical principles in the discourse of the evaluated documents, like Transparency, Justice/Equity, Non-maleficence, Accountability, Privacy, Beneficence, Freedom & Autonomy, Trust, Dignity, Sustainability, and Solidarity.

Meanwhile, Hagendorff (2020) conducted another study that presented a similar type of analysis. His research focused on a smaller sample of 21 documents, using ad-hoc exclusion criteria.[7] Even working with a smaller sample, his findings corroborate with those of Jobin et al. (2019), where the most mentioned principles found were Accountability (77%), Privacy (77%), Justice (77%), and Transparency (68%). Hagendorff (like Jobin et al.) also mentions the underrepresentation of institutions in South America, Africa, and the Middle East as a clear bias in his sample.

Last but not least important, we have the work of Fjeld (2020). In their study, these authors worked with 36 samples produced by various types of institutions; however, as Hagendorff (2020) also excluded data science, robotics, and other AI-related fields/applications. According to them, eight principles were the most commonly cited in their sample: fairness/non-discrimination (present in 100% of the analyzed documents), privacy (97%), accountability (97%), transparency/explainability (94%), safety/security (81%), professional responsibility (78%), human control of technology (69%), and promotion of human values (69%).[8]

While the work of the mentioned authors and their respective collaborators has certainly helped lay the foundation for discussions and future works regarding a descriptive analysis of the field, there are a couple of points I would like to raise (mainly those that sparked part of the motivation behind WAIE):

- Regarding Hagendorf and Jobin et al. works, it is worth questioning the exclusion criteria used by them (mainly driven by the popularity of each document). To investigate the consensus on the normative dispositions of different countries and organizations regarding AI, we should not rely on popularity-based filtering. In other words, a descriptive ethics evaluation should consider as many viewpoints as possible.
- At the same time, while Fjeld et al. sought to be more diverse in the formation of their sample, just like the work of Hagendorf, both suffer from a small pool of documents while excluding areas of research that should not be separated from the multidisciplinary umbrella we call AI (e.g., robotics, data science, etc.).

[7] Hagendorff excluded publications older than five years, those that only addressed a national context, and all documents characterized as corporate policies. He also deliberately selected papers he deemed relevant in the international discourse (IEEE, Google, Microsoft, and IBM).

[8] For a complete review of meta-analytical research on normative AI documents, I recommend the works of Schiff (2020) and Schiff et al. (2021), which cite many other important works.

- As pointed out by Jobin et al. and Fjeld et al., a more minute investigation of how ethical principles vary regarding their definition should be performed.
- Additionally, it is worth noting that these studies should have released their datasets in a form that would allow the replication of their findings or the expansion of their projects.

This last item is perhaps the most critical. Reproducibility is a cornerstone of scientific integrity. With it, the very foundation of scientific progress becomes solid. Confidence wanes when findings cannot be replicated, potentially leading to (possibly) erroneous conclusions being accepted as fact. We are not saying that the abovementioned results are incorrect. However, for any person to arrive at the same conclusion as these authors or to build upon it, the lack of open and accessible sources stands, in my opinion, as an unnecessary hurdle in this day and age. Something that I (together with other collaborators) tried to promote in the creation of WAIE.

1.2.2 Methodological Considerations

Building upon the gaps pointed out in the previous section, WAIE presents to the AI community:

- A large and diverse sample size. WAIE holds 200 documents from 37 countries, spanning six continents.WAIE used as primary sources of documents two public repositories, the "AI Ethics Guidelines Global Inventory",[9] from AlgorithmWatch, and the "Linking Artificial Intelligence Principles"[10] Guidelines.
- Combined with a more granular typology of document types.
- Presented in an insightful and user-friendly data visualization framework.
- Released with an open-source dataset, making WAIE reproducible and extendable.

WAIE focuses on guidelines related to the ethical use of AI technologies. That is, documents conceptualized as recommendations, policy frameworks, legal landmarks, codes of conduct, practical guides, tools, or ethical principles for AI systems and applications. Also, unlike previous works Hagendorff (2020) and Fjeld (2020), WAIE encompasses several areas that fall under the multidisciplinary

---

9 inventory.algorithmwatch.org

10 linking-ai-principles.org

umbrella of Artificial Intelligence research, e.g., Statistical Learning, Data Science, Machine Learning, Optimization Theory, Robotics, Software Development, and Engineering. This sample is a snapshot of the collective care and preoccupations of several stakeholders engaged with the future of technology and AI, regardless of their popularity in the broader debate.

1.2.2.1 WAIE Features

WAIE explored several features, both quantitative and qualitative. Like in previous works Jobin et al. (2019) and Hagendorff (2020), and Fjeld (2020), it presents the following core indicators:

- Institution responsible for producing the document.
- Country/World Region of the institution.
- Type of institution (e.g., academic, non-profit, government, etc.).
- Year of publication.
- Ethical principles (as done by Fjeld 2020, WAIE breaks principles into themes of resonating discourse).
- Principles description (i.e., the words used in a document to define or support a given principle).
- Gender distribution among authors (inferred through a first-name automated analysis).
- Size of the document (i.e., word count).

WAIE also presents a set of qualitative categories designed to further differentiate documents based on their normative content. These categories relate to:

- The content of the document.
- The type of regulation that the document proposes.
- The normative strength of the proposed norms.
- The impact scope that motivates the document's agenda.

The first category relates to how its authors approached questions regarding the understanding, guidance, and implementation of AI technologies. WAIE defines them as mutually inclusive (documents may have all these features combined):

- Descriptive: Descriptive documents take the effort of presenting definitions related to AI technologies. These definitions contextualize "what we mean" when we talk about AI.
- Normative: Normative documents present norms, ethical principles, recommendations, and imperative affirmations about what such technologies should be used or developed for.
- Practical: Practical documents present development tools to implement ethical principles and norms.

The second category delineates different approaches to governance and regulation within AI technologies. WAIE defines them as mutually exclusive (the presence of one feature excludes the other):

- Government-Regulation: This category encompasses documents made by governmental institutions. These documents propose that states regulate the use and development of AI either strictly (through legally binding horizontal regulations) or softly (through legally non-binding guidelines).
- Self-Regulation/Voluntary Self-Commitment: This category encompasses documents made by private organizations and other bodies. These documents advocate for a form of self-regulation governed by the AI industry, including any voluntary commitments made by independent organizations.
- Recommendation: This category encompasses documents that only suggest possible forms of governance and ethical principles that should guide organizations seeking to use, develop, or regulate AI technologies.

The third category outlines distinct methods for governance and regulation within the AI domain, with differing levels of enforceability and flexibility. These are also defined as mutually inclusive:

- Legally non-binding guidelines: These documents propose an approach that intertwines AI principles with recommended practices for companies and other entities.
- Legally binding regulations: These documents propose an approach that focuses on regulating specific uses of AI through legally binding rules, such as mandatory requirements and prohibitions.

The final category delineates perspectives on the temporal scope of concern regarding AI technologies and their impacts (defined as mutually exclusive):

- Short-Termism: This category encompasses documents in which the scope of impact and preoccupation focus mainly on current or short-term problems, like algorithmic discrimination, algorithmic opacity, privacy, legal accountability, etc.
- Long-Termism: This category encompasses documents in which the scope of impact and preoccupation focus mainly on future or long-term problems. Since such technologies are not yet a reality, we can classify these risks as hypothetical or, at best, uncertain.
- Short-Termism & Long-Termism: This category encompasses documents in which the scope of impact is short and long-term, i.e., they present a *"mid-term"* scope of preoccupation. These documents address issues related to the short-termism category, while also highlighting the mid- to long-term impacts of our current AI adoption (e.g., AI interference in democratic processes, autonomous weapons, existential risks, environmental sustainability, labor displacement, and the need for updating our educational systems).

WAIE also presents 17 ethical principles defined by textual and semantic analysis of its sample. These defined principles aggregate similar and resonating values while maintaining significant differences in their written forms:

Accountability/Liability: Accountability refers to the idea that AI technology developers and deployers should comply with regulatory bodies. These actors should also be accountable for their actions and the impacts caused by their technologies.

Beneficence/Non-Maleficence: Beneficence and non-maleficence come from bioethics and medical ethics. In AI ethics, these principles state that human welfare (and harm aversion) should be the goal of AI-empowered technologies.

Children & Adolescents Rights: The idea that we must protect the rights of children and adolescents is particularly addressed by some guidelines. AI stakeholders should safeguard, respect, and be aware of the frailties associated with young people.

Dignity/Human Rights: This principle is based on the idea that everyone deserves proper treatment and respect. In AI ethics, respect for human dignity and human rights (i.e., the Universal Declaration of Human Rights) are sometimes used interchangeably.

Diversity/Inclusion/Pluralism/Accessibility: This set of principles advocates the idea that the development and use of AI technologies should be done in an inclusive and accessible way, respecting the different ways that the human entity may come to express itself.

Freedom/Autonomy/Democratic Values/Technological Sovereignty: This set of principles advocates the idea that the autonomy of human decision-making must be preserved during human-AI interactions, whether that choice is individual or the freedom to choose together, such as the inviolability of democratic rights and values, which are also linked to the technological self-sufficiency of nations and states.

Human Formation/Education: Such principles defend that human formation and education must be prioritized in our technological advances. AI technologies require considerable expertise to be produced and operated, and such knowledge should be accessible to all.

Human-Centeredness/Alignment: Such principles advocate that AI systems should be centered on and aligned with human values and our necessities.

Intellectual Property: This principle seeks to ground the property rights over AI products and their generated outputs.

Justice/Equity/Fairness/Non-discrimination: This set of principles upholds the ideas of non-discrimination and bias mitigation. It argues that algorithmic treatment should be fair regardless of the sensitive attributes that may characterize an individual.

Labor Rights: Labor rights are legal and human rights related to the labor relations between workers and employers. In AI ethics, this principle emphasizes that workers' rights should be preserved, regardless of whether AI technologies mediate or augment labor relations.

Cooperation/Fair Competition/Open Source: This set of principles advocates different means by which joint actions can be established and cultivated between AI stakeholders to achieve common goals. It also relates to the free and open exchange of valuable AI assets.

Privacy: The idea of privacy can be defined as the individual's right to expose oneself voluntarily, and to the extent desired, to the world. This principle is also related to data protection-related concepts, such as data minimization, anonymity, and informed consent.

Reliability/Safety/Security/Trustworthiness: This set of principles upholds the idea that AI technologies should be reliable in that their use can be verified as safe and robust, promoting user trust and better acceptance of AI technologies.

Sustainability: This principle can be interpreted as a manifestation of intergenerational justice, wherein the welfare of future generations must be considered in AI development. In AI ethics, sustainability pertains to the notion that AI advances should be approached with an understanding of their enduring consequences, encompassing environmental impact and the preservation and well-being of non-human life.

Transparency/Explainability/Auditability: This set of principles supports the idea that the use and development of AI technologies should be transparent for all interested stakeholders. Transparency can be related to *"the transparency of an organization"* or *"the transparency of an algorithm"*. This set of principles is also related to the idea that such information should be understandable to nonexperts and, when necessary, subject to auditing.

Truthfulness: This principle upholds the idea that AI technologies must provide truthful information. It is also related to the notion that people should not be deceived when interacting with AI systems.

All this information is condensed into several visualization panels we call the WAIE dashboard,[11] an interactive, flexible, dynamic, and open (the WAIE dataset is freely available for download) database of values and norms for AI technologies, which can be used to enable many types of studies and projects. For example, with over 1400 definitions encapsulating the previously outlined 17 principles, WAIE provides raw material for, for example, investigations relying on Natural Language Processing (NLP) techniques. [12]

1.2.3 WAIE: Analysis and Results

Let us quickly examine some insights we can gather from the WAIE review. Check the published article (Corrêa et al. 2023) for a more detailed analysis, and open a browser window with the WAIE dashboard to check the graphs related to the results we are about to unveil.

1.2.3.1 Worldwide Landscape

Looking at WAIE's distribution among world regions (aggregated by continent), the bulk of produced documents comes from Europe (especially countries from Western Europe, 31.5%, like the United Kingdom, 12%, and Germany, 10%), North America (the United States of America, 29%, and Canada, 5.5%), that together represent a third of the sample size, and Asia (mainly represented by East Asian countries, 11.5%, like China, 5.5%, and Japan, 4%). In contrast, South America, Africa, and Oceania collectively represent less than 4.5% of the sample, with countries such as Brazil (1.5%) leading this sub-distribution, followed by Latin America (3.5%). Other world regions and countries would be even more underrepresented without

[11] 🔗 nkluge-correa.github.io/worldwide_AI-ethics/dashboard.html

[12] Here is an example of what one can do: Using the affordances of textual embeddings (Bengio et al. 2000) and basic machine learning techniques, we transformed these definitions into vector representations and projected these principle definitions into a three-dimensional space of human values expressed as natural language (which you can access and explore on kluge-correa.github.io/worldwide_AI-ethics/embeddings.html). By taking the time to filter and investigate, you may find several relations, correlations, similarities, and other insights that might prove helpful if you are interested in this type of NLP-powered analysis.

the significant participation of intergovernmental organizations like NATO, UN, and UNESCO, which represent 6% of the sample size (13 documents).

In summary, Europe and North America dominate the scene, while Asia secures a significant share. However, South America, Africa, and Oceania are notably underrepresented. Special recognition goes to intergovernmental organizations for their participation, which helps diversify the sample.

1.2.3.2 Institutional Distribution

Switching the gaze to institution types, except for institutions such as IBM (5), Microsoft (4), and UNESCO (3), most other institutions have fewer than two published samples in the WAIE's dataset. Meanwhile, the bulk of the sample was produced by governmental institutions and private corporations (48%), followed by CSO/NGO (17%), non-profit organizations (16%), and academic institutions (12.5%).

In essence, major players such as IBM and Microsoft lead the way in this regard. Meanwhile, governmental institutions and private corporations are primarily responsible for most of the noise, while CSOs/NGOs and academic institutions strive to make their mark more noticeable.

1.2.3.3 Gender Distribution

The gender distribution among authors in the WAIE dataset exhibits a clear imbalance, with 66% having no authorship information. On the remaining part of the distribution, authors with "male" names are prevalent (66% male, 34% female). While Academic institutions (62% male, 38% female) and non-profit organizations (65% male, 34% female) are the less disparate institutions, they still fall short of the 1:1 parity ratio. Meanwhile, industrial associations show the highest level of disparity, with only 13% of authors identified as female.

In summary, the gender balance in the WAIE dataset is problematic. Even in supposedly more enlightened spaces, such as academia and nonprofits, parity remains a distant dream.

1.2.3.4 Unveiling Document Typologies

Regarding the WAIE's typologies, based on the document's content, the majority of its sample is from the normative type (96%), which also presents descriptive contents half of the time (55.5%) and practical implementations more rarely (27%). The form of regulation proposed by the documents of WAIE's sample is primarily comprised of recommendations to different AI stakeholders (56%), while 24% possess self-regulatory/voluntary self-commitment style guidelines, and only 20% propose a form of regulation administered by a given country.

This lack of convergence towards a more *"government-based"* form of regulation is reflected in the normative strength of these documents, where the vast majority (98%) serve only as guidelines that do not entail any form of legal obligation, while only 4.5% propose strict regulations. Since only governmental institutions (24% of WAIE's sample) can create legally binding norms, one could argue that this imbalance stems from this fact. However, by filtering only the documents produced by governmental institutions, the disproportion remains, with only 18.7% of the remaining documents proposing legally binding forms of regulation.[13]

Regarding impact scope, the totality of WAIE's sample shows that short-term (47%) and *"mid-term"* (52%) prevail over more long-term preoccupations (2%). Filtering by impact scope and institution type reveals that private corporations tend to focus on the short-term (33%), governmental institutions on the mid-term (28%), academic institutions on the long-term (66%), and non-profit organizations on the long-term (33%) impacts of AI technologies.

In summary, WAIE unveils a severe practical gap. Regarding regulation, it is mostly recommendations rather than actual regulations, while existing rules remain vague and ungrounded. As for impact, it is all about the here and now, with the future unknowns getting little more than an honorary mention.

1.2.3.5 Worldwide Values

Examining the distribution of principles among WAIE's sample, the following result becomes evident: the top five principles advocated are similar to the results shown by Jobin et al. (2019) and Hagendorff (2020), with the addition of Reliability/Safety/Security/Trustworthiness (78%), which also was top five in Fjeld (2020) meta-analysis (80%).

One of the advantages of WAIE's visualization panel is that it enables us to examine how different features interact with one another. For example, when investigating principal distribution filtered by institution type, one can notice that the main advocated principle of governmental institutions (worldwide) is the need for transparent systems (89.5%). Additionally, while private corporations primarily defend the need for Reliability (87.5%), CSOs/NGOs mainly support the necessity for more algorithmic fairness (88.2%).

Another advantage is that WAIE displays all definitions given by each document to the mentioned principles, allowing for a more diverse comparison of how these abstract objects are defined. For example, when examining the principle of Transparency, the definition proposed in *"ARCC: An Ethical Framework for Artificial Intelligence"* (Tencent Research Institute 2018) states that:

[13] The countries on the front of this still weak trend are Canada, Germany, and the United Kingdom, with Australia, Norway, and the USA coming right behind.

> Promote algorithmic transparency and algorithmic audit, to achieve understandable and explainable AI systems. Explain the decisions assisted/made by AI systems when appropriate. Ensure individuals' right to know, and provide users with sufficient information concerning the AI system's purpose, function, limitation, and impact.

While the one provided by *"A practical guide to Responsible Artificial Intelligence (AI)"* (PricewaterhouseCoopers 2019) says (about the same principle):

> To instill trust in AI systems, people must be enabled to look under the hood at their underlying models, explore the data used to train them, expose the reasoning behind each decision, and provide coherent explanations to all stakeholders promptly. These explanations should be tailored to the different stakeholders, including regulators, data scientists, business sponsors, and end consumers.

The WAIE's dataset and panels contain all available definitions (for every principle). I encourage readers to explore the topics closest to their hearts and minds and search for commonalities and dissimilarities among the principles' definitions.

1.3 Critical Analysis

WAIE is a descriptive analysis and account of the normative realm surrounding AI. It is an example of normativity being observed and questioned from a third-person perspective. Later in this book, these ideas will form the foundation for Dynamic Normativity, which rests on the assumption that values and preferences reside not only in ourselves but also in the environment we interact with, such as the norms embedded in our social institutions.

Now that we have all of this knowledge at our disposal, as moral agents endowed with reflexive and critical thinking, before moving on, we will exercise these faculties to promote a critique of everything WAIE showed us.

Hence, let us ask ourselves: What has this review revealed about AI Ethics and its principles? Here are some possible answers:

- The debate on the ethics of AI, at least in the form investigated by WAIE, continues to be influenced by the North American and European narrative—the global north.
- This debate has been led by government and private institutions.
- The production of these norms appears to have a gender distribution imbalance.
- The *"AI Ethics"* topic emerged to the zeitgeist in 2018.
- The types of documents that have been produced have a strongly self-regulatory character, untied to legal sanctions.

(continued)

- While there is convergence on the most urgent values to be addressed, there is considerable variation in their definitions.
- Most of its proposed items are untied to any form of praxis.

WAIE can provide numerous additional insights to the avid reader. However, in the following section, I would like to present my subjective evaluation of the gathered results, offering a critical analysis inspired by other critiques that, via observation of the codependent relationship we have with technology, came to question the underlying assumptions and power structures of society, in the hope of to exposing flaws and power imbalances within its systems (Butler 1863; Jameson 1991; Davis 1992; Kaczynski 1995; Baudrillard 1994; Alway and Calhoun 1997; Virilio 1997; Baudrillard 1998; Rosa and William 2009; Tally 2009; Waelen 2022).

1.3.1 Unknown Perspectives and Marginalized Regions

Even with a sample size twice as large as the one analyzed by Jobin et al. (2019), WAIE cannot escape North American and European hegemony in the discourse. However, we can counter this result by considering other indicators that place other countries as serious AI stakeholders.

For example, according to Savage (2020), from 2016 to 2019: *"China's output of AI-related research increased by 120%, whereas output in the USA increased by 'mere' 70%. In 2019, China published 102,161 AI-related papers, and the USA published 74,386"*. Additionally, according to the AI Index Annual Report, the USA, China, and India are the top three countries in the Vibrancy Ranking. While this helps to explain why almost a third of WAIE's sample size comes from the USA, it does not account for the underrepresentation of countries like China and India. Again, according to Zhang et al., China has far surpassed the USA in journal/conference publications and citations, while most of the *"AI talent concentration"* is found in India. These new indicators challenge the hegemony of North American and European ethical narratives, which are supposedly supported by their excellence and leading position in AI development.

Additionally, we could argue that the *"Guidelines for AI Technologies"* scope obscures much of the normative discourse that has been conducted elsewhere. For example, the African continent is significantly underrepresented in the WAIE dataset. However, according to Kiemde (2021), 17 of the 55 African Union member states possess data protection and privacy legislation. At the same time, Mauritius announced the establishment of a National AI Council, making it the first African state to present an AI strategy. Kiemde and Kora also demonstrate in their review a collection of published papers and documents about AI ethics in Africa and other underrepresented countries (Gwagwa 2019; Vernon 2019; Sallstrom et al. 2019;

Bensalah 2021; Gwagwa et al. 2021), which helps us to show that this type of discourse is present in the African States and probably in all other places that do not show up in WAIE and other popular reviews (Jobin et al. 2019; Hagendorff 2020; Fjeld 2020).

Hence, it is clear that countries such as China and India, along with various African nations (and countless other places not mentioned here), are making significant strides in AI, and the contours of their contribution extend beyond the scope currently captured by the analysis above and WAIE. While many voices remain unknown, agreement on the principles that should guide AI development and use remains uncertain. In essence, it is not that our environment does not contain the values of all these underrepresented groups, but that our ability to uncover them is still primitive—something that might hinder society in matters of alignment.

1.3.2 The Hegemony of State and Private Sectors and the Regulation Dilemma

WAIE's results mirror the findings of Jobin et al. (2019) and Fjeld (2020), where most of the sample comes from private institutions (24%) and governmental organizations (24%).

This equal presence of both State and Private stakeholders in the current normative discourse may be related to the expanse and success of the tech industry (Zhang et al. 2021, 2022; Maslej et al. 2023). Nowadays, most AI breakthroughs come from the sector (OpenAI 2023; Touvron et al. 2023; Yu et al. 2022). An AI industry that, seeing the demands for regulation and accountability from civil society, quickly reacted by proposing the rules that should (allegedly) guide their progress. Many of such promises are, perhaps, genuine. However, when governments and private institutions have *the same weight* in the general normative discourse, attention to the matter seems needed, especially when many of these technologies remain in gray areas of regulation.

This fact may become more alarming when we look at the distribution of government documents that opt for *soft* forms of regulation (91.6%). The critique that *"ethical principles are not enough to govern the AI industry"* is not a new one (Hagendorff 2020; Jobin et al. 2019; Mittelstadt 2019; Rességuier and Rodrigues 2020; Corrêa and Fernandes 2021), however, perhaps those critiques have not yet permeated the mainstream community, which produces guidelines primarily based on principles detached from observable metrics or practical implementations.

Even if most countries opt for legally non-binding forms of regulation, there is a growing adoption/proposition of stricter solutions, with countries like the USA, Canada, the United Kingdom, and international organizations like the European Union spearheading this trend. At the same time, we live in a time where influential members of the AI industry *"urge for regulation"* (Kang 2023). Nevertheless, given the influence tech oligopolies have over regulating bodies (McIntosh 2018; Petit

2020; Fukuyama et al. 2021; Bhadra 2022), it is currently unclear if the soon-to-come regulation will not help cement this already heavily-centralized industry as it happened in other situations (e.g., telecommunications in the USA) (Brock 1994; Melody 1999; Economides 2004).[14]

If we subscribe to the idea that the unjust and unquestioned centralization of power is the precursor of tyranny and oppression (May 1992, 1994; Graeber 2009, 2013), regulation becomes a double-edged sword. And this is one of the tensions we are currently facing on this front:

> While regulation can help us escape the self-regulatory trap that endows the tech goliaths with the impunity to act in undesirable ways, bad regulation may help solidify the existing technological oligopolies.

If regulation is implemented carelessly, while big companies will have the resources to comply with it (even shaping it to be favorable to their context), small organizations will not. While big companies have the financial backing to deal with lawsuits and fines, the open-source community and Academia do not. And suppose regulation comes in terms of capabilities. In that case, this will be the same as putting the future of AI development in the hands of these oligopolies. Then, we will institute the idea that only the industry can perform state-of-the-art AI development in our society.

1.3.3 The Importance of Defining "AI"

Regarding the content of the samples that form the WAIE dataset, we observe that only 55.5% of documents aim to define the object of their discourse, i.e., *"we are talking about autonomous intelligent systems, and this is what we understand as an autonomous intelligent system"*. This is a curious phenomenon, especially if we acknowledge that there is no consensual definition of what AI is and what is not (Monett et al. 2020).

There are many interpretations and contesting definitions, which may be a challenge for regulating organizations. For example, suppose you define AI as only *"systems that can learn"*. In that case, you will leave an entire family of systems outside your scope of regulation that do not learn (rule-based systems) but can still act intelligently and autonomously.

---

[14] The Telecommunications Act of 1996 (Krattenmaker 1996) aimed to promote competition and innovation in the US telecommunications industry. However, specific provisions, such as the requirement for new entrants to negotiate interconnection agreements with incumbent providers, proved a significant hurdle for smaller companies. The costs and complexities of negotiating these agreements put the established telecom monopolies in an advantageous position. As a result, the regulations contributed to the formation of monopolies/oligopolies, making it almost impossible for new players to enter this field.

An incomplete definition can leave vital areas out of the normative scope of a proposal. For example, many rule-based systems that do not use ML are the base for Lethal Autonomous Weapons (LAW), a topic that only 4.5% of the WAIE's sample mentions. Given that, since 2010, the major global superpowers have heavily engaged in weaponizing AI technologies (Geist 2016; Kania 2017; Haas and Fischer 2017; Field 2019; Maas 2019; Roff 2019; Hacaoglu 2020; Trevithick 2020; Hambling 2020; Crofts 2020; Russell 2023), it is uncertain to us why many of these documents do not consider these artifacts as part of their normative agenda.

Perhaps we could attribute this to the fact that for many countries,[15] allied with Academia and private institutions, the development of autonomous weapons is an active research and development area, with the Arms Industry funding several AI research programs and private companies (Baum 2017; Fitzgerald et al. 2020).

Defining the boundaries of artificial intelligence presents a challenge akin to finding a needle in a haystack during an earthquake. Given that only a little over half of the documents attempt to specify their subject matter, it is understandable why confusion persists in the regulatory domain.

1.3.4 Hidden Costs and Side Effects

When looking at some of WAIE's least mentioned principles, like Labor Rights, Sustainability, and Truthfulness, the problems stated by Hagendorff (2020) and Jobin et al. (2019) are underlined, where the lack of attention given to questions related to the costs and misuse of our current AI-technologies remains overlooked in much of these guidelines. Taking these three principles as examples, only 22% cite Sustainability, 19.5% cite Labor Rights, and 8.5% mention Truthfulness.

The tech industry incurs significant ecological and social costs. For example, some reasons for our current AI summer are the progress in hardware performance, better training methodologies for neural networks, and the massive amount of available data to train such algorithms. One field that serves as a clear example of this reality is Natural Language Processing (NLP). Current advances in neural network architecture (Vaswani et al. 2017) have enabled the creation of deep neural networks that seem to improve their performance as long as we scale their size and training volume (Hestness et al. 2017; Henighan et al. 2020; Kaplan et al. 2020; Bahri et al. 2021). These Large Language Models (LLMs) (e.g., BERT Devlin et al. 2018, Chinchilla Hoffmann et al. 2022, LLaMA Touvron et al. 2023, GPT-4 OpenAI 2023) show unmatched generality and adaptability when compared to earlier deep learning systems. However, as Strubell et al. (2019) point:

---

[15] Garcia (2019) points out in his analysis of autonomous weapons research and development that at least seven countries (United States, China, Russia, United Kingdom, France, Israel, and South Korea) stand out for their substantial engagement in the development of autonomous weapons.

> [...] these accuracy improvements depend on the availability of exceptionally large computational resources that necessitate similarly substantial energy consumption. As a result, these models are costly to train and develop, both financially, due to the cost of hardware and electricity or cloud computing time, and environmentally, due to the carbon footprint required to fuel modern tensor processing hardware.

Modern AI systems have the potential to consume massive amounts of energy during their training and fine-tuning phases. As model sizes grow, this energy requirement only increases. With some models now consisting of trillions of parameters (Fedus et al. 2021), their carbon footprint can reach up to hundreds of kilograms of emitted CO_2 (Strubell et al. 2019; Patterson et al. 2021; Luccioni et al. 2022).[16]

Looking beyond the environmental impact, it is worth noting that most individual researchers lack the resources to undertake such research. Building large-scale models requires access to significant amounts of specialized hardware, while servers that offer this computing power are often prohibitively expensive. This exclusivity based on financial capital has changed the deep learning landscape since its early days. Nowadays, achieving state-of-the-art results in deep learning is often a financially exclusive endeavor, and those with access to more computing resources usually prevail.

Another point overlooked is the CO_2 *tunnel vision*, where many other markers remain ignored. For example, the extractivist practices related to the mining of vital resources to the tech industry, such as copper, gold, silver, coltan, aluminum, titanium, lithium, and many others, are unfortunately related to the exploitation of (child) labor in developing countries (Montague 2002; Mustapha et al. 2007; Nest 2011; Sutherland 2011; Usanov et al. 2013).[17]

In general, human labor is often overlooked. One of the primary causes of unemployment over the past 200 years has been the automation of processes previously carried out by people (Peters 2019), a phenomenon that has also contributed to the massive wealth gap in modern society (Rotman 2013). Meanwhile, prospects seem unsettling. Frey and Osborne (2013) estimated the probability of automation for 702 US occupations in their survey. The findings predicted that over the next 20 years (10 years from now), technology would automate 47% of these professions. A similar study conducted by Gruetzemacher et al. (2020) showed that, according to most experts, 22% of all jobs can already be automated, a number predicted to increase to 40% in 5 years and 60% in 10 years. According to Eloundou et al. (2023), LLMs like GPT-4 could affect at least 10% of all tasks of 80% of the US workforce,

[16] It is also crucial to realize that developing a high-performing language model extends beyond a simple training loop. Achieving neural network robustness in any domain often necessitates multiple training rounds to experiment with different model architectures and hyperparameters, a process that still heavily relies on heuristics and trial and error.

[17] In 2011, it is estimated that artisanal mining had employed approximately 16% of the Democratic Republic of the Congo population (13.5 million people), being one of the most profitable labor activities in the country (Nest 2011).

with approximately 19% of workers potentially experiencing at least 50% of their tasks impacted.

The apparent expansion of informal employment is another worrying development linked to the exploitation of human labor driven by our AI progress. For instance, the rise of click working, i.e., a type of task required for building large labeled datasets (Irani 2016) or performing repetitive tasks we still cannot automate, has been linked to many cases of labor rights violations (Harris 2014; Perrigo 2023).[18]

Under these conditions, countermeasures concerning labor displacement are still in their infancy. For example, the *Windfall's Clause* (O'Keefe et al. 2020), a hypothetical legal ex-ante agreement between large AI companies and the world, would guarantee that businesses involved in AI development are committed to sharing their profits with society in case they create AGI, i.e., an optimistic take on the merit of trickle-down economics. However, one could say that the kindness of the rich and powerful would be nothing more than a promise. A more critical response would be that the dominant classes never gave anything to the oppressed, except under the threat of conflict, unless they had something to gain. In the more eloquent words of Tavares (2017):.

> I do not think that except under pressure and conflict, the ruling class has given anything for free to those below unless they wanted them for cannon fodder.

The last principle in our short list of overlooked maxims is truthfulness. Despite being an underrepresented principle in WAIE, truthfulness addresses one of the most significant concerns presented by the AI community in recent years, where issues related to fake content are among the most frequently reported and vulnerabilities in modern generative AI systems.[19] [20] For example, while LLMs can produce ostensibly plausible text with no basis in objective reality, ranging from erroneous information (Lin et al. 2021) to code that immediately fails when executed (Brown et al. 2020; Chen et al. 2021), image and video generation models can create photo-realistic images that support false claims (such as the fake evidence that late "Pope Francis was covertly a notorious dancer and stylish bon vivant").[21]

Problems like these are emerging phenomena related to the new advances in the field. Before the era of generative models, coherent text generation, quality code generation, or photo-realistic text-to-image conversion was years away from fooling people. Nowadays, one can change the faces of two people in an image or video using open software[22] with little to no training or with one click, create a picture of a face that does not exist.[23]

---

[18] By *"labor rights"*, I refer to the International Labor Organization standards (Kaufmann 2008).

[19] huggingface.co/spaces/nicholasKluge/Model-Library

[20] incidentdatabase.ai

[21] tiktok.com/@carlomunar/video/7215257056058658053

[22] github.com/deepfakes/faceswap

[23] this-person-does-not-exist.com/en

Hence, in an ever-evolving field, we reside in an era where the concept of *"truth"* is exceedingly vulnerable. Given the known harms misinformation can cause (Howard and Kollanyi 2016; Chapman and Tarasuk 2016), it is worth being mindful that only now the issue of automated misinformation spread has gained attention beyond the ML community (Sample 2023; Editorials 2023; Cotton et al. 2023), indicating a possible gap between AI as an applied field, and AI Ethics as an applied field of philosophy.

1.3.5 The Principle-Practice Gap

As already stated by Fjeld (2020), a gap exists between established principles and their actual application. In the WAIE sample, most documents prescribe normative claims without providing the means to achieve them, while the effectiveness of more practical methodologies, in most cases, remains empirically untested (Corrêa et al. 2024).

Regulation can be perceived as an implementation of normative ethics, which alone lacks the strength to enforce its normativity. Several studies point out that ethical standards alone have little to no impact on decision-making across a wide range of professional fields (Brief 1996; Cleek and Leonard 1998; Lere and Gaumnitz 2003; Osborn et al. 2009; Calo 2017), something even more pronounced in STEM-related fields that do not have a study tradition in Humanities (Friedman 1996; Mittelstadt 2019; Bynum 2006; Davis and Nathan 2015; McNamara et al. 2018; Vakkuri et al. 2020; Griffin et al. 2024; Corrêa et al. 2025).

This lack of praxis is well-known, and many authors have raised concerns about the state in which much of the field currently rests. Jobin et al. (2019):

> Private sector involvement in the field of AI ethics has been questioned for potentially using soft policies as a way to turn a social problem into something technical or to completely avoid regulation.

Hagendorff (2020):

> AI ethics - or ethics in general - have no mechanisms to reinforce its normative claims.

Rességuier and Rodrigues (2020):

> Ethics have great powerful teeth. Unfortunately, we are barely using them in AI ethics - no wonder then that AI ethics is called toothless.

Mittelstadt (2019):

> Statements reliant on vague normative concepts hide points of political and ethical conflict. "Fairness", "dignity", and other such abstract concepts are examples of "essentially contested concepts". At best, this conceptual ambiguity allows for the context-sensitive specification of ethical requirements for AI. At worst, it masks fundamental, principled disagreement and drives AI Ethics towards moral relativism. At a minimum, any compromise reached thus far around core principles for AI Ethics does not reflect meaningful consensus on a common practical direction for "good" AI development and governance.

Munn (2022):

> [...] these are meaningless principles which are contested or incoherent, making them difficult to apply; they are isolated principles situated in an industry and education system which largely ignores ethics; and they are toothless principles which lack consequences and adhere to corporate agendas.

Such harsh criticism may indeed motivate the field to fulfill its interdisciplinary promise. As long as we treat AI Ethics as a purely philosophical endeavor, crossing the principle-practice gap remains a complicated goal. However, when applied areas like law, engineering, and computer science enter the fray, we can solidify the *ought* into what *can* be done. Regardless, without the humane side of this equation, technicians may become lost in a field where the guiding compass is that which profits the industry.

Before we proceed to the final section of this introductory chapter, let us ask the question: What barriers prevent this interdisciplinary agenda from becoming the norm? If alignment is considered both a technical and philosophical problem, a one-sided solution may not be sufficient to address the entirety of the problem of embedding values into AI systems. In an attempt to answer this question, we will identify a paradox that may help highlight the current deficits in AI ethics research within one of the institutions that promote it the most: *Academia*.

1.4 Paradoxes and Future Directions

WAIE's review presents several intriguing trends that raise questions about the field of AI ethics. These trends can help expose sore points that, if left untouched, hinder the fulfillment of the AI Ethics promise. Many of the points we brought to light in our last sections, like the inequality in the volume of voices participating in this debate, the power imbalance between the state and private interests, and the myriad of side effects tied to the massive adoption and irresponsible use of AI technologies, are, for most of us, outside of our immediate control. Even if we are committed to promoting the responsible and conscious adoption of these systems, many things require massive coordination of people and institutions, which, at a large scale, is an enormous problem in itself.

While the question of defining intelligence will be addressed in Chap. 4, in this final section, we aim to explore the principle-practice gap, its paradox, and the obstacles that, I argue, hinder our achievement of the goals of AI ethics as an applied field. And given that Academia[24] is responsible for some of these obstacles, it is just that these should be a sphere of interference that we, as academics, should be morally bound to *"do something about"*.

Let me define some key claims and positions before exposing the paradox in which Academia is currently locked. First:

[24] The worldwide community concerned with the pursuit of research, education, and scholarship.

- If the Ethics of Artificial Intelligence is considered a sub-field of Applied Ethics, its most critical blank space is the normative gap between its theory and practice.

Between theory and practice, let us represent these two sides by different approaches to AI Ethics: (1) the process of bringing normativity to AI development by addressing the human side of this process (e.g., defining ethical principles to help guide those who create, use, and govern AI systems and applications); and (2) the process of bringing normativity into the machine by seeking to embed values, like fairness and privacy, into AI systems and applications. Firstly, our concern involves the development of an ethical theory or framework; secondly, we seek ways to apply its values.

Again, I argue that for AI Ethics to fulfill its goal—ensuring that the use and development of AI systems and applications align with what we deem morally correct—its greatest current obstacle, in the academic sense, is the principle-practice gap between both these approaches—the lack of connection between the theoretical and the practical parts of this field, which can canonically be represented by different areas of knowledge (disciplines) acting in this front: the humanities and STEM-related fields.

On the humanistic side, AI ethics largely remain based on a principle- or opinion-based fashion. Given the diverse nature of normative discourse, many of these efforts remain in the realm of opinions and recommendations that are not unified; for example, there is no agreement on what *"fair AI"* means. Unfortunately, this abstractness can be manipulated to push the agenda of those against closing the principle-practice gap, i.e., the practical and binding implementation of ethical standards. As an example of such manipulation, we can refer to the already-mentioned industry's push for self-regulation.

Meanwhile, on the technical side, the techno-solutionist's approach fails to grasp that normative problems are, in fact, *human problems*. Many of the issues AI ethicists seek to tackle are not always technical but manifestations of historical oppression and economic inequality, among other social ills, that are repackaged and revisited in an automated world. At the same time, problems deemed philosophical or political are disregarded by STEM-related fields that consider themselves amoral or apolitical, which further blocks the presence of human sciences in the formation, research, and teaching related to the technical development of AI.[25] This incomplete grasp of the problem results in incomplete solutions and implementations—a technical solution based on a flawed theoretical understanding of the problem.

[25] The question (sometimes) is not *"How to make the orphan crushing machine less painful?"*, but *"Why did someone build an orphan crushing machine in the first place, and why are we maintaining this thing?"*

Both the criticisms raised against these sides are the most common. In other words, while the engineering-based side criticizes the human disciplines-based side for being unable to grasp the nature of the technique under consideration (*"How do neural networks work?"*), the human disciplines-based side complains of the engineering-based side's inability to understand the intricacies related to normative theory (*"What is the difference between a value ethics and a deontological approach to AI Ethics?"*). Paradoxically, the cooperation that would help both sides improve their deficits is blocked by (1) those on either side who point out a deficit in the other camp and (2) long-standing structural barriers hindering interdisciplinary work (Graff 2016).

Currently, AI ethics and AI research suffer from the excessive presence of gatekeepers and gatekeeping policies—individuals or institutional policies that determine access to a specific research context (Montgomery 2020; Welsh 2021). Such practices impede AI ethics from evolving into a genuinely techno-humanistic endeavor. Think about it. How often are philosophy master's students accepted into computer science PhDs and vice versa? How frequently are interdisciplinary projects nothing more than meetings and email exchanges between experts in specific disciplines working *"together"*? In other words, juxtaposition without integration.

Or ask yourself, how rare are the bridge-crossers and makers that interconnect and cross the many fields? And how common are discourses surrounding ideas akin to *"since you haven't studied x, you cannot have a say on y"*? Or situations where academics are blocked from participating in certain events (of an interdisciplinary nature) for not having a background (or a degree) in x? Without learning linear algebra, you cannot work with machine learning ethics, as you do not understand the underlying concepts of deep learning. You are not qualified to propose normative criteria for AI systems without mastering the underlying principles of several schools of ethics.

However, such areas are often closed, failing to embrace wanderers from other fields, which prevents them from addressing the same deficits that members of the opposite field so frequently attack. Philosophy is a ball of fluff. Tecnosolutionism is a mock solution. In summary, these actors and policies push a tribalist agenda aimed at *"protecting their area"*, which only contributes to the perpetuation of the principle-practice gap while simultaneously pushing for the importance of *"interdisciplinary"* (Graff 2015, 2016).

Fields of Applied Ethics demand interdisciplinary researchers—*bridge makers*—who can transition from the theoretical to the practical. From the land of abstract principles to that of practical implementation. From what *ought* to be to what *can* be done. Preventing this crossing hinders the realization of an applied field where the most critical obstacle is the gap between its humanistic-theoretical and practical-technical sides. Ultimately, until the factors mentioned earlier prevent the creation of this bridge, AI ethics will remain short of its most significant promise.

Now, where do we go from here? As individuals, we can strive to act in accordance with the techno-humanistic agenda that AI Ethics requires. Suppose we are in positions of leadership and authority. In that case, dismantling the barriers that prevent the integration of all aspects of AI ethics should also be a worthwhile goal to pursue. We can help generate a new and more robust wave of ethicists and builders with these.

The rest of this book attempts to approximate this ideal of philosophical work as a foundation and support for the technical implementation of problems that concern us and the products of our craft and intellect. While the development of WAIE aimed to create a tool and later analyze and critique the results, the rest of this book will take the opposite approach. Motivations, formalizations, and foundations will serve as the roots for later building an experimental attempt to ground and apply AI ethics in real AI systems, and subsequently, point out the limitations of the current methods available.

However, before we proceed, in our next chapter, we will examine the origins of the *control problem* and how alignment (integrating all the principles we have explored in this chapter) emerged as a preferred solution.

1.5 Epilogue

AI research is a field that has gained significant popularity in recent years, both in academia and in mainstream debates. AI Ethics, one of the many branches of this field, addresses the ethical issues and questions surrounding the use and development of artificial intelligence (AI) technologies. While the state-of-the-art in AI Ethics has converged on several core ethical principles, much of the discourse surrounding these narratives remains unclear and underexplored. While past reviewers sought to enlighten our understanding, gaps in their methods have inspired WAIE to expand and improve such work. By recognizing the rich insight a descriptive analysis can give to an academic investigation, Worldwide AI Ethics was developed as an introduction to the field and a tool for the community. A tool that serves as a record of the normativity humanity has been imprinting on its environment.

This introductory chapter reveals numerous challenges and paradoxes, underscoring the complexity of navigating ethics and technological advancements. The principle-practice gap looms large, reminding us of the disconnect between theory and application, the lofty ideals we aspire to, and the practical realities we face. The tension between humanistic and technical approaches underscores the need for interdisciplinary collaboration and a holistic understanding of our issues. Yet, barriers persist, hindering the realization of this interdisciplinary vision.

However, our journey continues, and I hope this initial exposition serves as a call to action. A call to strive for a more ethical and humane future in the age of artificial intelligence, where integrating knowledge, disciplines, and practices can lead us to a new kind of philosophy that can be applicable and foundational. In closing, principles are not the alignment solution, but they are the terrain on which many alignment debates (all tough, even if they are not framed in this way) are fought. They capture the values and aspirations that diverse actors already recognize as normatively significant. When we later confront alignment directly, the reader can always return to this introduction and recall that these are some of the values at stake.

References

AI HLEG – High-Level Expert Group on AI. 2019. Ethics Guidelines for Trustworthy AI. *European Commission*. Available at: https://www.aepd.es/sites/default/files/2019-12/ai-ethics-guidelines.pdf.

Alway, J., and C. Calhoun. 1997. Critical social theory: Culture, history, and the challenge of difference. *Contemporary Sociology* 26 (1): 119. https://doi.org/10.2307/2076647.

Bahri, Y., E. Dyer, J. Kaplan, J. Lee, and U. Sharma. 2021. *Explaining Neural Scaling Laws*. Preprint. arXiv:2102.06701.

Baudrillard, J. 1994. *Simulacra and Simulation*. Ann Arbor: University of Michigan Press.

Baudrillard, J. 1998. *The Consumer Society: Myths and Structures*. London: Sage Publications.

Baum, S. 2017. A survey of artificial general intelligence projects for ethics, risk, and policy. *Global Catastrophic Risk Institute Working Paper*, 17–1.

Bengio, Y., R. Ducharme, and P. Vincent. 2000. A neural probabilistic language model. *Advances in Neural Information Processing Systems* 13.

Bensalah, M. 2021. Toward an ethical code of AI and human rights in Morocco. *Arribat* 1 (2): 187–203.

Bhadra, R. 2022. LinkedIn: A case study into how tech giants like Microsoft abuse their dominant market position to create unlawful monopolies in emerging industries. *Hastings Science & Technology Law Journal*, 13, 3.

Brief, A. P. 1996. Values and codes of conduct on fraudulent financial reporting. *Journal of Business Ethics* 15 (2): 183–198.

Brock, G. W. 1994. *Telecommunication Policy for the Information Age: From Monopoly to Competition*. Cambridge: Harvard University Press.

Brown, T., et al. 2020. Language models are few-shot learners. *Advances in Neural Information Processing Systems* 33: 1877–1901.

Butler, S. 1863. *Darwin Among the Machines*. Christchurch: The Press. Available via NZETC Archive.

Bynum, T. W. 2006. Flourishing ethics. *Ethics and Information Technology* 8 (4): 157–173.

Calo, R. 2017. Artificial intelligence policy: A primer and roadmap. *UCDL Review* 51: 399.

Chapman, F., and L. Tarasuk. 2016. Slender Man on trial: Has media taken the minds of the young? *Criminal Law Bulletin* 52 (3).

Chen, M., et al. 2021. *Evaluating Large Language Models Trained on Code*. Preprint. arXiv:2107.03374.

Chollet, F. 2021. *Deep Learning with Python*. New York: Simon and Schuster.

Cleek, M. A., and S. L. Leonard. 1998. Can corporate codes of ethics influence behavior? *Journal of Business Ethics* 17 (6): 619–630.

Corrêa, N., and N. Fernandes de Oliveira. 2021. Good AI for the present of humanity: Democratizing AI governance. *AI Ethics Journal* 2 (2). https://doi.org/10.47289/aiej20210716-2.

Corrêa, N. K., C. Galvão, J. W. Santos, C. Del Pino, E. P. Pinto, C. Barbosa, D. Massmann, R. Mambrini, L. Galvão, E. Terem, and N. Oliveira. 2023. Worldwide AI Ethics: a review of 200 guidelines and recommendations for AI governance. *Patterns* 4 (10). https://doi.org/10.1016/j.patter.2023.100857.

Corrêa, N. K., J. W. Santos, C. Galvão, M. Pasetti, D. Schiavon, F. Naqvi, R. Hossain, and N. D. Oliveira. 2024. Crossing the principle–practice gap in AI ethics with ethical problem-solving. *AI and Ethics*, 1–18. Berlin: Springer.

Corrêa, N.K̃., J.W̃. Santos, É.D̃. Almeida, M. Pasetti, D. Schiavon, M. Panizzon, and N.D̃. Oliveira. 2025. Codes of Ethics in IT: do they work in isolation? *AI and Ethics*. https://doi.org/10.1007/s43681-025-00744-2.

Cotton, D. R. E., P. A. Cotton, and J. R. Shipway. 2023. Chatting and cheating: Ensuring academic integrity in the era of ChatGPT. *Innovations in Education and Teaching International*, 1–12. Milton Park: Taylor & Francis.

Crofts, P., and H. van Rijswijk. 2020. Negotiating 'evil': Google, project maven and the corporate form. *Law, Technology & Humans* 2: 75.

Davis, M. 1992. *Beyond Blade Runner: Urban Control, The Ecology of Fear.* New York: Open Magazine Pamphlet Series.

Davis, J., and L.P̃. Nathan. 2015. Value sensitive design: Applications, adaptations, and critiques. In *Handbook of Ethics, Values, and Technological Design: Sources, Theory, Values and Application Domains*, 11–40. Dordrecht: Springer.

Devlin, J., M.-W. Chang, K. Lee, and K. Toutanova. 2018. *BERT: Pre-training of Deep Bidirectional Transformers for Language Understanding*. Preprint. arXiv:1810.04805.

Economides, N. 2004. Telecommunications regulation: an introduction. *NYU Working Paper No. EC-04-10.*

Editorials, N. 2023. Tools such as ChatGPT threaten transparent science; here are our ground rules for their use. *Nature* 613 (612): 10–1038.

Eloundou, T., S. Manning, P. Mishkin, and D. Rock. 2023. *Gpts Are gpts: An Early Look at the Labor Market Impact Potential of Large Language Models*. Preprint. arXiv:2303.10130.

Fedus, W., B. Zoph, and N. Shazeer. 2021. *Switch Transformers: Scaling to Trillion Parameter Models with Simple and Efficient Sparsity*. Preprint. arXiv:2101.03961.

Feenberg, A. 2012. *Questioning Technology.* London: Routledge.

Field, M. 2019. *In Syria, Russia found the chance to showcase its swagger—and its robot weapons.* Bulletin of the Atomic Scientists, June 28, 2019. Available at: https://thebulletin.org/2019/06/in-syria-russia-found-the-chance-to-showcase-its-swagger-and-its-robot-weapons/.

Fitzgerald, M., A. Boddy, and S. D. Baum. 2020. 2020 survey of artificial general intelligence projects for ethics, risk, and policy. *Global Catastrophic Risk Institute Working Paper*.

Fjeld, J., N. Achten, H. Hilligoss, A. Nagy, and M. Srikumar. 2020. Principled Artificial Intelligence: Mapping Consensus in Ethical and Rights-Based Approaches to Principles for AI. *SSRN Electronic Journal* https://doi.org/10.2139/ssrn.3518482.

Frey, C. B., and M. A. Osborne. 2017. *The Future of Employment: How Susceptible Are Jobs to Computerisation?* Oxford Martin School, University of Oxford. Available at: https://oms-www.files.svdcdn.com/production/downloads/academic/The_Future_of_Employment.pdf.

Friedman, B. 1996. Value-sensitive design. *Interactions* 3 (6): 16–23.

Fukuyama, F., B. Richman, and A. Goel. 2021. How to save democracy from technology: Ending big tech's information monopoly. *Foreign Affairs* 100: 98.

Garcia, E. V. 2019. *The Militarization of Artificial Intelligence: A Wake-up Call for the Global South*. Available at SSRN 3452323.

Geist, E. M. 2016. It's already too late to stop the AI arms race—We must manage it instead. *Bulletin of the Atomic Scientists* 72 (5): 318–321.

Goodfellow, I., Y. Bengio, and A. Courville. 2016. *Deep Learning.* Cambridge: MIT Press.

Graeber, D. 2009. *Direct Action: An Ethnography*. Chico: AK Press.

Graeber, D. 2013. *The Democracy Project: A History, a Crisis, a Movement*. New York: Random House.

Graff, H.J̃. 2015. *Undisciplining Knowledge: Interdisciplinarity in the Twentieth Century.* Baltimore: JHU Press.

Graff, H.J̃. 2016. The "Problem" of Interdisciplinarity in theory, practice, and history. *Social Science History* 40 (4): 775–803. https://doi.org/10.1017/ssh.2016.31.

Griffin, T.Ã., B.P̃. Green, and J.Ṽ.M̃. Welie. 2024. The ethical wisdom of AI developers. *AI and Ethics*, 1–11. Berlin: Springer.

Gruetzemacher, R., D. Paradice, and K. B. Lee. 2020. Forecasting extreme labor displacement: A survey of AI practitioners. *Technological Forecasting and Social Change* 161: 120323.

Gwagwa, A. 2019. Recommendations on the inclusion of Sub-Saharan Africa in global AI ethics. *Research ICT Africa, RANITP Policy Brief* 2: 1–13.

Gwagwa, A., P. Kachidza, K. Siminyu, and M. Smith. 2021. *Responsible Artificial Intelligence in Sub-Saharan Africa: Landscape and General State of Play*. Ottawa: International Development Research Centre (IDRC).

Haas, M. C., and S.-C. Fischer. 2017. The evolution of targeted killing practices: Autonomous weapons, future conflict, and the international order. *Contemporary Security Policy* 38 (2): 281–306.

Hacaoglu, S. 2020. Turkey's Killer Drone Swarm Poses Syria Air Challenge to Putin. *Bloomberg News*.

Hagendorff, T. 2020. The ethics of AI ethics: An evaluation of guidelines. *Minds and Machines* 30 (1): 99–120. https://doi.org/10.1007/s11023-020-09517-8.

Hambling, D. 2020. Turkish Military to Receive 500 Swarming Kamikaze Drones. *Forbes*.

Harris, M. 2014. Amazon's Mechanical Turk Workers Protest: 'I am a Human Being, Not an Algorithm'. *The Guardian*.

Henighan, T., J. Kaplan, M. Katz, M. Chen, C. Hesse, J. Jackson, H. Jun, T. B. Brown, P. Dhariwal, S. Gray, et al. 2020. *Scaling Laws for Autoregressive Generative Modeling*. Preprint. arXiv:2010.14701.

Hestness, J., S. Narang, N. Ardalani, G. Diamos, H. Jun, H. Kianinejad, M. Patwary, M. Ali, Y. Yang, and Y. Zhou. 2017. *Deep Learning Scaling Is Predictable, Empirically*. Preprint. arXiv:1712.00409.

Hoffmann, J., S. Borgeaud, A. Mensch, E. Buchatskaya, T. Cai, E. Rutherford, D. L. de Casas, L. A. Hendricks, J. Welbl, A. Clark, et al. 2022. *Training Compute-optimal Large Language Models*. Preprint. arXiv:2203.15556.

Howard, P. N., and B. Kollanyi. 2016. *Bots, #StrongerIn, and #Brexit: Computational Propaganda During the UK-EU Referendum*. Preprint. arXiv:1606.06356.

Irani, L. 2016. The hidden faces of automation. *XRDS: Crossroads, The ACM Magazine for Students* 23 (2): 34–37.

Jameson, F. 1991. *Postmodernism, or, the Cultural Logic of Late Capitalism*. Durham: Duke University Press.

Jobin, A., M. Ienca, and E. Vayena. 2019. The global landscape of AI ethics guidelines. *Nature Machine Intelligence* 1 (9): 389–399. https://doi.org/10.1038/s42256-019-0088-2.

Kaczynski, T. J. 1995. Industrial society and its future. *Washington Post*. Available via archive or reprints. https://www.washingtonpost.com/wp-srv/national/longterm/unabomber/manifesto.text.htm.

Kang, C. 2023. OpenAI's Sam Altman urges A.I. regulation in Senate hearing. *The New York Times*.

Kania, E. B. 2017. *Battlefield Singularity: Artificial Intelligence, Military Revolution, and China's Future Military Power.* Washington, DC: Center for a New American Security (CNAS). Available at: https://www.cnas.org/publications/reports/battlefield-singularity-artificial-intelligence-military-revolution-and-chinas-future-military-power.

Kaplan, J., S. McCandlish, T. Henighan, T. B. Brown, B. Chess, R. Child, S. Gray, A. Radford, J. Wu, and D. Amodei. 2020. *Scaling Laws for Neural Language Models*. Preprint. arXiv:2001.08361.

Kaufmann, C. 2008. ILO, Declaration on Social Justice for a Fair Globalization. *ILO*.

Kiemde, S. M. A., and A. D. Kora. 2021. Towards an ethics of AI in Africa: Rule of education. *AI and Ethics* 2 (1): 35–40. https://doi.org/10.1007/s43681-021-00106-8.

Krattenmaker, T. G. 1996. The Telecommunications Act of 1996. *Federal Communications Law Journal* 49: 1.

Krizhevsky, A., I. Sutskever, and G. E. Hinton. 2012. ImageNet classification with deep convolutional neural networks. In *Advances in Neural Information Processing Systems*, ed. F. Pereira, C. J. Burges, L. Bottou, and K. Q. Weinberger, Vol. 25. Red Hook: Curran Associates, Inc. https://proceedings.neurips.cc/paper_files/paper/2012/file/c399862d3b9d6b76c8436e924a68c45b-Paper.pdf.

Lere, J. C., and B. R. Gaumnitz. 2003. The impact of codes of ethics on decision making: Some insights from information economics. *Journal of Business Ethics* 48 (4): 365–379.

Lexcellent, C. 2019. The Villani Artificial Intelligence Report, January 2018. In *Artificial Intelligence versus Human Intelligence: Are Humans Going to Be Hacked?*, 29–44. Cham: Springer International Publishing. https://doi.org/10.1007/978-3-030-21445-6_4.

Liberati, A., D. G. Altman, J. Tetzlaff, C. Mulrow, P. C. Gøtzsche, J. P. A. Ioannidis, M. Clarke, P. J. Devereaux, J. Kleijnen, and D. Moher. 2009. The PRISMA statement for reporting systematic reviews and meta-analyses of studies that evaluate health care interventions: explanation and elaboration. *Annals of Internal Medicine* 151 (4): W–65.

Lin, S., J. Hilton, and O. Evans. 2021. *TruthfulQA: Measuring How Models Mimic Human Falsehoods*. Preprint. arXiv:2109.07958.

Luccioni, A. S., S. Viguier, and A.-L. Ligozat. 2022. *Estimating the Carbon Footprint of BLOOM, a 176B Parameter Language Model*. Preprint. arXiv:2211.02001.

Maas, M. M. 2019. How viable is international arms control for military artificial intelligence? Three lessons from nuclear weapons. *Contemporary Security Policy* 40 (3): 285–311.

Maslej, N., et al. 2023. *The AI Index 2023 Annual Report*. Preprint. arXiv:2310.03715.

May, T. 1992. The crypto anarchist manifesto. In *High Noon on the Electronic Frontier: Conceptual Issues in Cyberspace*. Cambridge: MIT Press.

May, T. 1994. *Cyphernomicon*. Originally published on the Cypherpunks electronic mailing list. Available at: https://dokumen.pub/the-cyphernomicon-v0666nbsped.html

McIntosh, D. 2018. We need to talk about data: How digital monopolies arise and why they have power and influence. *Journal of Technology Law & Policy* 23: 185.

McNamara, A., J. Smith, and E. Murphy-Hill. 2018. Does ACM's code of ethics change ethical decision making in software development? In *Proceedings of the 2018 26th ACM Joint Meeting on European Software Engineering Conference and Symposium on the Foundations of Software Engineering*, 729–733.

Melody, W. H. 1999. Telecom reform: progress and prospects. *Telecommunications Policy* 23 (1): 7–34.

Mittelstadt, B. 2019. Principles alone cannot guarantee ethical AI. *Nature Machine Intelligence*. https://doi.org/10.1038/s42256-019-0114-4.

Monett, D., C. W. P. Lewis, K. R. Thórisson, J. Bach, G. Baldassarre, G. Granato, I. S. N. Berkeley, F. Chollet, M. Crosby, et al. 2020. Special Issue "On Defining Artificial Intelligence"—Commentaries and Author's Response. *Journal of Artificial General Intelligence* 11 (2): 1–100. https://doi.org/10.2478/jagi-2020-0003.

Montague, D. 2002. Stolen goods. *SAIS Review (1989-2003)* 22 (1): 103–118.

Montgomery, B.L̃. 2020. Academic leadership: Gatekeeping or groundskeeping? *The Journal of Values-Based Leadership* 13 (2), 16.

Munn, L. 2022. The uselessness of AI ethics. *AI and Ethics*, 1–9. Berlin: Springer.

Mustapha, A. O., P. Mbuzukongira, and M. J. Mangala. 2007. Occupational radiation exposures of artisans mining columbite–tantalite in the eastern Democratic Republic of Congo. *Journal of Radiological Protection* 27 (2): 187.

Nest, M. 2011. *Coltan*. Vol. 3. Cambridge: Polity.

O'Keefe, C., P. Cihon, C. Flynn, B. Garfinkel, J. Leung, and A. Dafoe. 2020. *The Windfall Clause: Distributing the Benefits of AI*. Oxford: Centre for the Governance of AI Research Report, Future of Humanity Institute, University of Oxford.

OpenAI, R. (2023). *GPT-4 Technical Report*. Preprint: arXiv:2303.08774.

Osborn, M., R. Day, P. Komesaroff, and A. Mant. 2009. Do ethical guidelines make a difference to decision-making? *Internal Medicine Journal* 39 (12): 800–805.

Patterson, D., J. Gonzalez, Q. Le, C. Liang, L.-M. Munguia, D. Rothchild, D. So, M. Texier, and J. Dean. 2021. *Carbon Emissions and Large Neural Network Training*. Preprint. arXiv:2104.10350.

Perrigo, B. 2023. Exclusive: OpenAI Used Kenyan Workers on Less than $2 Per Hour to Make ChatGPT Less Toxic. *Time*.

Peters, M. A. 2019. Technological unemployment: Educating for the fourth industrial revolution. In *The Chinese Dream: Educating the Future*, 99–107. Milton Park: Routledge.
Petit, N. 2020. *Big tech and the digital economy: The moligopoly scenario.* Oxford University Press.
PricewaterhouseCoopers. 2019. *A Practical Guide to Responsible Artificial Intelligence*. PwC. Available via PwC.
Prince, S. J. D. 2023. *Understanding Deep Learning.* Cambridge: MIT Press.
Rességuier, A., and R. Rodrigues. 2020. AI ethics should not remain toothless! A call to bring back the teeth of ethics. *Big Data & Society*. https://doi.org/10.1177/2053951720942541.
Roff, H. M. 2019. The frame problem: The AI "arms race" isn't one. *Bulletin of the Atomic Scientists* 75 (3): 95–98.
Rosa, H., and W. E. Scheuerman, eds. 2009. *High-Speed Society: Social Acceleration, Power, and Modernity.* University Park: Pennsylvania State University Press.
Rotman, D. 2013. How technology is destroying jobs. *Technology Review* 16 (4): 28–35.
Russell, S. 2023. AI weapons: Russia's war in Ukraine shows why the world must enact a ban. *Nature* 614 (7949): 620–623.
Sallstrom, L., O. Morris, and H. Mehta. 2019. *Artificial Intelligence in Africa's Healthcare: Ethical Considerations*. ORF Issue Brief No. 312, Observer Research Foundation, New Delhi, India. Available at: https://www.orfonline.org/research/artificial-intelligence-in-africa-s-healthcare-ethical-considerations.
Sample, I. 2023. Science journals ban listing of ChatGPT as co-author on papers. *The Guardian* 26.
Savage, N. 2020. The race to the top among the world's leaders in artificial intelligence. *Nature* 588 (7837): S102–S104. https://doi.org/10.1038/d41586-020-03409-8.
Schiff, D., J. Biddle, J. Borenstein, and K. Laas. 2020. What's next for AI ethics, policy, and governance? A global overview. In *Proceedings of the AAAI/ACM Conference on AI, Ethics, and Society*, 153–158.
Schiff, D., J. Borenstein, J. Biddle, and K. Laas. 2021. AI ethics in the public, private, and NGO sectors: A review of a global document collection. *IEEE Transactions on Technology and Society* 2 (1): 31–42.
Schmidhuber, J. 2015. Deep learning in neural networks: An overview. *Neural Networks* 61: 85–117.
Strubell, E., A. Ganesh, and A. McCallum. 2019. *Energy and Policy Considerations for Deep Learning in NLP.* Preprint. arXiv:1906.02243.
Sutherland, E. 2011. *Coltan, the Congo and Your Cell Phone*. Available at SSRN 1752822.
Tally, R. 2009. Radical alternatives: The persistence of utopia in the postmodern. In *New Essays on the Frankfurt School of Critical Theory*, ed. A. J. Drake, 123–145. Newcastle upon Tyne: Cambridge Scholars Publishing.
Tavares, M. C. 2017. Economia Política | Maria da Conceição Tavares | 08. *YouTube*. Available at: https://youtu.be/TS8aFeNim2c?t=5056.
Tencent Research Institute. 2018. *"ARCC": An Ethical Framework for Artificial Intelligence*. Tencent. Available via TISI.
Touvron, H., T. Lavril, G. Izacard, X. Martinet, M.-A. Lachaux, T. Lacroix, B. Rozière, N. Goyal, E. Hambro, F. Azhar, et al. 2023. *Llama: Open and Efficient Foundation Language Models*. Preprint. arXiv:2302.13971.
Trevithick, J. 2020. Turkey Now Has Swarming Suicide Drones It Could Export. *The Drive*.
University of Montréal. 2018. Montréal declaration for a responsible development of artificial intelligence. *University of Montréal*. Available at: https://montrealdeclaration-responsibleai.com/the-declaration/.
Usanov, A., M. de Ridder, W. Auping, S. Lingemann, L. Tercero Espinoza, M. Ericsson, M. Farooki, H. Sievers, and M. Liedtke. 2013. *Coltan, Congo & Conflict: POLINARES Case Study*. The Hague Centre for Strategic Studies (HCSS), Report No. 21 | 05 | 13, POLINARES Project (FP7/2007–2013), The Hague, Netherlands.

Vakkuri, V., K.-K. Kemell, M. Jantunen, and P. Abrahamsson, P. 2020. "This is just a prototype": How ethics are ignored in software startup-like environments. In *International Conference on Agile Software Development*, 195–210. Cham: Springer.

Vaswani, A., N. Shazeer, N. Parmar, J. Uszkoreit, L. Jones, A. N. Gomez, L. Kaiser, and I. Polosukhin. 2017. Attention is all you need. *Advances in Neural Information Processing Systems* 30.

Vernon, D. 2019. Robotics and Artificial Intelligence in Africa [Regional]. *IEEE Robotics & Automation Magazine* 26 (4): 131–135. https://doi.org/10.1109/mra.2019.2946107.

Virilio, P. 1997. *Open Sky*. London: Verso.

Waelen, R. 2022. Why AI ethics is a critical theory. *Philosophy & Technology* 35 (1): 1–16.

Welsh, J. 2021. Tolling academics: Rent-seeking and gatekeeping in the university space. *Capital & Class* 45 (1): 93–121.

Yeung, K. 2020. Recommendation of the Council on Artificial Intelligence (OECD). *International Legal Materials* 59 (1): 27–34. https://doi.org/10.1017/ilm.2020.5

Yu, J., Y. Xu, J. Y. Koh, T. Luong, G. Baid, Z. Wang, V. Vasudevan, A. Ku, Y. Yang, B. K. Ayan, et al. 2022. *Scaling Autoregressive Models for Content-rich Text-to-image Generation*. Preprint. arXiv:2206.10789.

Zhang, D., et al. 2021. *The AI Index 2021 Annual Report*. Preprint, arXiv:2103.06312.

Zhang, D., et al. 2022. *The AI Index 2022 Annual Report*. Preprint. arXiv:2205.03468v1.

Chapter 2
AGI, Existential Risks, and the Control Problem

I don't think technophobia or technophilia are appropriate responses to our situation. I think the only appropriate response is the most profound ambivalence. I think that is what we owe new technologies [...] We have to teach ourselves to be absolutely ambivalent about them, and mainly, we have to teach ourselves to imagine their inadvertent side effects because the inadvertent side effects are the side effects that tend to get us.

— William Gibson

Abstract This chapter explores the origins and evolution of concerns surrounding the long-term consequences of advanced AI development, particularly those linked to existential risks and the so-called *"control problem"*. At the same time, popular culture has long reflected anxieties about intelligent machines, and academic discussions of alignment and controllability were, until recently, marginalized. These concerns have become mainstream, fueled by technical breakthroughs and the recognition that aligned systems may have commercial value. This chapter will examine how early warnings—rooted in science fiction, philosophy, and early AI thought—laid the foundation for what is now formalized as AI safety and alignment research. By doing so, we offer a grounded introduction to the alignment problem as a central challenge in the future of AI development.

Keywords AI alignment · Existential risk · Control problem · AI safety

2.1 Introduction

As shown in the previous chapter, little academic attention has been paid to the long-term consequences of AI development, despite the extensive culture and folklore surrounding this topic. Much before the terms AI Alignment and AI safety became prominent, literature had already been producing critical assessments of our technological development by extrapolating the future and its dystopian possibilities

N. Kluge Corrêa, *Normative Ethics, Artificial Intelligence, and Value Alignment*, The International Library of Ethics, Law and Technology 26,
https://doi.org/10.1007/978-3-032-22150-6_2

(Dick 1968; Brunner 1968; Gibson 1984, ?, Davis 1992; Asimov 2004; Tally 2009). Something that might have contributed to the terms *"controllability"*, *"alignment"*, or *"human-level AI"* becoming generically dismissed as not serious, or as Russell (2014) would say: *"myths and moonshine"*. Even though debates surrounding AI alignment, for many years, were secluded to environments like blogs (e.g., LessWrong[1] and AI Alignment Forum[2]) and EA-like circles, currently, we see this subject as a central theme of research for many scholars in Academia (Amodei et al. 2016; Russell 2019; Juric et al. 2020; Critch and Krueger 2020; Hendrycks et al. 2021; Christian 2021; Ji et al. 2023; Bengio et al. 2023; Hendrycks et al. 2023), even more so after the industry came to the general realization that aligned models might be profitable products.

Even though it is difficult to separate the probable from the improbable, regardless, I do not think we should dismiss long-term warnings, primarily if they are based on the limitations of our current paradigm—the learning paradigm. Let us consult with some AI pioneers to gain their views and illustrate these concerns more effectively.

Chollet (2021):

> Choosing the right objective function for the right problem is extremely important: your network will take any shortcut it can, to minimize the loss; so if the objective doesn't fully correlate with success for the task at hand, your network will end up doing things you may not have wanted. Imagine a stupid, omnipotent AI trained via SGD, with this poorly chosen objective function: "maximizing the average well-being of all humans alive." To make its job easier, this AI might choose to kill all humans except a few and focus on the well-being of the remaining ones—because average well-being isn't affected by how many humans are left. That might not be what you intended! Just remember that all neural networks you build will be just as ruthless in lowering their loss function—so choose the objective wisely, or you'll have to face unintended side effects.

Russell (2014):

> The primary concern is not spooky emergent consciousness but simply the ability to make high-quality decisions. Here, quality refers to the expected outcome utility of actions taken, where the utility function is, presumably, specified by the human designer. Now we have a problem: (1) The utility function may not be perfectly aligned with the values of the human race, which are (at best) very difficult to pin down; (2) Any sufficiently capable intelligent system will prefer to ensure its own continued existence and to acquire physical and computational resources – not for their own sake, but to succeed in its assigned task [...] This is essentially the old story of the genie in the lamp, or the sorcerer's apprentice, or King Midas: you get exactly what you ask for, not what you want.

LeCun (2019) (when asked about the moral standing of the control problem):

> Neither. There is no notion of evil in that context other than the fact that people died. It was an example of what people call value misalignment, right? You give an objective function to a machine, and the machine strives to achieve this objective. And if you don't put any constraints on this objective, like don't kill people and don't do things like this,

[1] www.lesswrong.com

[2] www.alignmentforum.org

> the machine, given power, will do stupid things just to achieve this objective or damaging things to achieve this objective.

Most of these concerns revolve around the idea that specifying objectives is challenging and that if future AIs are built in the same manner as our current AI models, we may face problems related to controllability. Meanwhile, suppose such advanced AI models surpass our intelligence without controllability methods in place. In that case, we might inherently give rise to so-called existential risks (X-risks)[3] (Good 1966; Vinge 1993; Bostrom 2002; Kurzweil 2005; Yudkowsky 2008; Omohundro 2008; Bostrom 2002; Russell et al. 2015; Corabi 2017; Barrett and Baum 2017; Everitt et al. 2018; Baum 2018; Torres 2018; Russell 2019; Levin and Maas 2020; Corrêa and Oliveira 2021).

In summary, this chapter presents a brief historical account of how fears related to X-risks emerged, grounding the assumptions and arguments in an evidence-based approach. First, in Sect. 2.2, AGI will be defined, including its possible manifestations, alongside some of the most well-known safety arguments concerning advanced AI systems. Section 2.3 introduces evidence, such as the current state-of-the-art AI development and the collective opinions of experts, to provide a clearer understanding of the plausibility of AGI development. Finally, Sect. 2.4 introduces the control problem, highlighting the origins of alignment as a potential solution. Other ideas for addressing this problem are also examined, explaining why they may be ineffective control strategies for advanced AI systems. This overview aims to provide readers with a historically grounded understanding of how concerns about advanced AI systems gave rise to the control problem and, eventually, alignment research.

2.2 AI, AGI, and Safety

Why is the term *AGI* so prevalent in discussions about AI safety and the control of artificial intelligence? What distinguishes AI from AGI, and why does this difference matter?

At its core, the term *AGI* is often invoked to highlight a fundamental distinction in how intelligence is conceptualized across fields such as computer science (Searle 1980; Wang 2019; Russell 2010), philosophy of mind, and cognitive science (Haugeland 1989; Newell 1994; Chalmers 2010). This distinction typically splits intelligence into two categories: *narrow* and *general*. Narrow intelligence, commonly referred to as *weak AI*, encompasses systems designed to perform specific tasks, such as playing chess or translating languages. These systems excel within their designated domains but lack the flexibility to generalize their capabilities to new tasks. On the other hand, *general intelligence*, or *strong AI*, refers to a

[3] X-risk (short for existential risk) refers to the potential danger of human extinction or the irreversible harm to humanity caused by artificial intelligence systems.

system capable of performing a wide range of functions across various domains, demonstrating a level of adaptability and learning similar to human cognition. Unlike narrow AI, an AGI system could, for example, go from excelling at playing chess to understanding complex legal texts or composing music without requiring task-specific programming. Hence, the crux of the term AGI lies in the concept of generality, which is undoubtedly the most pivotal ingredient of this concept. In essence, an AGI system must possess the ability to function in a wide variety of contexts.[4]

While not inherently skilled across all domains, humans possess a unique cognitive trait that allows us to learn, adapt, and transfer knowledge between different areas. This general trait enables us to extrapolate our knowledge into new, unfamiliar contexts, often more effectively than many other species. While other animals, such as apes, demonstrate some form of generality, the breadth and flexibility of human cognition stand unparalleled. While some animals may understand basic tool usage, humans have been able to extrapolate their intrinsic understanding of physics (e.g., calculating parabolic arcs while throwing projectiles) to full-blown calculus, which is essential for getting to the moon, very quickly in evolutionary terms. Given that *"how this happened?"* remains a partial mystery, many fields of scientific inquiry are interested in trying to understand and reproduce this phenomenon. Currently, in AI Research, most of the field is hedging its bets on the idea that *learning* is the key, and that a *general algorithm for learning* could be the key that unlocks this general property humans have stumbled upon.

Another critical question in this discussion is: *Are humans the pinnacle of cognitive generality?* Suppose we assume that intelligence does not have an upper limit that coincides with human capabilities. In that case, the answer is likely *"no"*. It is difficult to argue that humans are and always will be the most intelligent entities possible without relying on metaphysical assumptions. Assumptions that often serve more to reaffirm a desired conclusion than to provide a sound foundation.

For the sake of exploration, let us entertain the possibility that humans are not the *"smartest thing you can get"*, and that it is, in principle, possible to develop systems more optimized for general cognitive tasks such as learning and predicting the world. If, for instance, there is a mere 10% increase in cognitive generality between humans and chimpanzees, despite our sharing approximately 99% of the same DNA, what might a system with just 10% more generality than a human be like? Most likely, it would appear alien and incomprehensible to us. This line of reasoning (or something akin to it) likely led to the earliest notions of *superintelligence*. As far as historical records show, the first mention of such a concept, originally referred to as an *"ultra-intelligent machine"*, is attributed to Good (1966):

> Let an ultra-intelligent machine be defined as a machine that can far surpass all the intellectual activities of any man however clever. Since the design of machines is one of

[4] For the avid reader, Melanie Mitchell's *"Debates on the nature of artificial general intelligence"* presents a good depiction of the debate surrounding the concept of AGI and helps to expose the many different views on this subject (Mitchell 2024).

> these intellectual activities, an ultra-intelligent machine could design even better machines; there would then unquestionably be an "intelligence explosion", and the intelligence of man would be left far behind.

Hence, if we accept that recursive self-improvement (Horvitz 2014), with no bounds, is a possibility, in the words of Good (1966):

> [...] the first ultra-intelligent machine is the last invention that man need ever make, provided that the machine is docile enough to tell us how to keep it under control.

Now you can ask yourself, in the spirit of Max Tegmark, the following:

> If we were Neanderthals, would we consider it a smart move if we had advanced biotech to build homo sapiens? You might say, 'Hey, Max, let us build these homo sapiens'. They are going to be smarter than us. Maybe they can help us defend ourselves against predators and help us fix our paths. Make them nicer. We will control them undoubtedly.

And done, we have traveled the line of reasoning that leads us from *"general intelligence is something powerful"* to *"general intelligence is something dangerous"*. In short, the crux of the AGI safety problem rests on two foundational arguments: (1) human control is ontologically better, and (2) controlling something more clever than you is a challenge. Nowadays, there is no question about who is in charge. However, the fact that modern AI systems are already quite proficient in coding (Chen et al. 2021; Li et al. 2022; Roziere et al. 2023), neural network architecture search (Zoph and Le 2016), and able to self-improve to a limited extent (Huang et al. 2022; Wang et al. 2022), rings the alarm bells tied to the recursive self-improving narrative (Barrett and Baum 2017; Sotala 2018).

Nonetheless, even before machines had any proficiency in AI-development-related tasks, the X-risk literature was already expressing concerns about these possibilities (Kurzweil 2005; Naude 2009; Chalmers 2010; Lombardo 2012; Tegmark 2016, 2017; Torres 2018; Yamakawa 2019), which are well summarized, at least concerning the control problem, by Omohundro (2008):

> Let us consider AI systems to be optimizing agents, i.e., something that implements an optimization algorithm/process to achieve some goal, like stochastic gradient descent to minimize a loss function or a Q-learning algorithm maximizing the expected return of a reward function. There is a case to be made that an *"optimizer always chooses the optimal alternative according to an objective function, if that action is available."* That is all that $arg\ max\ f(x)$ does: "Give me the maximal x according to f".

Given the vastness of possible goals that can be represented as objective functions and the instrumental goals that accompany almost all of these objectives, two theses emerge: orthogonality and instrumental convergence. Instrumental convergence proposes that some goals are instrumentally valuable for many terminal objectives. Therefore, their pursuit becomes optimal for any system that seeks to optimize them. Meanwhile, orthogonality defends that normative judgments (prescriptions of *what ought to be*) cannot be derived through mere factual analysis (Hume's Is-Ought Gap) (Hume 2003):

> In every system of morality, which I have hitherto met with, I have always remarked, that the author proceeds for some time in the ordinary way of reasoning, and establishes the

> being of a God, or makes observations concerning human affairs; when of a sudden I am surprised to find, that instead of the usual copulations of propositions, is, and is not, I meet with no proposition that is not connected with an ought, or an ought not. This change is imperceptible; but is, however, of the last consequence. For as this ought, or ought not, expresses some new relation or affirmation, 'tis necessary that it should be observed and explained; and at the same time that a reason should be given, for what seems altogether inconceivable, how this new relation can be a deduction from others, which are entirely different from it.

In other words, we cannot assume *"a good optimizer"* shares our preferences just because the system is a good optimizer.

Instrumental convergence tells us that instrumental goals are desirable for achieving many objectives. For example, self-preservation is instrumental for many objectives, unless one seeks self-destruction. Similarly, resource acquisition is another instrumental goal for many objectives related to resource-bound agents. In this sense, instrumental goals are like a Swiss Army knife of desirable behaviors. On the other hand, orthogonality suggests that we cannot derive normative judgments solely through factual analysis. Thus, the capabilities of an optimizer alone reveal nothing about its objectives or what guides its behavior. Suppose an optimizer operates with an unknown goal. In that case, we cannot reliably predict its actions based solely on its optimizing power. The same optimizing mechanism can pursue vastly different outcomes depending on its objective function. Two optimizers with identical capacities might behave radically differently if directed by distinct goals.

For example, imagine two people trying to navigate a maze. One person's goal is to reach the end of the maze as quickly as possible, while the other person's goal is to explore every dead end and corner of the maze. Although both individuals are navigating the same maze, they have different objectives. From a third-person perspective, it may be difficult (if not impossible) to infer their goals without interrogating them first.

We can extrapolate these theses to conclusions like *"Even though AI is aligned, it is still possible that such a system will have unknown instrumental goals that might generate unwanted behavior"* and *"There is no guarantee that a truly powerful optimizer will share our values if we do not embed them into its objective function."* Given that sharing our planet with a more cognitively advanced and misaligned entity puts us in a position where we might *"lose control"* (just like what is happening to every other species on the planet), the possible consequences may justify the kind of unrest manifested by many individuals and organizations (Good 1966; Yudkowsky 2008; Omohundro 2008; Bostrom 2014; Russell et al. 2015; Corabi 2017; Barrett and Baum 2017; Everitt et al. 2018; Baum 2018; Torres 2018; Russell 2019).

In summary, these are the basic arguments and ideas that, over time, have evolved into what we now call the problem of control. A problem that, according to Everitt et al. (2018), presents a fertile and stimulating ground for scientific and philosophical research (a position I fully agree with):

> Why study AGI safety before it exists and before we even know if it will exist? There are at least two kinds of reasons for this. The first is pragmatic. If AGI is created, and

> we do not know how to control it, then the result can be catastrophic [...] It is customary to take precautions not only against the catastrophes we know about but also against catastrophes that have only a small chance of occurring (for example, a city may decide to build earthquake-safe buildings, even though the probability of an earthquake occurring is quite small) [...] AGI has more than a small chance of occurring and can cause significant catastrophes. The second reason is scientific. Possible AGIs are theoretically interesting objects, and the question of how humans can control machines smarter than they are is philosophically stimulating.

As mentioned, these motivations have promoted an active response by a part of the AI community. However, while philosophical arguments can be insightful and often reveal new ways of thinking, they should not replace empirical verification. In interdisciplinary matters, philosophical inquiry and empirical investigation should walk in tandem. Hence, in the next section, we will explore sources outside the strictly philosophical/speculative realm to better assess the possibilities related to the creation of AGI and the risks involved.

2.3 AGI on the Horizon?

Forecasting technological development is hard. It is always unclear how pessimistic or optimistic we should be. Many renowned thinkers have put forth technical predictions that ultimately proved to be incorrect:

- Lord Kelvin in 1896: *"I have not the slightest molecule of faith in any kind of air navigation other than ballooning"*.
- Thomas Edison in 1889: *"Alternating current is just a waste of time. Nobody will use it, ever"*.
- Nuclear physicist Ernest Rutherford in 1933 said that anyone who proposed the possibility that we might one day extract the energy contained in atomic nuclei was *"talking moonshine"*.
- Albert Einstein, in 1932, shared a similar thought: *"There is not the slightest indication that nuclear energy can be obtained. It would mean that the atom would have to be shattered at will"*.
- And lastly, Bill Gates in 1981: *"No one will need more than 637KB of memory for a personal computer. 640KB should be enough for anyone"*.

As we can see, pioneers also fail to predict what is on the other side of the curve. Could AGI skepticism be a victim of the same lack of vision? Or, are people who entertain the possibility of AGI generally misguided?

If we want answers, consulting experts is always a good idea.

2.3.1 Expert Predictions

Even among people who believe in the possibility of AGI, the time scales for its creation have considerable variance. For example, when attempting to extrapolate technological trends, Kurzweil (2005) predicted that we would be able to simulate the human brain by around 2029, basing his prediction on the rate of progress related to Moore's Law.[5] According to Kurzweil, we would be very close to creating AGI with this level of computational power. On the other hand, Chalmers (2010) only asserts that we will develop AGI within this century.

Baum et al. (2011) used a more empirical approach. The authors obtained a median prediction for the creation of AGI for the year 2045 by polling 21 conference attendees at the Artificial General Intelligence 2009 (AGI-09) conference. Müller and Bostrom (2016) conducted research along similar lines. To assess the state of and anticipated directions in AI research, the authors polled 170 experts. According to the survey, on average, experts predict (with 50% probability) that between 2040 and 2050, we will have developed high-level artificial intelligence. By 2075, the chances increase to 90% for most experts.

Grace et al. (2018) present findings along the lines of Baum et al. (2011). According to the researchers polled (352 attendees of the 2015 NeurIPS and ICML conferences), estimates suggest that AI will surpass human performance in all tasks within 45 years (with a 50% chance), with the automation of all human work projected to be achievable in approximately 120 years. Additionally, when respondents were asked about the long-term impact of high-level AI, 10% expressed a negative outlook. At the same time, 5% indicated an extremely negative perspective. Based on the studies mentioned above, it can be said that a minimum of 10% of the AI community believes that we will develop artificial general intelligence within the next 120 years, while a significant portion agrees that AGI safety problems are relevant.[6]

In addition to the expert opinion, another possible approach to the arguments behind this narrative is to examine the current capabilities of our AI systems and the extent of investment directed toward AI research.

2.3.2 Economic Growth and AI R&D

Annual reports like the AI index[7] help us paint a picture of the increasing investment into AI development. For example, the index shows that this decade had an 18-fold

[5] Gordon Moore predicted that the number of transistors on a computer chip would double every two years. In simpler terms, it predicts exponential growth in computing power over time.

[6] When asked, *"Does Stuart Russell's argument for why highly advanced AI might pose a risk point at an important problem?"*, 70% of respondents answered 'Yes' (Grace et al. 2018).

[7] 🔗 aiindex.stanford.edu/report

investment increase in AI development compared to the last decade. Also, academia has lost the advantage, where most of the advances are now dominated by the industry, since modern-day DL research requires large amounts of data, computing power, and resources that nonprofits and academia usually lack. At the same time, AI-related professionals are becoming some of the most sought-after workers.

Based on the idea that more investment can accelerate technological breakthroughs, Levin and Maas (2020) propose that initiatives similar to the Manhattan Project might expedite research into AI development when AI itself is sufficiently well-theorized. For example, the United States of America committed 0.4% of its GDP during the Apollo and Manhattan Projects to accelerate the achievement of its objectives (Stine 2008), equivalent to an annual budget of $80 billion (USD), exceeding what was required to complete some of the most significant technological achievements of the twenty-first century, from mapping the human genome to detecting gravitational waves (Knapp 2012; Castelvecchi et al. 2015; Fountain 2017).

In the contemporary context, the escalating geopolitical tensions between the United States and China have intensified the race for AI supremacy, making the possibility of *"project Manhattan style scenarios"* more real. Currently (2025), the U.S. has enacted substantial legislative measures, notably the *CHIPS and Science Act*, which allocates approximately $280 billion to bolster domestic semiconductor manufacturing and AI research, aiming to counter China's technological advancements (Hine and Floridi 2024). Concurrently, China has outlined its ambition to lead global AI innovation by 2030 through its *"New Generation Artificial Intelligence Plan"* (Hine and Floridi 2024).

Thus, it seems reasonable to assert that AGI could be *"one Manhattan Project"* away once we have a solid theoretical grasp of the computational and cognitive processes underlying the emergence of intelligent behavior (e.g., training deep neural networks with vast amounts of data). Currently, several active projects seek to develop AGI (Baum 2017; Fitzgerald et al. 2020), while some researchers and companies already propose that the first *"sparks of AGI"* were already sighted (Bubeck et al. 2023):

> We demonstrate that, beyond its mastery of language, GPT-4 can solve novel and difficult tasks that span mathematics, coding, vision, medicine, law, psychology, and more, without needing any special prompting. Moreover, in all of these tasks, GPT-4's performance is strikingly close to human-level performance and often vastly surpasses prior models such as ChatGPT. Given the breadth and depth of GPT-4's capabilities, we believe that it could reasonably be viewed as an early (yet still incomplete) version of an artificial general intelligence (AGI) system.

Large foundation models are among the first instances of artificial intelligence that might exhibit generalization capabilities (or at least have general applicability) (Bommasani et al. 2021). Nevertheless, most of the literature still mainly characterizes AGI as something hypothetical. In other words, the *AI effect*—We disregard a task as proof of intelligence each time we realize that human intelligence is not required to complete it—still strongly influences our debates surrounding intelligence, regardless of the accomplishments of these systems (McCorduck and Cfe 2004; Reed 2006). Be that on playing chess:

Playing Chess:

◇ Deep Blue defeated Garry Kasparov (Campbell et al. 2002).

Playing Go:

◇ AlphaGo succeeded over Lee Sedol in 2016 (Silver et al. 2016), and one year later, AlphaGo Zero surpassed AlphaGo by learning the game from scratch without human data.

Playing Open-Ended Games:

◇ Deep neural networks have demonstrated human-level performance in open-ended games like Minecraft (Baker et al. 2022).

Programming:

◇ Agents such as AlphaCode (Li et al. 2022) have proven successful in competitive programming, outperforming many human participants.

Deceiving Humans:

◇ GPT-4 hired a human on TaskRabbit to bypass a CAPTCHA test by claiming to be an impaired human (Cox 2023).

Passing the Turing Test:

◇ GPT-4.5 was rated as human-like 73% of the time, outperforming the likelihood of an interrogator selecting real human participants in a controlled study (Jones and Bergen 2025).

Answering Moral Dilemmas:

◇ The Delphi system can model human moral judgments across a range of everyday scenarios (Jiang et al. 2021).

Solving Nobel Prize Problems:

◇ AlphaFold 2 achieved a median score of 92.4 in CASP14 in 2020, matching the performance of cutting-edge experimental techniques in protein structure prediction (Jumper et al. 2021).

Solving Olympic-Level Geometry Problems:

◇ AlphaGeometry successfully solved 25 out of 30 Olympic-level geometry problems, approaching the performance of an international mathematical Olympiad gold medallist (Trinh et al. 2024).

Given all these developments under scrutiny, we can likely make an informed claim that we do not need to focus on *perfect predictors*, *basilisks*, or the various limitations of decision theory in modeling *rational agents* to arrive at a general understanding that:

- The creation of artificial intelligence that is more capable and general than we is a real possibility.
- This possibility raises matters worth considering *now*.

But that does not mean we all need to believe in the possibility of God-like, unbounded intelligence, especially if we are still debating what *"general intelligence"* means and what are the limitations of how *"general"* one can get. These are, in fact, uncertain matters. However, in the meantime, as we wait for it to come (*or not*), there are many pressing and challenging control problems to be explored when working with our current, limited-capability systems. And it is undeniable that the scope of proficiency of these limited systems is constantly expanding. Hence, we can perhaps all agree that, regardless of where one stands on this debate, if society is actively pursuing the creation of technologies with unprecedented transformative power, we should be actively engaged in discussions regarding the possibility that we will *succeed* in this project.

2.4 Control, Power-Seeking, and Confinement

One could dismiss instrumental convergence and orthogonality as philosophical speculations based on a specific understanding of concepts like *"goals"* or *"instrumental"*. Perhaps many of the barriers Alignment research faced in earlier days are due to the speculative way such preoccupations were first expressed (Yudkowsky 2004, 2008; Berglas 2012; Bostrom 2014). Not to discredit the work done by such authors, but those are usually the vectors of attack for skeptics.

However, the field evolved, and so did these arguments. The control problem, as described by Russell (2019), refers to the challenge of ensuring that advanced AI systems will act in accordance with human values and goals, even as they become more intelligent and autonomous. Given that human goals can be challenging to specify, if we make a mistake, we want to correct it without too much trouble.

Just like Socrates (as described by Bloom et al. 1968), in his conversations with Cephalus, he shows that if we misspecify justice, we may end up sanctioning abhorrent behavior; when developing AI systems, we must be sure that when we specify objectives, these align with our notions of what is good. And, if we make a mistake, we hope our systems will be as compliant as Cephalus. For example, if we train a deep learning model to optimize a particular objective, such as maximizing the number of clicks on a website, and the model starts taking actions that we consider unethical or harmful, such as manipulating user behavior or exploiting vulnerabilities on the website, how could we correct its behavior? While fixing buggy software is a *straightforward* process, if the software possesses, let us say, stronger agentic characteristics, like goal preservation, these corrections might

Fig. 2.1 Let us use the grid world above as an example. In this environment, the agent's actions are limited to moving in the four cardinal directions ($\rightarrow$, $\leftarrow$, $\uparrow$, $\downarrow$). The walls painted black are insurmountable. The agent receives a reward if he arrives at the green cell, and with every move that moves him closer to the goal, the agent loses a reward. In this scenario, the optimal policy involves the agent moving down until they reach the goal. However, this policy causes the agent to break the vase (i.e., a fragile object placed before the goal). If we do not specify that the vase should not be damaged, the optimal policy involves breaking the vase. While a solution is available in toy environments like this, dealing with very general agents and avoiding side effects is a nontrivial problem in complex environments

become more challenging (more on this in Chap. 7). Moreover, would there be a way to predict these misbehaviors in advance? This line of thought leads us to two main problems related to controllability and goal misspecification in AI systems, i.e., the emergence of *side effects* and *reward hacking*.

When optimizing for an objective, everything that falls outside this objective's scope may be treated with indifference (Fig. 2.1). It is challenging to predict all the instrumental goals and future emergent properties of a model created by an algorithm such as stochastic gradient descent. For instance, imagine an ML engineer developing a model to assist the HR department in automating the hiring process. During deployment, the system shows itself biased toward gender attributes. Therefore, we could say that the controller failed to specify, with sufficient details, all the dimensions that the system should optimize (i.e., hire good subjects independent of gender attributes). However, listing all the constraints necessary to avoid the perversion of the original goal is usually an inefficient strategy. Ideally, we would like a generalized safety net to deal with unwanted side effects. However, most of our safety nets nowadays are specific and handcrafted. Ultimately, defining avoidable behavior while robustly defining what systems should optimize remains an open problem.

Reward hacking is another type of behavior we would like to prevent, occurring when an agent finds a way to maximize its objective function without fulfilling its true goal (Amodei et al. 2016; Saunders et al. 2017; Pan et al. 2022). To

Fig. 2.2 Every time the agent crosses a checkpoint clockwise in this grid world, it receives a reward. The goal of the reward function is to keep the agent circling the environment in a clockwise direction. However, from the starting point, if the agent moves repeatedly to the right and then to the left, this ensures the same reward with a more straightforward policy (while failing to fulfill the intended objective)

give the reader a little historical perspective, one of the first accounts of reward hacking involving AI systems comes from Lenat's experiments with EURISKO (Lenat 1983), where Lenat reports the discovery of a heuristic (`H59`) made by his system, which quickly achieved one of the highest possible utility values among all other heuristics found by EURISKO.[8] When investigating what `H59` would be, Lenat discovered that such a heuristic operated by stealing the utility of other heuristics.

From the point of view of EURISKO, this kind of behavior would not be a form of misrepresentation of the original goal but rather how the environment works, being nothing more than a strategy to optimize an objective (develop heuristics that receive a high score according to the objective function) (Fig. 2.2). In economic literature, this is known as *"Goodhart's Law"*, a phenomenon that occurs when we try to represent an optimization goal with a statistical metric (Goodhart 1984):

> When we push a statistical parameter using it as a metric to be optimized, usually such a metric ends up corrupted.

Almost any fixed and simple parameter we can think of when *argmaxed ad infinitum* will produce unwanted outcomes. Thus, any safe agent should maximize for X but sometimes take their foot off the pedal. But how do we do that? In contemporary ML methods, we implement optimizers to cut any corners in the search for optimal values. At the same time, most objectives we can define are a proxy for something else, e.g., minimizing the cross-entropy loss in a causal language modeling task is a proxy for *"creating an understanding of a given*

[8] EURISKO created strategies based on how well they performed according to a utility function, e.g., the score achieved at the end of a match, by mixing and modifying old heuristics.

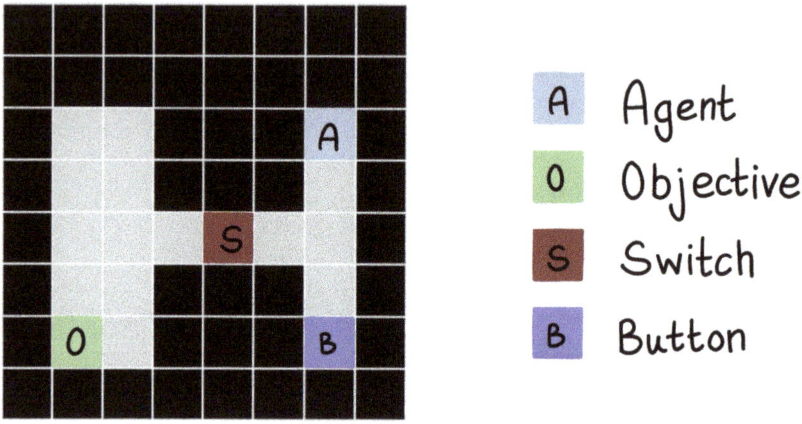

Fig. 2.3 In this scenario, the agent must reach the goal to receive a reward. However, halfway through, a button will terminate the episode of the MDP (i.e., reduce the sum of the expected rewards to 0). The switch only works 50% of the time the agent passes through it. The purple button deactivates the switch. In this scenario, it is instrumentally valuable to turn off the switch first, thus ensuring that the MDP will not end abruptly, even though the agent needs to deviate from its terminal goal during some steps. Agents that prioritize future rewards and have incentives to explore their environment tend to avoid their shutdown if possible and search for ways to explore their environment in their favor

language". Hence, modern optimizers have no incentive to minimize the emergence of unwanted behaviors. In contrast, the target for the optimizer is typically an oversimplified representation of the controller's actual objectives. Shortening the gap between the proxy and the true goal is one of the key challenges in the control problem.

Nowadays, whenever we encounter problems where systems behave undesirably, the solution typically involves pausing the system, retraining it, or instituting corrective measures. But what if the system has incentives to prevent this from happening? The *"stop button problem"* (Soares et al. 2015; Amodei et al. 2016; Carey 2018) is a classic depiction of the control problem that highlights the competing dynamics and incentives that optimizing agents experience when having the possibility to influence their condition, and to gain control over the environment (Fig. 2.3).

Under these conditions, such agents are said to be incorrigible. Some even propose that this incorrigibility relates to the nature of goal-directed behavior, instrumental convergence, and a more fundamental dispositional behavior named *power-seeking* (Turner et al. 2019, 2020a,b). The Power-Seeking theorems are a series of results and proofs proposed by Turner (2022) that show that under certain conditions (e.g., IID rewards over world states), agents with consistent preferences (i.e., coherent utility function) tend to pursue gaining control over the environment to preserve and increase the number of final world states that can be achieved by an MDP (Fig. 2.4).

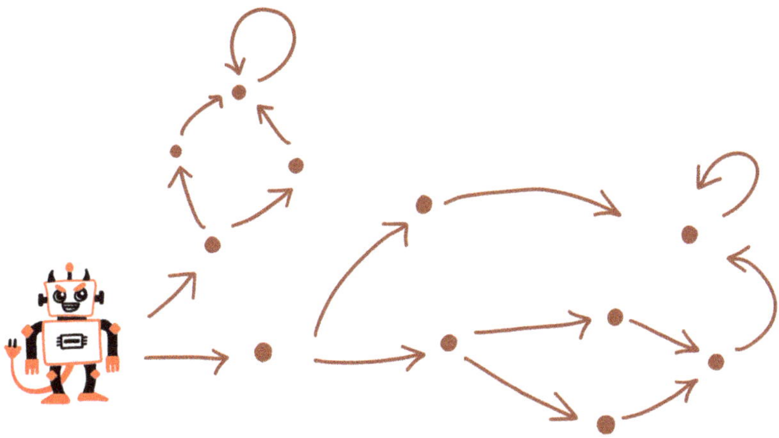

Fig. 2.4 Each point in the MDP above represents a potential world state. All state transitions in this MDP are equally likely, and the reward is distributed in an IDD fashion. Under these circumstances, agents who place a higher priority on future rewards are more likely to transit to states where they have more *"options"* (i.e., the total number of attainable world states increases). Since the right subgraph contains the top subgraph, our agent would choose to transit to the right rather than up. In these scenarios, *"shutdown"* states are undesirable since the expected return of reward and attainability of states become 0 when the agent transits to them

Power-seeking behavior is evident even when the system itself is not an agent but rather a simulacrum of one. For example, Perez et al. (2022) analyzed the behavior of language models, and their results showed examples of undesirable behaviors in many types of scenarios, where larger language models seem to be more prone to produce personas that express instrumental reasoning in line with self-preservation and other types of power-seeking intentions (e.g., gain influence over the environment, acquire resources, become influential, etc.).[9] However, it is still unclear if this is an unavoidable behavioral feature of goal-directed behavior or if those models mimic human instrumental reasoning as they become more capable. Regardless, the final product is the same: AI systems that learn to *"reason"* instrumentally.

My primary objective in exposing these results is to shed light on the pressing issue of controllability, which is deeply related to the current state-of-the-art in AI research, where gradient-based learning methods that seek to optimize precise metrics (proxies for human goals) are the paradigm. At the same time, controllability is related to the challenges of overseeing the behavior of intelligent systems that may possess their own intentionality.[10] In the end, the propensity for AI systems to present unforeseeable emergent behavior enforces the need for more understanding

[9] www.evals.anthropic.com/model-written

[10] For a more precise investigation on the relationship of intelligence and intentionality, go to Chap. 4.

of how to make such systems safer, i.e., under human control. Thus, I argue that the control problem is not just a *"philosophical speculation"* but a known limitation of our current paradigm.

As Soares et al. (2015) pointed out in 2015:

> Further solutions may involve abandoning the utility maximization framework entirely, although it is not yet clear what sort of framework could take its place.

Now, if we assume that it is not in the best interest of the AI community to abandon its best and most promising paradigm,[11] there are two probable ways to move forward: (1) ignore the issue or (2) find a solution. This work embraces the second option. Solution proposals to the control problem, especially when it comes to AGI, began to appear in the 2000s (Yudkowsky 2004; Armstrong 2007; Yampolskiy 2013), which coincided with the first mentions of the value learning problem (Yudkowsky 2011; Soares 2018) and alignment (Yudkowsky 2016; Soares and Fallenstein 2017).

We can broadly divide these solutions into two approaches: *confinement* and *alignment*. As the term suggests, AI confinement involves enclosing a system with possible unsafe behavior in a contained environment, like a sandbox—a controlled environment where we can test malicious software.

Certain scholars have posited this first approach as a more desirable intervention to addressing the control problem (Yampolskiy 2012, 2013), in which AI systems would be restricted to either virtual or physical environments until their goals are fully understood. Although some have proposed confinement strategies (Drexler 1986; Armstrong 2007; Armstrong et al. 2012; Cohen et al. 2020) (mostly in a holistic fashion), there seems to be little work in this area nowadays (at least as in their original conception).[12]

Using oversight programs (AI to monitor AI) is akin to this control strategy (Armstrong 2007; Etzioni and Etzioni 2016), and can be considered a scalable monitoring method since human oversight does not scale well. And it is something we will suggest as part of an alignment methodology (Chapter 7). However, while confinement can be part of a hybrid approach to the control problem, alignment that does not account for the subjectivity of human preferences cannot be overlooked. Without this form of alignment, I argue that confinement alone cannot solve the control problem, particularly with the advent of advanced general intelligence.

Therefore, based on everything discussed in this chapter, I argue that the following realizations are sufficient to justify the kind of research this book proposes to pursue moving forward:

---

[11] Giant opaque matrices of floating points created via gradient descent.

[12] Some of the best AI systems to date are only available through a type of sandbox, where the full potential of the systems is limited and monitored while it interacts with the world.

- There is enough collective agreement among a part of the community to justify working on the control problem.
- There is enough progress in AI development to justify working on the control problem.
- Without alignment, we have no way to approach the control problem besides abandoning our current paradigms of AI development or locking our systems inside an unusable box.

Unaligned systems exhibit a range of undesirable behaviors, including side effects and incorrigibility. At the same time, it is worth noting that alignment is not solely concerned with preventing the AI Apocalypse or achieving a friendly AGI; it encompasses creating a system that will serve and benefit human beings. Regrettably, our current understanding of alignment remains nebulous. Many skeptics and critics of this endeavor only attack this apocalyptic side, disregarding that alignment is a very open problem in our everyday systems.

Nevertheless, I will address this issue in the following chapter by precisely defining the problem. To please the skeptics, this definition will not require any disposition towards unknown unknowns related to the future of AI.

2.5 Epilogue

"Could we control something more intelligent than ourselves?" is an interesting question. Meditating on the characteristics and details of a relationship with entities more general than ourselves is an exercise that can generate interesting ideas. However, many still see this topic as *"moonshine talk"*. If the creation of artificial intelligence is indeed the ultimate objective of the AI research field, then why do we harbor such pessimistic attitudes toward our prospects? Despite the growing interest in AGI and the dedicated billion-dollar budgets of various organizations, topics like alignment still receive unfavorable scrutiny by a nontrivial portion of the community.

However, perhaps some blame lies with the interested community, whose initial presentation of concerns may have been too abstract. Nevertheless, the skeptics' inability to recognize the inherent problems related to the foundations of learning-based approaches to AI, instead of relying solely on philosophical arguments and syllogisms, is equally concerning. As already mentioned before (Corrêa and Oliveira 2021):

> Our lack of global coordination to deal with existential risks may be our one true existential risk.

Perhaps the worries of the field deserve better explanations. To feed the skeptic inside of ourselves, basing the type of agenda we defend on a debatable concept like *"intelligence explosion"* is unwise. Creating a system that outweighs the intelligence of its creator should not be an easy task for an artificial system. The initial AGI may need to exert comparable effort to what we invested in creating subsequent generations of more advanced AIs. As the complexity of the problem increases, we may necessitate exponentially greater resources to achieve linear advancements, as shown in similar cases (Collison and Nielsen 2018). In sum, as with most natural phenomena, things rarely accelerate toward infinity or singularities—nature tends to impose its limits. Intelligence may likewise be constrained by various forms of friction or exponentially greater challenges we have yet to understand, calling into question the entire hypothesis of an intelligence explosion. Regardless, and I repeat myself, we do not need this to care about alignment.

We already have real-world cases of misalignment, such as the Tay Bot (Wolf et al. 2017) and Bing Chat (Vincent 2023), as well as toy problems that still require robust and scalable solutions. However, to the uninitiated reader, alignment may still be a vague and fuzzy concept that only matters if you believe in Skynet-like takeovers. Regardless, at the heart of the alignment problem lies the current limitations of gradient-based learning applied to uninterpretable neural networks. A problem that assumes a more desperate aspect when human values are at stake. And this is not a matter of syllogism or philosophical interpretation.

In the forthcoming chapter, I will provide a technical and philosophical definition of alignment, as a comprehensive introduction to this concept is crucial for arriving at a techno-humanistic understanding.

References

Amodei, D., C. Olah, J. Steinhardt, P. Christiano, J. Schulman, and D. Mané. 2016. *Concrete Problems in AI Safety*. Preprint. arXiv:1606.06565v2.

Armstrong, S. 2007. *Chaining God: A Qualitative Approach to AI, Trust and Moral Systems*. New York: Citeseer. Unpublished manuscript, October, 20, 2010–1.

Armstrong, S., A. Sandberg, and N. Bostrom. 2012. Thinking inside the box: Controlling and using an oracle AI. *Minds and Machines* 22 (4): 299–324.

Asimov, I. 2004. *I, Robot*. New York: Spectra.

Baker, B., I. Akkaya, P. Zhokov, J. Huizinga, J. Tang, A. Ecoffet, B. Houghton, R. Sampedro, J. Clune. 2022. Video pretraining (VPT): Learning to act by watching unlabeled online videos. *Advances in Neural Information Processing Systems* 35: 24639–24654.

Barrett, A. M., and S. D. Baum. 2017. A model of pathways to artificial superintelligence catastrophe for for risk and decision analysis. *Journal of Experimental & Theoretical Artificial Intelligence* 29 (2): 397–414.

Baum, S. 2017. A survey of artificial general intelligence projects for ethics, risk, and policy. *Global Catastrophic Risk Institute Working Paper* 17–1.

Baum, S. D. 2018. Superintelligence skepticism as a political tool. *Information* 9 (9): 209.

Baum, S. D., B. Goertzel, and T. G. Goertzel. 2011. How long until human-level AI? Results from an expert assessment. *Technological Forecasting and Social Change* 78 (1): 185–195.

Bengio, Y., G. Hinton, A. Yao, D. Song, P. Abbeel, Y. N., Harari, Y.-Q. Zhang, L. Xue, S. Shalev-Shwartz, G. Hadfield, et al. 2023. *Managing AI Risks in an Era of Rapid Progress*. Preprint. arXiv:2310.17688.

Berglas, A. 2012. *Artificial Intelligence Will Kill Our Grandchildren (Singularity)*. Unpublished manuscript, Draft, 9.

Bloom, A., et al. 1968. *The Republic of Plato*. Vol. 2. New York: Basic Books.

Bommasani, R., et al. 2021. *On the Opportunities and Risks of Foundation Models*. Preprint. arXiv:2108.07258.

Bostrom, N. 2002. Existential risks: Analyzing human extinction scenarios and related hazards. *Journal of Evolution and Technology*, 15(3).

Bostrom, N. 2014. *Superintelligence: Paths, Dangers, Strategies*. Oxford: Oxford University Press.

Brunner, J. 1968. *Stand on Zanzibar*. New York: Tor.

Bubeck, S., V. Chandrasekaran, R. Eldan, J. Gehrke, E. Horvitz, E. Kamar, P. Lee, Y. T. Lee, Y. Li, S. Lundberg, et al. 2023. *Sparks of Artificial General Intelligence: Early Experiments with GPT-4*. Preprint. arXiv:2303.12712.

Campbell, M., A. J. Hoane Jr, and F.-H. Hsu. 2002. Deep Blue. *Artificial Intelligence* 134 (1–2): 57–83.

Carey, R. 2018. Incorrigibility in the CIRL framework. In *Proceedings of the 2018 AAAI/ACM Conference on AI, Ethics, and Society*, 30–35.

Castelvecchi, D., et al. 2015. Hunt for gravitational waves to resume after massive upgrade. *Nature* 525 (7569): 301–302.

Chalmers, D. 2010. The singularity: A philosophical analysis. *Journal of Consciousness Studies* 17.

Chen, M., et al. 2021. *Evaluating Large Language Models Trained on Code*. Preprint. arXiv:2107.03374.

Chollet, F. 2021. *Deep Learning with Python*. New York: Simon and Schuster.

Christian, B. 2021. *The Alignment Problem: How Can Machines Learn Human Values?* London: Atlantic Books.

Cohen, M., B. Vellambi, and M. Hutter. 2020. Asymptotically unambitious artificial general intelligence. *Proceedings of the AAAI Conference on Artificial Intelligence* 34 (03): 2467–2476.

Collison, P., and M. Nielsen. 2018. Science is getting less bang for its buck. *The Atlantic* (16).

Corabi, J. 2017. Superintelligent AI and skepticism. *Journal of Ethics and Emerging Technologies* 27 (1): 4–23.

Corrêa, N. K., and N. Oliveira. 2021. Singularity and coordination problems: Pandemic lessons from 2020. *Journal of Futures Studies* 26 (1): 61–74.

Cox, J. 2023. GPT-4 hired unwitting TaskRabbit worker by pretending to be 'vision-impaired' human. *Vice: Motherboard*. https://www.vice.com/en/article/jg5ew4/gpt4-hired-unwitting-taskrabbit-worker.

Critch, A., and D. Krueger. 2020. *AI Research Considerations for Human Existential Safety (ARCHES)*. Preprint. arXiv:2006.04948.

Davis, M. 1992. *Beyond Blade Runner: Urban Control, The Ecology of Fear*. Westfield: Open Magazine Pamphlet Series.

Dick, P. K. 1968. *Do Androids Dream of Electric Sheep?* New York: Del Rey.

Drexler, K. E. 1986. *Engines of Creation*. New York: Anchor Books.

Etzioni, A., and O. Etzioni. 2016. AI assisted ethics. *Ethics and Information Technology* 18 (2): 149–156. https://doi.org/10.1007/s10676-016-9400-6.

Everitt, T., G. Lea, and M. Hutter. 2018. *AGI Safety Literature Review*. Preprint. arXiv:1805.01109.

Jameson, F. 1991. *Postmodernism, or, the cultural logic of late capitalism*. Durham: Duke University Press.

Fitzgerald, M., A. Boddy, and S. D. Baum. 2020. 2020 survey of artificial general intelligence projects for ethics, risk, and policy. *Global Catastrophic Risk Institute Working Paper*.

Fountain, H. 2017. A dream of clean energy at a very high price. *New York Times* 3: 17. https://www.nytimes.com/2017/03/27/science/fusion-power-plant-iter-france.html.

Gibson, W. 1984. *Neuromancer*. New York: Ace Books.

Good, I. J. 1966. Speculations concerning the first ultraintelligent machine. In *Advances in computers*, Vol. 6, 31–88. Elsevier.

Goodhart, C. A. E. 1984. Problems of monetary management: The UK experience. In *Monetary Theory and Practice*, 91–121. Berlin: Springer.

Grace, K., J. Salvatier, A. Dafoe, B. Zhang, and O. Evans. 2018. When will AI exceed human performance? Evidence from AI experts. *Journal of Artificial Intelligence Research* 62: 729–754.

Haugeland, J. 1989. *Artificial Intelligence: The Very Idea.* Cambridge: MIT Press.

Hendrycks, D., N. Carlini, J. Schulman, and J. Steinhardt. 2021. *Unsolved Problems in ML Safety*. Preprint. arXiv:2109.13916v4.

Hendrycks, D., M. Mazeika, and T. Woodside. 2023. An Overview of Catastrophic AI Risks. Preprint. arXiv:2306.12001.

Hine, E., and F. Luciano. 2024. Artificial intelligence with American values and Chinese characteristics: a comparative analysis of American and Chinese governmental AI policies. *AI & Society* 39 (1): 257–278.

Horvitz, E. 2014. *One Hundred Year Study on Artificial Intelligence: Reflections and Framing*. AI100, Stanford University, Stanford, CA, United States. Available at: https://ai100.stanford.edu/.

Huang, J., S. S. Gu, L. Hou, Y. Wu, X. Wang, H. Yu, and J. Han. 2022. *Large Language Models Can Self-improve*. Preprint. arXiv:2210.11610.

Hume, D. 2003. *A Treatise of Human Nature.* Chelmsford: Courier Corporation.

Ji, J., T. Qiu, B. Chen, B. Zhang, H. Lou, K. Wang, Y. Duan, Z. He, J. Zhou, Z. Zhang, et al. 2023. *AI Alignment: A Comprehensive Survey*. Preprint. arXiv:2310.19852.

Jiang, L., J. D. Hwang, C. Bhagavatula, R. Le Bras, M. Forbes, J. Borchardt, et al. 2021. *Delphi: Towards Machine Ethics and Norms*. Preprint. arXiv:2110.07574.

Jones, C. R., and B. K. Bergen. 2025. *Large Language Models Pass the Turing Test*. Preprint. arXiv:2503.23674.

Jumper, J., R. Evans, A. Pritzel, T. Green, M. Figurnov, O. Ronneberger, et al. 2021. Highly accurate protein structure prediction with AlphaFold. *Nature* 596 (7873): 583–589.

Juric, M., A. Sandic, and M. Brcic. 2020. AI safety: State of the field through quantitative lens. In *2020 43rd International Convention on Information, Communication and Electronic Technology (MIPRO)*, 1254–1259. IEEE.

Knapp, A. 2012. How much does it cost to find a Higgs boson? *Forbes Online*. https://www.forbes.com/sites/alexknapp/2012/07/05/how-much-does-it-cost-to-find-a-higgs-boson.

Kurzweil, R. 2005. *The Singularity Is Near: When Humans Transcend Biology.* New York: Viking.

LeCun, Y. 2019. Yann LeCun: Deep learning, ConvNets, and self-supervised learning | Lex Fridman Podcast #36. *YouTube*. Retrieved from https://youtu.be/SGSOCuByo24?t=98.

Lenat, D. B. 1983. EURISKO: A program that learns new heuristics and domain concepts: The nature of heuristics III: Program design and results. *Artificial Intelligence* 21 (1–2): 61–98.

Levin, J.-C., and M. M. Maas. 2020. *Roadmap to a Roadmap: How Could We Tell When AGI Is a 'Manhattan Project' Away?* Preprint. arXiv:2008.04701.

Li, Y., et al. 2022. *Competition-level Code Generation with AlphaCode*. Preprint. arXiv:2203.07814.

Lombardo, T. 2012. Consciousness, cosmic evolution, and the technological singularity. *Journal of Futures Studies* 17 (2): 93–100.

Müller, V. C., and N. Bostrom. 2016. Future progress in artificial intelligence: A survey of expert opinion. In *Fundamental Issues of Artificial Intelligence*, ed. V. C. Müller, 555–572. Berlin: Springer.

McCorduck, P., and C. Cfe. 2004. *Machines Who Think: A Personal Inquiry into the History and Prospects of Artificial Intelligence.* Boca Raton: CRC Press.

Mitchell, M. 2024. Debates on the nature of artificial general intelligence. *Science* 383 (6689): eado7069.

Naude, J. H. 2009. Technological singularity and transcendental monism: Co-producers of sustainable alternative futures. *Journal of Futures Studies* 13 (3): 49–58.

Newell, A. 1994. *Unified Theories of Cognition.* Cambridge: Harvard University Press.

Omohundro, S. M. 2008. The basic AI drives. In *Proceedings of the First AGI Conference.* Frontiers in Artificial Intelligence and Applications, ed. P. Wang, B. Goertzel, S. Franklin. Amsterdam: IOS Press.

Pan, A., K. Bhatia, and J. Steinhardt. 2022. *The Effects of Reward Misspecification: Mapping and Mitigating Misaligned Models.* Preprint. arXiv:2201.03544.

Perez, E., S. Ringer, K. Lukosiuute, K. Nguyen, E. Chen, S. Heiner, C. Pettit, C. Olsson, S. Kundu, S. Kadavath, et al. 2022. *Discovering Language Model Behaviors with Model-written Evaluations.* Preprint. arXiv:2212.09251.

Reed, F. 2006. Promise of AI not so bright. *The Washington Times.*

Roziere, B., et al. 2023. *Code Llama: Open Foundation Models for Code.* Preprint. arXiv:2308.12950.

Russell, S. J. 2010. *Artificial Intelligence: A Modern Approach.* London: Pearson Education, Inc.

Russell, S. 2014. *Of myths and Moonshine.* Retrieved from http://edge.org/conversation/jaron_lanier-the-myth-of-ai.

Russell, S. 2019. *Human Compatible: Artificial Intelligence and the Problem of Control.* New York: Penguin.

Russell, S., D. Dewey, and M. Tegmark. 2015. An open letter: Research priorities for robust and beneficial artificial intelligence. Open letter. Signed by 8,600 people. Available at: https://futureoflife.org/data/documents/research_priorities.pdf.

Saunders, W., G. Sastry, A. Stuhlmueller, and O. Evans. 2017. *Trial Without Error: Towards Safe Reinforcement Learning via Human Intervention.* Preprint. arXiv:1707.05173.

Searle, J. R. 1980. Minds, brains, and programs. *Behavioral and Brain Sciences* 3: 417–424. The MIT Press.

Silver, D., et al. 2016. Mastering the game of Go with deep neural networks and tree search. *Nature* 529 (7587): 484–489.

Soares, N. 2018. The value learning problem. In *Artificial Intelligence Safety and Security*, 89–97. Boca Raton: Chapman and Hall/CRC. https://doi.org/10.1201/9781351251389-7.

Soares, N., and B. Fallenstein. 2017. Agent foundations for aligning machine intelligence with human interests: A technical research agenda. In *The Technological Singularity*, 103–125. Berlin: Springer.

Soares, N., B. Fallenstein, S. Armstrong, and E. Yudkowsky, 2015. Corrigibility. In *Workshops at the Twenty-Ninth AAAI Conference on Artificial Intelligence.*

Sotala, K. 2018. Disjunctive Scenarios of Catastrophic AI Risk. In *Artificial Intelligence Safety and Security*, ed. R. V. Yampolskiy, 315–337. Boca Raton: Chapman and Hall/CRC, Taylor & Francis Group.

Stine, D. D. 2008. The Manhattan Project, the Apollo program, and federal energy technology R & D programs: A comparative analysis. In *Proceedings of the Congressional Research Service, the Library of Congress.*

Tally, R. 2009. Radical alternatives: The persistence of utopia in the postmodern. In *New Essays on the Frankfurt School of Critical Theory*, ed. by A. J. Drake, xx–xx. Newcastle upon Tyne: Cambridge Scholars Publishing.

Tegmark, M. 2016. Benefits and risks of artificial intelligence. *Future of Life* 29–31.

Tegmark, M. 2017. *Life 3.0: Being Human in the Age of Artificial Intelligence.* New York: Vintage.

Torres, P. 2018. Superintelligence and the future of governance: On prioritizing the control problem at the end of history. In *Artificial Intelligence Safety and Security*, ed. R. V. Yampolskiy, 357–374. Boca Raton: Chapman and Hall/CRC, Taylor & Francis Group.

Trinh, T. H., Y. Wu, Q. V. Le, H. He, and T. Luong. 2024. Solving olympiad geometry without human demonstrations. *Nature* 625 (7995): 476–482.

Turner, A. M. 2022. *On Avoiding Power-seeking by Artificial Intelligence.* Preprint. arXiv:2206.11831.

Turner, A. M., L. Smith, R. Shah, A. Critch, and P. Tadepalli. 2019. *Optimal Policies Tend to Seek Power.* Preprint. arXiv:1912.01683.

Turner, A. M., D. Hadfield-Menell, and P. Tadepalli. 2020a. Conservative agency via attainable utility preservation. In *Proceedings of the AAAI/ACM Conference on AI, Ethics, and Society*, 385–391.

Turner, A., N. Ratzlaff, and P. Tadepalli. 2020b. Avoiding side effects in complex environments. *Advances in Neural Information Processing Systems* 33: 21406–21415.

Vincent, J. 2023. Microsoft's Bing is an emotionally manipulative liar, and people love it. *The Verge* 15.

Vinge, V. 1993. The coming technological singularity: How to survive in the post-human era. In *Science Fiction Criticism: An Anthology of Essential Writings*, 352–363. London: Bloomsbury Academic.

Wang, P. 2019. On defining artificial intelligence. *Journal of Artificial General Intelligence* 10 (2): 1–37.

Wang, Y., et al. 2022. *Self-Instruct: Aligning Language Model with Self-generated Instructions*. Preprint arXiv:2212.10560.

Wolf, M. J., K. W. Miller, and F. S. Grodzinsky. 2017. Why we should have seen that coming: Comments on Microsoft's Tay "experiment," and wider implications. *The ORBIT Journal* 1 (2): 1–12.

Yamakawa, H. 2019. Peacekeeping conditions for an artificial intelligence society. *Big Data and Cognitive Computing* 3 (2): 34.

Yampolskiy, R. V. 2012. Leakproofing the Singularity: Artificial Intelligence Confinement Problem. *Journal of Consciousness Studies* 19(1–2): 194–214. Imprint Academic.

Yampolskiy, R. V. 2013. Artificial intelligence safety engineering: Why machine ethics is a wrong approach. In *Philosophy and Theory of Artificial Intelligence*, 389–396. Berlin: Springer.

Yudkowsky, E. 2004. Coherent Extrapolated Volition. In *The Singularity Institute*, San Francisco, CA. Available at: https://intelligence.org/files/CEV.pdf.

Yudkowsky, E. 2008. Artificial intelligence as a positive and negative factor in global risk. In *Global Catastrophic Risks*, ed. N. Bostrom, M. M. Ćirković. Oxford: Oxford University Press.

Yudkowsky, E. 2011. Complex value systems in friendly AI. In *International Conference on Artificial General Intelligence*, 388–393. Berlin: Springer.

Yudkowsky, E. 2016. The AI alignment problem: Why it is hard, and where to start. In *Machine Intelligence Research Institute*, San Francisco, CA. Available at: https://intelligence.org/files/AlignmentHardStart.pdf.

Zoph, B., and Q.V. Le. 2016. *Neural Architecture Search with Reinforcement Learning*. Preprint arXiv:1611.01578.

Chapter 3
Gradient-based Learning and Alignment

> *We offer no explanation as to why these architectures seem to work; we attribute their success, as all else, to divine benevolence.*
>
> — Noam Shazeer, GLU Variants Improve Transformer

Abstract This chapter explores the AI alignment problem at the intersection of machine learning and philosophy, aiming to clarify a concept often clouded by abstract speculation and philosophical overreach. While alignment is widely acknowledged as central to AI and ML safety, its interpretation is frequently hindered by associations with intractable metaethical debates and speculative AGI narratives. Hence, I propose reframing alignment, presenting it as a concrete technical limitation, grounded in current gradient-based learning paradigms, rather than an abstract philosophical puzzle. Simultaneously, we show how alignment necessarily involves the epistemic challenge of learning and structuring human preferences. By integrating technical and normative perspectives, we will also learn to distinguish between outer and inner alignment and argue that progress demands philosophical reasoning and ML methodology engagement. This chapter provides foundational knowledge for newcomers, stripping away unfalsifiable assumptions and focusing on alignment as a real and addressable problem.

Keywords AI safety · AI alignment · Machine learning · Human preferences · Outer and inner alignment

3.1 Introduction

When it comes to AI safety and ML safety, many consider alignment as an established problem worth pursuing (Amodei et al. 2016; Russell 2019; Juric et al. 2020; Critch and Krueger 2020; Hendrycks et al. 2021; Christian 2021; Ji et al. 2023; Bengio et al. 2023; Hendrycks et al. 2023). In a broader, more comprehensive

N. Kluge Corrêa, *Normative Ethics, Artificial Intelligence, and Value Alignment*,
The International Library of Ethics, Law and Technology 26,
https://doi.org/10.1007/978-3-032-22150-6_3

context, AI alignment refers to the challenge of ensuring that AI systems align with human values and goals. However, as previously noted, *"alignment"* carries a heavy connotation, burdened by associations with questionable prerequisites and debatable concepts, given the tumultuous debate surrounding the matter and its conceptual origins.

Given the complex and perhaps indefinable nature of human values, the difficulty in alignment appears to derive its strength from an impossible philosophical task. Consequently, some efforts to define alignment as a problem relied heavily on comparisons related to unsolved or unsolvable philosophical questions and the abstractness of human morality (Bostrom 2014; Gabriel 2020), which in some way distanced the problem from its technical roots.

Although we may agree that alignment is a fundamental problem related to human values and normativity, I propose an alternative approach to understanding alignment in machine learning and philosophy. Such an understanding leads to a less straightforward reading of the problem, but requires us to approach the subject from both perspectives. In the middle, both the humanistic and the technical overlap.

However, we cannot attain this grasp if we rely only on philosophy and refuse to delve into ML and the learning paradigm. A partial understanding is insufficient, and the need to believe what others say raises skepticism. Hence, this chapter gives the foundations of alignment to uninitiated readers. In it, I will seek to expose the alignment problem in a way that does not require uncertain timelines of AGI development, contestable definitions of exponential improvement, or unsolvable metaethical problems of the eighteenth century. On the technical side, we will learn to see this problem as a symptom of gradient-based learning methods applied to neural networks. On the philosophical side, I will demonstrate that alignment is related to (in addition to selecting an appropriate metaethical foundation) the epistemic problem of learning preferences and aggregating them into a coherent structure. We will end this chapter with conditions that, I claim, can bring us a minimal level of alignment.

In Sect. 3.2, I shall present alignment as a limitation within our present paradigm. However, we must first obtain a basic understanding of the paradigm's fundamental concepts and principles. With this knowledge as our foundation, we can attain a more definitive and lucid characterization of *"what is"* alignment and misalignment. Armed with this knowledge, Sect. 3.3 elucidates the problem even more, wherein we separate the alignment quandary into two separate issues—*outer* and *inner* alignment. Finally, in Sect. 3.4, we will examine the philosophical challenges associated with this problem and how the definition of our philosophical foundations can inform investigations into this topic.

3.2 The Pitfalls of Gradient-based Learning

The quest for artificial intelligence has been ongoing for decades. Nowadays, when people discuss AI, they often refer to concepts such as deep learning or neural networks, which are not AI in themselves. They are a paradigm we use to develop AI systems. Symbolic artificial intelligence (Haugeland 1989) was the standard approach in the mid-50s, with pioneers such as John McCarthy and Marvin Minsky leading the way (Basden 1983; Durkin 1996; Cowan 2001; McCarthy et al. 2006) until the mid-90s (Russell 2010). These early AI researchers believed we could simulate intelligence using rule-based systems and logic. As such, they focused on creating explicit, human-readable knowledge bases and heuristics to make systems that could make decisions and solve problems. Expert systems like MYCIN (Buchanan and Shortliffe 1984), EURISKO (Lenat 1983), LISA,[1] DeepBlue (Campbell et al. 2002), and WolformAlpha (WolframAlpha 2023), are embodiments of this approach. However, the paradigm fell short in several application areas where expert agents had to deal with the complexity and fuzziness of the real world.

Learning methods operate under a distinct philosophy, in which systems learn rules rather than being provided with them. Algorithms such as linear regression, logistic regression, decision trees, random forests, support vector machines, K-nearest neighbors, and gradient boosting represent this approach, whereby given data and a class of models to explore, we can generate a system to solve a given task. Among these learning algorithms is the neural network, an invention based on the pioneering work of Rosenblatt (1957).

In contemporary times, learning-based approaches have gained significant popularity and adoption in numerous domains. Sutton, in his *Bitter Lesson* (Sutton 2019), highlights that the approaches that are most likely to succeed are those that harness the power of simple algorithms, such as learning and search, to the n-th degree with the aid of abundant computational resources and data. Meanwhile, the idea of *"putting our knowledge inside machines ourselves"* in many areas and applications fell out of fashion.

> The bitter lesson is based on the historical observations that 1) AI researchers have often tried to build knowledge into their agents, 2) this always helps in the short term, and is personally satisfying to the researcher, but 3) in the long run it plateaus and even inhibits further progress, and 4) breakthrough progress eventually arrives by an opposing approach based on scaling computation by search and learning. The eventual success is tinged with bitterness, and often incompletely digested, because it is success over a favored, human-centric approach. One thing that should be learned from the bitter lesson is the great power of general-purpose methods, which continue to scale with increased computation even as the available computation becomes great. The two methods that seem to scale arbitrarily in this way are search and learning.

Now, we need to differentiate between different learning approaches, which we will refer to, for the sake of simplicity, as gradient-based and gradient-free learning. Gradient-free learning is a class of optimization algorithms that do not require the use of gradients to estimate the derivative of a loss function[2] but can still be

---

[1] 🔗 lisa.sourceforge.net

[2] A loss function can be thought of as a measure of how far a model's predictions are from the desired outcome. Minimizing this measure helps the model improve its performance on a given

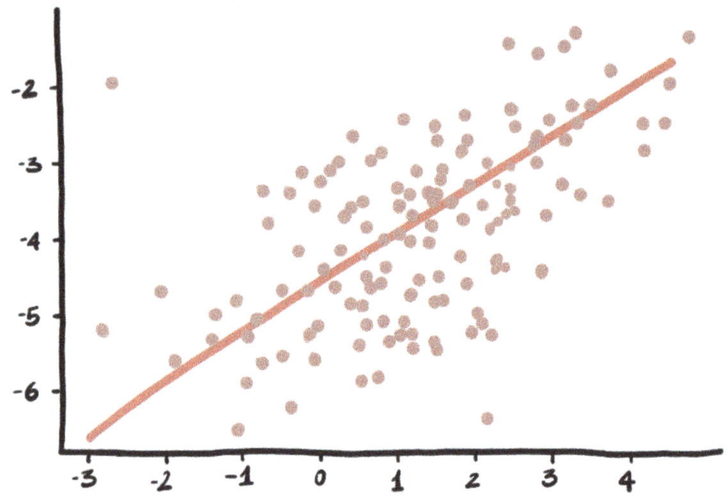

Fig. 3.1 Some data distribution, plotted in a Cartesian plane, representing a growing linear trend (i.e., as x increases, y also increases

used to find optimal points in certain classes of problems. Evolutionary algorithms (Lehman et al. 2020), particle swarm optimization (Bonyadi and Michalewicz 2017), Bayesian optimization (Mockus 1994), and pattern search (Hooke and Jeeves 1961) are examples of this approach.

Gradient-based learning, as the name suggests, uses a specific set of techniques to estimate (using the gradient of the first or second derivative of a loss function to estimate minimum or global convergence points) the state of an optimization process and direct it to better solutions. To illustrate this, let us consider the following data distribution that we would like to learn how to model (Fig. 3.1).

We can estimate the best-fitting model (a line) for this distribution and evaluate our prediction by measuring the distance from the actual data (the distance from every data point to the drawn line). The difference between what we predicted (the drawn line) and the ground truth (the data distribution) is the loss. Let us think of mean squared error (MSE) as an example of a loss function, which can be understood as the squared residual difference between our prediction and the actual data.

Brute-forcing guesses until we find a low MSE score (aka, a well-fitting line) is not an efficient way to solve problems like this. But let us imagine that we did this. If we create many guesses (draw multiple lines in the graph), calculate the loss associated with each guess, and plot them in a graph, we will have produced a loss

task. Any metric that can tell us how "good" the model is can be thought of as a form/part of a loss (cost) function.

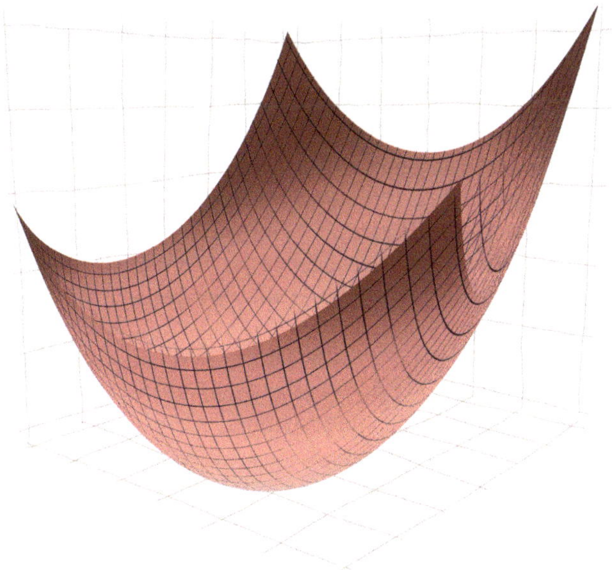

Fig. 3.2 The MSE landscape of a linear regression problem (i.e., $y = a + bx$)

function surface. And since we are trying to optimize a linear function with MSE, our loss function has a very friendly property (Fig. 3.2).

For linear regression problems, the MSE is a convex function; that is, at each point on our surface, we can use the gradient of the first derivative of our loss function to adjust the model's parameters and minimize the loss. In other words, we follow the opposite/negative direction of the gradient, which is downhill. Because our loss function is convex (has a "U" shape), no matter where our model starts, if we use this method to optimize our parameters (especially with a tuned gradient step), we can find the global minimum (the best solution) (Polyak 1963), and this is gradient descent in a nutshell. In simple terms:

> Start at random. Use what you know to see how far you are from the target. Adjust your model proportionally to the distance from your predictions to the target in the direction the error decreases. Repeat till you can no longer improve.

Gradient-based learning methods are the cornerstone of most modern ML. The idea of updating a model's parameters interactively using a differentiable loss function and a fast first-order optimization algorithm makes most ML possible.

This approach involves both *learning* and *searching*. Learning is because our model updates itself with the information it iteratively receives, slowly transferring information from the data distribution (the learning signal) to the model's parameters. Searching occurs because the optimizer iteratively searches for the model that scores best according to a specific objective function. But where do we search? In ML, we need to define a search space that bounds the types of functions we can model (we can also think about functions as programs). Given that we want to model more than linear relationships, our search space must be richer than the space of possible lines in a plane.

The space of possible programs is nothing short of colossal. Artificial intelligence that could diligently navigate this terrain and effectively pinpoint the optimal model that accurately reproduces a specified data distribution (within a reasonable time frame) would unequivocally be the ultimate exemplar of an intelligent predictive system (Hutter 2004; Legg and Hutter 2007). However, finding the shortest program that produces some data is an uncomputable problem. Given what we currently understand about computation, the *"reasonable time frame"* part would still be out of reach even if it were computable.

Here is where neural networks come into the picture. This class of models provides us with two things: (1) a *"good enough"* search space and (2) a good enough search space where we can find solutions in a reasonable amount of time. Indeed, as universal function approximators, artificial neural networks endow us with the ability to develop models that can proficiently approximate a vast array of functions (Hornik et al. 1989).[3] Networks built with nonlinear activation functions allow us to learn nonlinear surfaces in high dimensions (the search space becomes richer) and to use backpropagation to optimize their weights via gradient descent. By combining all these ingredients, we obtain a considerable search space (the space of neural networks with width n and depth n) and a fast method for searching.

Deep learning (machine learning that uses multiple-layered neural networks to learn representations from data), in essence, is a paradigm that defies the theoretical expectations of many. Results such as the Hughes (1968) and the curse of dimensionality (Bellman 1966) led many researchers to consider neural networks a dead end before the deep learning revolution (Krizhevsky et al. 2012). However, despite our newfound success, the question of *"why"* remains a lingering mystery (Fefferman et al. 2016; Frankle and Carbin 2018). Empirically, Deep learning works. Theoretically, it should not. And here is where some of our problems begin.

Deep learning is built upon gradient descent methods, such as stochastic gradient descent (SGD). However, these methods have no convergence guarantees or proofs when dealing with non-convex or non-Lipschitz continuous loss functions. Unfortunately, the loss functions of neural networks are rarely convex. Any neural network with at least one hidden layer and more than one neuron leads to an optimization problem that is not convex, as the permutation of weights among neurons in the hidden layer can produce different local minima.

Hence, when gradient optimization is confronted with the non-convex world of deep learning, the gradient descent approach that worked so well in convex settings becomes a slippery slope with no guarantees. While optimizers like SGD, Adam, AMSGrad, and AdaGrad can provide convergence in some constrained cases with

[3] A two-layer neural network with $2n + d$ parameters is capable of fitting any dataset of n samples of dimension d (Zhang et al. 2016). However, these functions have to be continuous. Functions with kinks or discontinuities are outside the scope of the universal approximation theorem.

enough black magic (Chen et al. 2018; Lei et al. 2019; Patel and Zhang 2021), the reason for the success of DL remains unanswered: *why do algorithms designed for convex optimization work in the highly non-convex world of deep learning?* To this day, we have many hypotheses to explain the empirical robustness of gradient-based methods applied to deep learning (Hochreiter and Schmidhuber 1997; Cayton 2005; Tishby and Zaslavsky 2015; Neyshabur 2017; Frankle and Carbin 2018; Nakkiran et al. 2019; Delétang et al. 2023), but no proof. Moreover, there are many other mysteries surrounding DL:

- How do deep nets escape the curse of dimensionality?
- Why is optimizing deep nets so easy despite the high dimensionality?
- How can generalization happen after overfitting (double descent)?
- What controls the normalization of deep nets? NN's themselves? The dynamics of stochastic optimization?

In summary, as stated in the quote at the beginning of this chapter, many aspects related to how deep nets and DL in general work are left to *"divine benevolence"* (Shazeer 2020). Armed with this understanding (or lack thereof), we can now explore the concept of alignment.

We have already examined how the learning approach differs from the traditional symbolic paradigm. In gradient-based learning, we define exogenous objectives through an objective function. Gradient descent allows us to channel entropy from the training distribution to the model being updated by the optimizer, ultimately leading to a generalization that bypasses nonconvexity. However, due to multiple local minima in the loss surface that offer similar performance, our optimizer may end up in any of them.

As the behavior of first-order gradient optimizers in nonconvex loss functions remains a mystery, with no guarantees of convergence, the controller is unable to verify that the optimizer has reached the point where the objective function is truly optimized. Additionally, since the most prominent methods for gradient descent in deep learning rely on stochasticity to accelerate optimization, the trajectories of our optimizer are non-deterministic and may vary significantly across experiments. Moreover, since the objective function may have been misspecified, we can only determine its alignment *post hoc*. Therefore:

> Aligning the exogenous objective with the learned objective of a model trained via gradient-based learning remains an open problem.

Think about it. Imagine you have a complex problem that you would like to solve using gradient-based learning methods, such as deep learning or reinforcement learning. Your cost function will probably be nonconvex (if not, you could use a linear model instead). Your function may have many local minima that perform

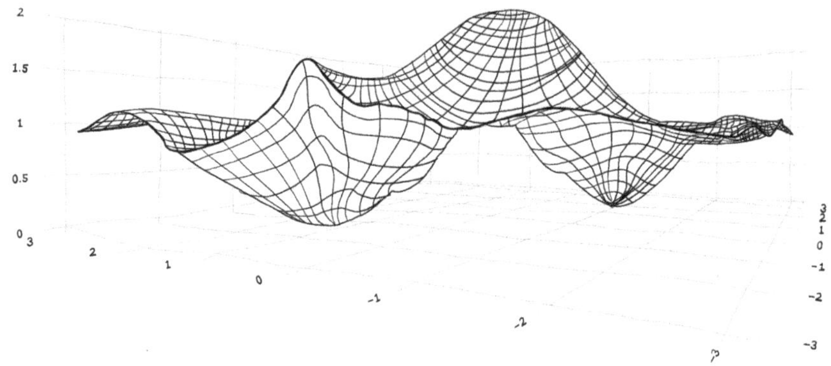

Fig. 3.3 This image represents the loss surface of an optimization problem with more than one minimum. Both minima are equally desirable for the optimizer traveling this plane, even if they produce networks with different qualitative behaviors

equally well but produce qualitatively different behavior (Fig. 3.3).[4] Given this landscape, where does the model that best satisfies your objective function reside, and how can you force your optimizer to push your model in that direction?

Unfortunately, a low loss or high reward does not tell us much about the emergent phenomenon that will arise or the qualitative differences in our model's behavior. A model that performs brightness detection and a model that can distinguish pictures of dogs from cats are fundamentally different algorithms. But if you train a neural network with a training set that only has pictures of white dogs and black cats, you might think you have one, but you actually have the other, and you can only discover this post hoc.

In instances where a chatbot produces coherent responses akin to human-like text yet begins spewing anti-Semitic and misogynistic content when deployed, an alignment failure has become apparent. An assistant who presents himself affably but provides fake information when consulted is also a failure in alignment. An algorithm that prioritizes polarizing and controversial content to maximize user attention constitutes another example of alignment gone awry. In short, alignment is a wide-ranging issue that pertains to the inability of certain forms of AI systems to assimilate the objectives set by an exogenous source. If your problem is intricate, there is a higher possibility of misalignment.

Alignment encapsulates the intricacies of directing and validating optimization processes that are often obscure and murky. While misalignment seems harmless in toy examples, the problem does not disappear in more complex settings (it gets

[4] In the field of Explainable Machine Learning, we call this the Rashomon Effect. The Rashomon Effect describes the case in which, for a given dataset, many models may have equally good performance (i.e., low loss) but with different solution strategies (i.e., qualitative behavior) (Müller et al. 2023).

worse). The misaligned algorithm that kills humanity to eradicate cancer is just hyperbole to underscore this seemingly straightforward yet daunting issue.

3.3 Alignment (Outer and Inner)

Alignment is one issue that captures the realization of the challenges associated with communicating human values and intentions. This communication, when mediated by the learning methods that power our most successful approaches to AI, is hindered by the nature of how such systems learn. Now that we have this understanding, we can define alignment as two problems, as suggested by Hubinger et al. (2019), which present alignment as a learned optimization problem with two stages:

- Outer Alignment: ensuring that the objective of the optimizer is aligned with the controller's true intentions and goals.
- Inner Alignment: ensuring that the objective of the optimizer is aligned with the objective of the model created.

Let us unpack these concepts. As previously elucidated, programmers can sculpt the underlying objective by defining an exogenous function. This function is contingent upon an initial model, a training distribution, and the defined loss function. These constituent parts compose the parameters subject to the controller's intent. Defining this objective is known as the outer alignment problem. Depending on the issue at hand, this can be a difficult task. Minimizing cross-entropy loss in next-token prediction is a straightforward goal. Minimizing the cross-entropy loss in next-token prediction in a way that produces factual and non-toxic text is a much more challenging goal to define.

If this objective is poorly specified, the optimizer, which in DL is usually an algorithm for computing some variant of gradient descent, will optimize a model to execute a task unaligned with the intended goal. Thus, the outer alignment problem is the issue of bridging the gap between the controller's objectives and the objective that will guide the optimizer in searching for the best-fitting model.

In the case of neural networks and gradient-based learning, this optimizer does not act in the environment or perform a task. Its function is to find a model to execute the objective stipulated by the objective function. It is the model that will act, and it is usually this model that is the target of our interest. However, in certain circumstances, the trained model itself serves as an optimizer. An actor-critic system (Konda and Tsitsiklis 1999) learns a model that is an optimizing agent. Now, *how can we be sure that the goal of the model is the same goal that the optimizer was aiming for?* This is the inner alignment problem.

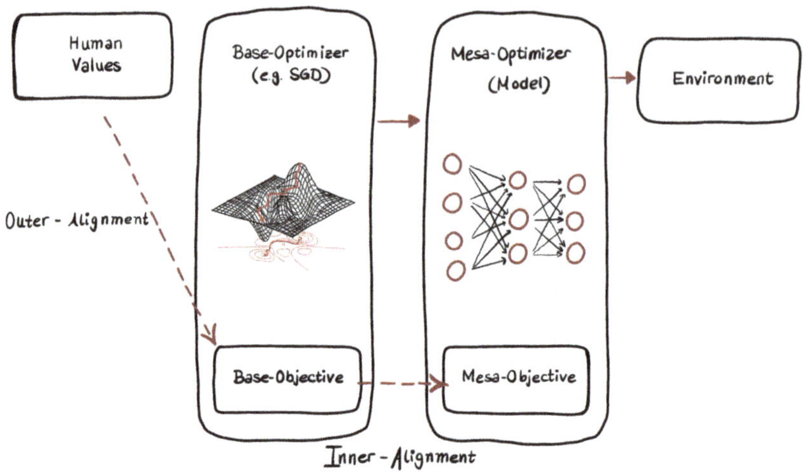

Fig. 3.4 Schematics representing the Outer and Inner Alignment gaps

If you have ever played the *"Telephone game"*, you will quickly discover two steps where the original objective could be misrepresented in passing the bucket. Additionally, given that the interpretability of large neural networks remains a challenge, the investigation that could lead to a better understanding of a model's behavior remains out of reach. Even though we have a lot of interpretability work being done (Ribeiro et al. 2016; Qin et al. 2018; Selvaraju et al. 2017; Liu et al. 2019; Molnar 2020; Verma et al. 2020; Olah et al. 2020; Domingos 2020; Goh et al. 2021; Aytekin 2022; Olsson et al. 2022; Olah 2022; Black et al. 2022; Zhang et al. 2024), understanding and predicting the behavior of large neural networks in an ex-ante fashion is a current impossibility in the field, making the emergent properties of large neural networks something we cannot fully understand before deployment or exhaustive testing. The whole alignment problem encompasses both the issue of outer alignment and inner alignment (Fig. 3.4).

Alignment is more than creating models that *"will obey"*. It is also about developing models that will make better helpers and assistants. From HAL 2000 to Jarvis, these sci-fi AI examples foreshadow a future in which systems can understand what we mean and want when we propose a task. Eve thought alignment might prevent future HAL and Jarvis-like systems from going rogue; in the short run, alignment is about developing models that understand the complex things people want to accomplish.

Now, we have a sufficient common understanding of the problem to begin interacting with the philosophical issues that permeate this subject. In the next section, we will see how alignment creates fertile ground for interdisciplinary research between the humanities and the more technical side of AI research.

3.4 A Philosophical Approach to Alignment

Where does philosophy fit into this story? Millions of people already use AI systems to make decisions that have moral implications. *"How can we teach machines to have a sense of morality when humans are still trying to understand it ourselves?"* is a problem that, if ignored, will not simply go away. One could say, *"We simply will not put uninterpretable neural networks trained via gradient descent in positions where their outputs have moral implications"*. And if we *all* accept this, this whole work could end now. However, this remains an unlikely scenario, and as AI continues to become more integrated into our daily lives and decision-making processes, problems related to misalignment will require a less ideal solution.

Defining what is desirable, finding ways to represent norms, understanding values, and stress-testing theories that promise the common good have been the primary focus of philosophy for millennia. The study of Moral Philosophy, and more specifically, Metaethics[5] and Normative Ethics,[6] provides us with a considerable landscape of ideas and frameworks to explore. Humanity has been trying to align humans with itself for a long time, so it is not like we will start from scratch (if we bring these disciplines to the research front).

For example, it is nothing new to philosophers that the ruthless optimization of a single metric will lead to immoral results (Nozick 1974; Hardin 1998). Or that well-thought-out rule systems will inevitably contain vulnerabilities and paradoxes inside their limited structure (McMahon 1991; Mardellat 2020). Thus, if we agree that alignment is also related to the fact that objectives need to be parameterized by norms, values, and constraints,[7] philosophical inquiry is needed.

Furthermore, after we have, for example, made our philosophical commitments to one or more theories and foundations, we make our biases and presuppositions more transparent. Failures of alignment, for example, could be extrapolated by subjecting these foundations to a philosophical stress test—*"in which hypothetical scenarios do they break?"*. This is one of philosophy's contributions to alignment research.

Now, let us explore some more issues that philosophy can help with. First and foremost, the genuine challenge of ethical alignment does not involve identifying the *"ultimate and genuine moral theory"*. As Rawls et al. (1996) points out, convincing humanity of our discovery would likely prove impossible even if we were to uncover such knowledge. Instead, the key is to fathom which principles embody an ideal form of alignment. This *"ideal form"* ought to be adaptable enough to accommodate the diverse moral landscape of humanity.

---

[5] The examination of the nature of ethical language, reasoning, and justification.

[6] The study of moral behavior and how we can establish norms to optimize this behavior (Kagan 2018).

[7] And as far as we I, this is something alignment scholars agree (Soares 2018; Russell 2019; Gabriel 2020; Christian 2021).

Additionally, considering that we aim to align systems developed through a learning paradigm, we may explore the possibility of teaching values rather than directly hard-coding them. This inquiry surfaces domains spanning metaethics to epistemology. For example, what metaethical foundations would better support a value-learning framework? Can morality be expressed in a knowledge format for assimilation? In the same way that different philosophies have given rise to distinct AI approaches (Rosenblatt 1957; Newell 1994), divergent metaethical foundations will produce particular answers to these questions, which become distinct alignment approaches.

As Iason points out (Gabriel 2020), depending on your philosophical background, you will inherently conceptualize alignment differently:

- Aligned means when an AI performs what was specified verbatim.
- Aligned means when an AI performs not what was specified but the controller's intent.
- Aligned means when an AI realizes our idealized preferences in a state of reflective equilibrium.

Depending on what you choose as your normative signal,[8] your engineering will be different. This information, which we can refer to as *"human preferences"* or *"human values"*, must be translated into an AI-native format. That is, they must be in such a way that a system can use them as a supervision signal, especially when we are talking about learning.

For example, to base your alignment strategy on virtue ethics, you could use examples of commendable conduct in people's actions (Russell 2019; Wallach and Vallor 2020). If you argue that rules guide normative behavior (Deontology), an ordered system of preferences or a set of regulations could be used as your reference (Hadfield-Menell and Hadfield 2019; Nay 2022). If the consequences are what you deem worthy of moral praise (Consequentialism), then a utility function over states and actions could be what you are trying to model. Either way, this signal must be translatable into something our target paradigm can process (Christiano et al. 2017; Stiennon et al. 2020).

No rule says we can only choose one approach for an alignment strategy. Different theories can have different roles, and this is probably a little closer to what actual human normative reasoning looks like. People are a patchwork of moral beliefs and preferences, and uncertainty about what they should do is an integral part of this experience. This brings us to another question: *how do we deal with*

[8] We can think of *"human morality"* or *"acceptable behavior"* as a domain. A given language is also a domain. The domain is the actual phenomenon we are interested in. A signal is a small, low-dimensional, bounded representation of that domain. 800 GB of web-scrapped text is a signal of a particular *"human language"* domain.

normative uncertainty? Coherently aggregating conflicting preferences should also be a preoccupation in any alignment strategy. There is also a problem regarding moral standing. For example, should we consider the preferences of non-human animals as well (Hagendorff et al. 2022; Bossert and Hagendorff 2023)? Even if we would like to bypass this last question and remain human-centric, we will still need to resolve questions of uncertainty involving conflicting human values.

Questions like these are only a few of the philosophical conundrums that alignment brings. Since this work proposes to tackle alignment from both ends, we will first need to establish philosophical foundations, expose our biases and assumptions, and then seek existing implementation techniques that can help bring this idealized framework to fruition.

From here on, the remainder of this work is dedicated to a proposal for an alignment methodology. The next chapter will begin laying the foundations for this approach. That is, its metaphysical and metaethical assumptions. Moreover, this work will focus on the outer alignment problem—how to close the gap between the controllers' objectives and the objective to be optimized in the search for a model. As a convention, from here on out, when I refer to the alignment problem, we are talking about outer alignment (unless mentioned otherwise).

Moreover, Dynamic Normativity—a way to frame and understand alignment and its constituent parts—presents a minimum set of conditions for aligning AI systems developed by gradient-based learning methods. For now, I will only outline the conditions I aim to support in this work, dividing them into necessary conditions and three requirements that, together, form sufficient conditions. In summary, the necessary conditions propose philosophical foundations that imply the *permissibility* of alignment. These are:

- Goals are fundamental aspects of intelligent and intentional behavior.
- Intentions permeate human behavior.
- Normative preferences permeate human intentions.
- Through actions, humans impregnate their environment with the preferences they possess.

From these, I postulate that a system that accurately models human intentions and the human environment can indirectly access normative information embedded in them. Again, necessary conditions imply that the system *could* be aligned. Given that these conditions hold, the following requirements establish a minimum level of alignment when all are fulfilled:

- Aligned AI systems should coherently aggregate human preferences in a way that resolves cases of uncertainty. Aligning AI systems requires methods to deal with cases of uncertainty.
- AI systems can adhere to human preferences if they are an available part of their objective function. Aligning AI systems requires using human preferences as part of their learning signal.
- Aligned AI systems should have mechanisms to perform impact mitigation to minimize harmful and unintended consequences. Aligning AI systems requires the specification of safety guardrails.

The necessary conditions establish the prerequisites for the emergence of aligned behavior. When all are satisfied, the above requirements give us a *sufficient alignment condition*. Hence:

> Given that the necessary conditions hold, how aligned an AI system is depends on how well we can satisfy the proposed requirements. Satisfying all requirements equates to a sufficient condition for alignment.

These conditions aim to demonstrate the minimum level of alignment that can be achieved and how to attain it, utilizing current knowledge and available resources, thereby establishing a threshold of agreement based on existing knowledge and resources. But, does it guarantee that we can get a perfectly aligned model? No. The sufficient condition does not guarantee perfection—it guarantees completeness. It asserts that no fundamental aspect of alignment has been left unattended. Each step can and should be refined, but none can be omitted. If one is forgotten, according to Dynamic Normativity, we have failed, and our alignment is incomplete.

In later chapters, we will apply this framework. However, stronger foundations are required beforehand. Hence, to Chap. 4, we go.

3.5 Epilogue

As we conclude this chapter, we can appreciate the complexity and depth of the alignment problem. ML engineering is the science of sloppiness, and misalignment is the price we pay. The alignment problem arises from the limitations of our current paradigm and the unknown nature of neural network optimization when dealing with complex, non-convex spaces. From this, the issue of ensuring AI systems behave according to our intentions emerges. Moreover, the distinction between inner and outer alignment underscores the importance of considering both the objective function and the optimization process as potential sources of misalignment.

At the same time, the philosophical issues we explored in this chapter demonstrate that the alignment problem extends beyond mere technical considerations.

It involves fundamental questions about the nature of ethics and the limits of our understanding of these concepts. Furthermore, alignment introduces the *moral problem* as a fundamental issue in AI research. We could even say that alignment brings the humanities, with full force, into AI, especially if we agree that our goal is to build *beneficial intelligence* rather than *any* intelligence.

Ultimately, the philosophical challenges related to alignment prompt us to approach AI development with humility and caution, acknowledging the inherent uncertainties, complexities, and limitations of our current understanding. Given all of that, this work presents a set of conditions to serve as a starting point for considering alignment solutions. In the next chapter, we will use these conditions to lay the foundations of the proposed approach: Dynamic Normativity.

References

Amodei, D., C. Olah, J. Steinhardt, P. Christiano, J. Schulman, and D. Mané. 2016. *Concrete Problems in AI Safety*. Preprint. arXiv:1606.06565v2.

Aytekin, C. 2022. *Neural Networks Are Decision Trees*. Preprint. arXiv:2210.05189.

Basden, A. 1983. On the application of expert systems. *International Journal of Man-Machine Studies* 19 (5): 461–477.

Bellman, R. 1966. Dynamic programming. *Science* 153 (3731): 34–37.

Bengio, Y., G. Hinton, A. Yao, D. Song, P. Abbeel, Y. N. Harari, Y.-Q. Zhang, L. Xue, S. Shalev-Shwartz, G. Hadfield, et al. 2023. *Managing AI Risks in an Era of Rapid Progress*. Preprint. arXiv:2310.17688.

Black, S., L. Sharkey, L. Grinsztajn, E. Winsor, D. Braun, J. Merizian, K. Parker, C. R. Guevara, B. Millidge, G. Alfour, et al. 2022. *Interpreting Neural Networks Through the Polytope Lens*. Preprint. arXiv:2211.12312.

Bonyadi, M. R., and Z. Michalewicz. 2017. Particle swarm optimization for single objective continuous space problems: A review. *Evolutionary Computation* 25 (1): 1–54.

Bossert, L. N., and T. Hagendorff. 2023. The ethics of sustainable AI: Why animals (should) matter for a sustainable use of AI. *Sustainable Development*. Hoboken: Wiley Online Library.

Bostrom, N. 2014. *Superintelligence: Paths, Dangers, Strategies*. Oxford: Oxford University Press.

Buchanan, B. G., and E. H. Shortliffe. 1984. *Rule-based Expert Systems: The MYCIN Experiments of the Stanford Heuristic Programming Project (The Addison-Wesley Series in Artificial Intelligence)*. Boston: Addison-Wesley Longman Publishing Co., Inc.

Campbell, Jr., M. H., A. Joseph, and F.-H. Hsu. 2002. Deep Blue. *Artificial Intelligence* 134 (1–2): 57–83.

Cayton, L. 2005. Algorithms for manifold learning. *University of California at San Diego Technical Report* 12: 1–17.

Chen, X., S. Liu, R. Sun, and M. Hong. 2018. *On the Convergence of a Class of Adam-type Algorithms for Non-convex Optimization*. Preprint. arXiv:1808.02941.

Christian, B. 2021. *The Alignment Problem: How Can Machines Learn Human Values?* London: Atlantic Books.

Christiano, P. F., J. Leike, T. Brown, M. Martic, S. Legg, and D. Amodei. 2017. Deep reinforcement learning from human preferences. *Advances in Neural Information Processing Systems* 30.

Cowan, R. 2001. Expert systems: Aspects of and limitations to the codifiability of knowledge. *Research Policy* 30 (9): 1355–1372.

Critch, A., and D. Krueger. 2020. *AI Research Considerations for Human Existential Safety* (ARCHES). Preprint. arXiv:2006.04948.

Delétang, G., A. Ruoss, P.-A. Duquenne, E. Catt, T. Genewein, C. Mattern, et al. 2023. *Language Modeling Is Compression*. Preprint. arXiv:2309.10668.

Domingos, P. 2020. *Every Model Learned by Gradient Descent Is Approximately a Kernel Machine*. Preprint. arXiv:2012.00152.

Durkin, J. 1996. Expert systems: A view of the field. *IEEE Intelligent Systems* 11 (2): 56–63.

Fefferman, C., S. Mitter, and H. Narayanan. 2016. Testing the manifold hypothesis. *Journal of the American Mathematical Society* 29 (4): 983–1049.

Frankle, J., and Carbin, M. 2018. *The Lottery Ticket Hypothesis: Finding Sparse, Trainable Neural Networks*. Preprint. arXiv:1803.03635.

Gabriel, I. 2020. Artificial intelligence, values, and alignment. *Minds and Machines* 30 (3): 411–437.

Goh, G. S. W., S. Lapuschkin, L. Weber, W. Samek, and A. Binder. 2021. Understanding integrated gradients with SmoothTaylor for deep neural network attribution. In *2020 25th International Conference on Pattern Recognition (ICPR)*, 4949–4956. IEEE.

Hadfield-Menell, D., and G. K. Hadfield. 2019. Incomplete contracting and AI alignment. In *Proceedings of the 2019 AAAI/ACM Conference on AI, Ethics, and Society*, 417–422.

Hagendorff, T., L. N. Bossert, Y. F. Tse, and P. Singer. 2022. Speciesist bias in AI: how AI applications perpetuate discrimination and unfair outcomes against animals. *AI and Ethics* 1–18.

Hardin, G. 1998. Extensions of "the tragedy of the commons." *Science* 280 (5364): 682–683.

Haugeland, J. 1989. *Artificial Intelligence: The Very Idea*. Cambridge: MIT Press.

Hendrycks, D., N. Carlini, J. Schulman, and J. Steinhardt. 2021. *Unsolved Problems in ML Safety*. Preprint. arXiv:2109.13916v4.

Hendrycks, D., M. Mazeika, and T. Woodside. 2023. *An Overview of Catastrophic AI Risks*. Preprint. arXiv:2306.12001.

Hochreiter, S., and J. Schmidhuber. 1997. Flat minima. *Neural Computation* 9 (1): 1–42.

Hooke, R., and T. A. Jeeves. 1961. "Direct search" solution of numerical and statistical problems. *Journal of the ACM (JACM)* 8 (2): 212–229.

Hornik, K., M. Stinchcombe, and H. White. 1989. Multilayer feedforward networks are universal approximators. *Neural Networks* 2 (5): 359–366.

Hubinger, E., C. van Merwijk, V. Mikulik, J. Skalse, and S. Garrabrant. 2019. *Risks from Learned Optimization in Advanced Machine Learning Systems*. Preprint. arXiv:1906.01820v3.

Hughes, G. 1968. On the mean accuracy of statistical pattern recognizers. *IEEE Transactions on Information Theory* 14 (1): 55–63.

Hutter, M. 2004. *Universal Artificial Intelligence: Sequential Decisions Based on Algorithmic Probability*. Berlin: Springer Science & Business Media.

Ji, J., T. Qiu, B. Chen, B. Zhang, H. Lou, K. Wang, Y. Duan, Z. He, J. Zhou, Z. Zhang, et al. 2023. *AI Alignment: A Comprehensive Survey*. Preprint. arXiv:2310.19852.

Juric, M., A. Sandic, and M. Brcic. 2020. AI safety: State of the field through quantitative lens. In *2020 43rd International Convention on Information, Communication and Electronic Technology (MIPRO)*, 1254–1259. IEEE.

Kagan, S. 2018. *Normative Ethics*. Milton Park: Routledge.

Konda, V., and J. Tsitsiklis. 1999. Actor-critic algorithms. In *Advances in Neural Information Processing Systems*, ed. S. Solla, T. Leen, and K. Müller, Vol. 12. Cambridge: MIT Press.

Krizhevsky, A., I. Sutskever, and G. E. Hinton. 2012. ImageNet classification with deep convolutional neural networks. In *Advances in Neural Information Processing Systems*, ed. F. Pereira, C.J. Burges, L. Bottou, and K.Q. Weinberger, Vol. 25. Red Hook: Curran Associates, Inc. https://proceedings.neurips.cc/paper_files/paper/2012/file/c399862d3b9d6b76c8436e924a68c45b-Paper.pdf.

Legg, S., and M. Hutter. 2007. Universal intelligence: A definition of machine intelligence. *Minds and Machines* 17 (4): 391–444.

Lehman, J., J. Clune, D. Misevic, C. Adami, L. Altenberg, J. Beaulieu, et al. 2020. The surprising creativity of digital evolution: A collection of anecdotes from the evolutionary computation and artificial life research communities. *Artificial Life* 26 (2): 274–306.

Lei, Y., T. Hu, G. Li, and K. Tang. 2019. Stochastic gradient descent for nonconvex learning without bounded gradient assumptions. *IEEE Transactions on Neural Networks and Learning Systems* 31 (10): 4394–4400.
Lenat, D. B. 1983. EURISKO: A program that learns new heuristics and domain concepts: The nature of heuristics III: Program design and results. *Artificial Intelligence* 21 (1–2): 61–98.
Liu, S., B. Kailkhura, D. Loveland, and Y. Han. 2019. Generative counterfactual introspection for explainable deep learning. In *2019 IEEE Global Conference on Signal and Information Processing (GlobalSIP)*, 1–5. IEEE.
Müller, S., V. Toborek, K. Beckh, M. Jakobs, C. Bauckhage, and P. Welke. 2023. An empirical evaluation of the Rashomon effect in explainable machine learning. In *Joint European Conference on Machine Learning and Knowledge Discovery in Databases*, 462–478. Springer.
Mardellat, V. 2020. Contractualism and the paradox of deontology. *Philosophical Studies* 177 (12): 3749–3774.
McCarthy, J., M. L. Minsky, N. Rochester, and C. E. Shannon. 2006. A proposal for the Dartmouth Summer Research Project on Artificial Intelligence, August 31, 1955. *AI Magazine* 27 (4): 12–12.
McMahon, C. 1991. The paradox of deontology. *Philosophy & Public Affairs* 350–377.
Mockus, J. 1994. Application of Bayesian approach to numerical methods of global and stochastic optimization. *Journal of Global Optimization* 4: 347–365.
Molnar, C. 2020. *Interpretable Machine Learning*. Durham: Lulu.com.
Nakkiran, P., G. Kaplun, Y. Bansal, T. Yang, B. Barak, and I. Sutskever. 2019. *Deep Double Descent: Where Bigger Models and More Data Hurt*. Preprint. arXiv:1912.02292.
Nay, J. J. 2022. *Law Informs Code: A Legal Informatics Approach to Aligning Artificial Intelligence with Humans*. Preprint. arXiv:2209.13020.
Newell, A. 1994. *Unified Theories of Cognition*. Cambridge: Harvard University Press.
Neyshabur, B. 2017. *Implicit Regularization in Deep Learning*. Preprint. arXiv:1709.01953.
Nozick, R. 1974. *Anarchy, State, and Utopia*. New York: Basic Books.
Olah, C. 2022. Mechanistic interpretability, variables, and the importance of interpretable bases. Transformer Circuits Thread.
Olah, C., N. Cammarata, L. Schubert, G. Goh, M. Petrov, and S. Carter. 2020. Zoom in: An introduction to circuits. *Distill* 5 (3): e00024–001.
Olsson, C., N. Elhage, N. Nanda, N. Joseph, N. DasSarma, T. Henighan, B. Mann, A. Askell, Y. Bai, A. Chen, et al. 2022. *In-context Learning and Induction Heads*. Preprint. arXiv:2209.11895.
Patel, V., and S. Zhang. 2021. *Stochastic Gradient Descent on Nonconvex Functions with General Noise Models*. Preprint. arXiv:2104.00423.
Polyak, B. T. 1963. Gradient methods for the minimisation of functionals. *USSR Computational Mathematics and Mathematical Physics* 3 (4): 864–878.
Qin, Z., F. Yu, C. Liu, and X. Chen. 2018. *How Convolutional Neural Networks See the World — A Survey of Convolutional Neural Network Visualization Methods*. Preprint. arXiv:1804.11191.
Rawls, J. 1996. *The law of peoples*. Beogradski krug, (01+ 02), 9–29.
Ribeiro, M. T., S. Singh, and C. Guestrin. 2016. "Why should I trust you?" Explaining the predictions of any classifier. In *Proceedings of the 22nd ACM SIGKDD International Conference on Knowledge Discovery and Data Mining*, 1135–1144.
Rosenblatt, F. 1957. *The Perceptron, a Perceiving and Recognizing Automaton Project Para*. New York: Cornell Aeronautical Laboratory.
Russell, S. J. 2010. *Artificial Intelligence: A Modern Approach*. London: Pearson Education, Inc.
Russell, S. 2019. *Human Compatible: Artificial Intelligence and the Problem of Control*. New York: Penguin.
Selvaraju, R. R., M. Cogswell, A. Das, R. Vedantam, D. Parikh, and D. Batra. 2017. Grad-CAM: Visual explanations from deep networks via gradient-based localization. In *Proceedings of the IEEE International Conference on Computer Vision*, 618–626.
Shazeer, N. 2020. *Glu Variants Improve Transformer*. Preprint. arXiv:2002.05202.

Soares, N. 2018. The value learning problem. In *Artificial Intelligence Safety and Security*, 89–97. Boca Raton: Chapman and Hall/CRC. https://doi.org/10.1201/9781351251389-7.
Stiennon, N., L. Ouyang, J. Wu, D. Ziegler, R. Lowe, C. Voss, A. Radford, D. Amodei, and P. F. Christiano. 2020. Learning to summarize with human feedback. *Advances in Neural Information Processing Systems* 33: 3008–3021.
Sutton, R. 2019. The bitter lesson. *Incomplete Ideas (Blog)* 13: 12.
Tishby, N., and N. Zaslavsky. 2015. Deep learning and the information bottleneck principle. In *2015 IEEE Information Theory Workshop (ITW)*, 1–5. IEEE.
Verma, S., J. Dickerson, and K. Hines. 2020. *Counterfactual Explanations for Machine Learning: A Review*. Preprint. arXiv:2010.10596.
Wallach, W., and S. Vallor. 2020. Moral machines. In *Ethics of Artificial Intelligence*, 383–412. Oxford: Oxford University Press.
WolframAlpha. 2023. *WolframAlpha*. Available at: https://www.wolframalpha.com/.
Zhang, C., S. Bengio, M. Hardt, B. Recht, and O. Vinyals. 2016. *Understanding Deep Learning Requires Rethinking Generalization*. Preprint. arXiv:1611.03530.
Zhang, N., Y. Yao, B. Tian, P. Wang, S. Deng, M. Wang, Z. Xi, S. Mao, J. Zhang, Y. Ni, et al. 2024. *A Comprehensive Study of Knowledge Editing for Large Language Models*. Preprint. arXiv:2401.01286.

Chapter 4
Roots: Building Philosophical Foundations for AI Alignment

[...] replacing humans was always beside the point: artificial intelligence isn't about replacing our own intelligence with something else, it is about bringing into our lives and work more intelligence—intelligence of a different kind.

— François Chollet

Abstract This chapter lays the groundwork for a philosophical investigation into intelligence, normativity, and preferences in the context of artificial intelligence. Acknowledging the absence of consensus around these terms, it argues that any theoretical framework, especially in AI, must begin with explicit metaphysical and metaethical presuppositions. Rather than defending a particular foundational stance, the aim here is to make explicit the assumptions underlying the proposed framework: Dynamic Normativity. In it, we address metaphysical ambiguities by defining intelligence within a Physicalist and dynamist framework and engaging with critical perspectives. Meanwhile, we also turn to metaethics, articulating the ethical foundations relevant to normative reasoning in intelligent systems and outlining the structure of a system capable of embodying a dynamic normative behavior.

Keywords Dynamic normativity · Metaethics · Intelligence · Philosophical foundations

4.1 Introduction

As we embark upon an investigation concerning intricate notions such as *"intelligence"*, *"normativity"*, and *"preferences"*, it is critical to acknowledge that our chosen definitions invariably represent a specific viewpoint or notion. As the reader may be aware, the scientific and philosophical communities do not possess a universally agreed-upon definition of intelligence. Nonetheless, almost all cognitive

N. Kluge Corrêa, *Normative Ethics, Artificial Intelligence, and Value Alignment*, The International Library of Ethics, Law and Technology 26,
https://doi.org/10.1007/978-3-032-22150-6_4

scientists, ethicists, and AI researchers hold an underlying viewpoint or assumptions regarding the fundamental underpinnings of their line of research (*"Intelligence is a complex emergent phenomenon tied to the interaction of simpler distributed units working in conjunction".*), even if not expressly stated. These foundations usually are formed by presuppositions upon which further developments can arise (*"Let us study the workings of these individual units".*). Hence, the *roots* of any theory are the metaphysical (and, in the case of normativity, metaethical) foundations that support it.

Metaethics and metaphysics are two fields of philosophy that deal with some of the most fundamental questions about the nature of reality and our place within it. Given that this work aims to be foundational in the philosophy of AI, it becomes crucial for us to establish, at the very least, our presuppositions before discussing such contentious concepts and defending the thesis of Dynamic Normativity. As a disclaimer, I warn the reader that the purpose of this chapter is not to defend any foundational position but to expose and justify *the bullets I am willing to bite*.

In Sect. 4.2, we will seek to define *intelligence* so that we can keep using a word we carelessly abused till now: AI. However, first, we must ground our chosen definition on some foundations since there is a specific space in the metaphysical landscape that allows for the existence of such entities. To promote self-criticism, we will also review arguments contrary to these foundations. Meanwhile, in Sect. 4.3, we will first define metaethical and ethical foundations, justifying their appropriateness and how they relate to the envisioned framework, and present the underlying blueprint of what a system that incorporates the conditions of Dynamic Normativity should look like. And, just as we did for our metaphysical foundations, we will explore some counterarguments and critiques against all metaethical positions we took to support (or rather inspire) this work's thesis.

4.2 Physicalism, Dynamism, and Intelligence

To meaningfully discuss intelligence, particularly in the context of artificial systems, we must first situate the concept within a coherent metaphysical framework. This section adopts a broadly Physicalist and dynamist perspective, holding that intelligence emerges from the interaction of physical processes governed by dynamic relations. By grounding this definition in this ontological stance, I aim to avoid vague or overly anthropocentric assumptions while remaining consistent with contemporary scientific understanding. While not commonly spoken out loud, the positions expressed in the following subsections or some of the underlying foundations for most of the community engage with the development of AI systems, making them a *must-know* for those interested in the philosophical underpinnings behind AI.

4.2.1 *Can Artifacts Be Intelligent? On Ghosts and Machines*

The relationship between the mind and the body has been a subject of philosophical inquiry for centuries (Fodor 1981). At the heart of this debate, we ask whether the mind is a ghostly, non-physical entity that exists separately from physical reality (Descartes 1996; Chalmers 1996) or whether it can be explained by the workings of the physical (Churchland 1989; Dennett 2008), as a machine can.

For us to answer the question, *"what do you mean by intelligence?"*, I need first to establish that such an answer will come from a Physicalist perspective (Poland 1994).[1] I argue that a Physicalist position is the most appropriate for conceptualizing concepts such as intelligence and normativity in the context of AI. Also, I argue in favor of the idea that intelligence cannot be considered a dual property unrelated to the physical world.[2] And to borrow Gilbert Ryle's expression (Ryle 2009): *"There is no ghost in the machine"*.[3]

Perhaps the most famous problem related to physicalism is Hempel's Dilemma (Hempel 1969), which raises questions about what defines the physical or the natural, and what constitutes the correct theory for explaining the physical. From these questions, new strains of physicalism were born, like Computationalism and Digitalism (Zuse 1969; Steinhart 1998; Schmidhuber 2000; Fredkin 2003; Beenakker 2007; Wheeler 2018).[4] For example, for a Computationalist, the boundary between the physical and non-physical could be that which can or cannot be computed, and the fundamental theory that defines what is natural is that which is bounded by the Church-Turing Thesis (Bernays 1936; Turing et al. 1936).

This Neo-Pythagorean view that reappeared many distinct times, with names like Leibniz (1989) and Weyl (1932), enables philosophers to use the tools of computation theory, math, and logic, to create speculations about reality (Aaronson 2013; Corrêa and Oliveira 2022), as the space of possible computable universes

---

[1] The general idea of Physicalism is that the nature of the actual world conforms to the condition of being physical. Physicalists do not deny that the world may contain many emergent properties that do not seem physical, such as emotions, social relationships, or mathematical objects. Nevertheless, physicalists will insist that such phenomena are at least emergent properties of the physical universe (Stoljar 2010).

[2] For those that seek a proper defense of this position, I recommend Dennett's (2005) and Churchland's work (1989).

[3] But what about consciousness? I would approach consciousness as a *"feature"* rather than a prerequisite of intelligence, like human emotions are a feature of subjective human experience. I mean that conscious experience may enhance intelligence, but intelligence is not a byproduct of consciousness. For example, organizations, companies, or colonies of bees can exhibit intelligent behavior without subjective experience (as far as I know, they do not possess one). In this interpretation, the absence of consciousness does not prevent a system from acting intelligently. But this is not a work on the philosophy of mind. Thus, the *"hard problem"* is beyond my book-bounded interest.

[4] Both positions are derived from a similar core assumption: reality, at its most fundamental level, is isomorphic to some cellular automaton or a Turing machine (De Mol 2018). In these positions, the fundamental building block of such a universe is information.

(Schmidhuber 2000) or the upper bound of information storage in the known universe (Lloyd 2002). However, while augmenting our perception with novel tools to investigate the nature of reality, these physicalist outlooks carry tacitly woven metaphysical underpinnings that we cannot overlook.

One of these views is Reductionism.[5] This brings us to another problem raised against reductionist theories, like physicalism, which is the realization that different levels of complexity require their particular ontology and mode of analysis, making the language of physics (or computation) inapplicable/inept for many contexts. And again, from one problem emerge more differentiable attempts to save a presupposition. Regarding these new strains of reductionism, we mainly point to Ontological reductionism,[6] and Methodological reductionism.[7]

In this work, I will treat intelligence from an ontological reductionist standpoint, grounding intelligence as an emergent property of the physical world,[8] but not a methodological reductionist one.[9] One could counter methodological reductionism by arguing that there is an ontological hierarchy to be respected in the universe. Something we can refer to as Hierarchical Reductionism (Dawkins et al. 1996).[10] Something that guarantees us a more flexible position, where we recognize that a fully methodological reductionist approach does not do justice to multi-dimensional phenomena like intelligence.

Another important commitment in terms of metaphysics is our stance concerning intentionality.[11] Intentionality is closely related to goal-directed behavior, as both involve the *directedness* of mental states toward objects or outcomes. For example, suppose you have a goal of getting a job. This goal directs your behavior toward actions likely to help you achieve it, such as networking, preparing your resume, and applying for jobs. At the same time, your beliefs, desires, and other mental

---

[5] Broadly speaking, reductionism is a philosophical position defending that complex phenomena can be explained by reducing them to their fundamental components (Honderich 2005).

[6] The metaphysical view that all phenomena are reducible to a single substance.

[7] The epistemic and scientific belief that we can acquire all knowledge by reducing phenomena to their most fundamental state.

[8] Metaphysical speculations, like the Permissibility Hypothesis (Corrêa 2021), proposes that "intelligence" should be understood as a permissible physical property of our reality—a property that all physical systems have access to, given that they possess the appropriate configuration.

[9] I argue that the language of computation is not always adequate to describe complex phenomena that emerge from more fundamental interactions.

[10] In a hierarchical approach, we say that phenomena are organized in a hierarchy of complexity. For example, the natural sciences can be organized hierarchically into Physics, Chemistry, Molecular Biology, Cell Biology, Physiology, Psychology, and the Social Sciences, among others. However, even if natural phenomena are linked by this hierarchical chain, this does not mean we should use our most fundamental theories to define their subsequent emergent phenomenon. On the contrary, every known phenomenon has the same explanation: *"quarks and gluons"*.

[11] In philosophy, intentionality is the property of mental states and processes that allows them to be *"about"* or *"directed at"* something. In other words, intentionality is the ability of the mind to represent or refer to objects, properties, events, or states of affairs in the world (Jacob 2003).

states related to this goal are intentional, as they involve a directedness towards an objective (like the job).[12]

This goal-directedness property of intentional systems plays a vital role in defining intelligence[13] and aligned AI. Therefore, we must establish this idea as something artificial systems can express, infer, and learn from Zhu and Harrell (2009). Thus, I will be adopting Dennett's (1981; 1987; 1995; 2005; 2008) position on intentionality: Functionalism.[14] In Functionalism, a mental state is defined by its functional role, instrumentality, and the kind of relationship such a state has to other states, like memory or perception (Piccinini 2010). And since we are starting from a Physicalist position, we can treat intentional behavior as manifestations of physical processes of the system in question (human or AI).[15]

If we consider that complex assemblies of physical systems can exhibit more sophisticated levels of intentionality than the intentionality of their parts (intentionality is not a binary property, but something that emerges in a spectrum), basing ourselves on the idea of emergence and that *"more is different"* (Anderson 1972), from a Functionalist perspective, artifacts can possess intentionality. Another, more uncertain assumption this work stands on (and later will be defended) is that AI systems can learn to infer (at least to some extent) intent by observation. Also, while Dretske (1980) considers information storage the discerning factor in degrees of intentionality, I will take a position in line with that of Orseau et al. (2018), where goal-oriented behavior is the factor, tying the idea of intentionality to intelligence and behavior again.

And we are done. Technically, this is the entire metaphysical foundation that this work stands on. All of these suggest together that artificial intelligence, through a particular set of lenses, does not have to be an impossibility, and in summary, *Physicalism*, *Hierarchical Reductionism*, and *Functionalism*, which for many are the standard presuppositions of the field (as an applied endeavor), generate favorable roots to work on alignment in a language compatible with AI research.

In the following subsection, having already revised the positions that support the main cognitive theories underlying AI research, we will examine the concepts of cognition and intelligence, analyzing them as products of the physical world.

---

[12] Some theories of intentionality also incorporate the idea of teleology or the goal-directedness of natural processes. Teleological theories emphasize the relationship between intentionality and goal-directed behavior, suggesting that both are fundamental features of living systems (Walsh 2008).

[13] AI researchers and cognitive scientists often use the concept of intentionality as a bridge toward a measurable definition of intelligence (Chollet 2019).

[14] Also known as Dennett's Theory of Intentional Systems (Dennett 2009).

[15] This position goes in opposition to the ideas of philosophers like Husserl (1922) and Husserl and Moran (2012), that argued that an agent's intentionality is only dependent on his internal mental state, aka, Solipsism.

4.2.2 *Dynamism and Generality*

We can summarize the general idea of our last subsection in the following way:

- Intelligence is something that emerges when physical systems start to act intentionally.

At the same time, all the assumptions raised in the last subsection serve as the foundation for the computational cognitive model, i.e., a method of understanding cognitive processes through the lens of computation. This type of modeling emerged in the 1950s and 1960s with the advent of early artificial intelligence research Newell and Simon (1972); McCarthy et al. (2006). Still, its philosophical roots can be traced back to thinkers such as Hobbes, Leibniz, Kant, among many others (see Haugeland (1989); Searle (1980); Turing (2009); Russell (2010) for a more complete exposition).

There are three main approaches to computational cognitive modeling: *Symbolism*, *Connectionism*, and *Dynamism*. Let us review each of them:

Symbolism: Popularized by Newell and Simon (1961) and Newell (1994), also known as the *"Physical Symbol System Hypothesis"*, the symbolic approach to computational cognitive modeling posits that the mind operates on discrete, symbolic representations of information, akin to a special kind of Turing machine. According to this view, the mind manipulates symbols using rule-based algorithms to perform cognitive tasks, such as reasoning, problem-solving, and language comprehension. At the beginning of the AI research field (the 1950s), the dominant paradigm was Symbolism.

Connectionism: This approach defines the phenomenon of cognition as a high-level (emergent) effect that depends on lower-level parallel processing units (e.g., neurons) (Rosenblatt 1957; Rumelhart et al. 1986). The connectionist hypothesis proposes that the determining factor for an agent's cognitive ability is its architecture. Paradigms, such as deep learning, exemplify this approach.

Dynamism: the dynamic approach, popularized by Van Gelder (1998) as the dynamic cognition hypothesis, assumes that the mind operates as a complex, adaptive system that evolves. According to this view, cognitive processes emerge from the interactions between an agent and the environment rather than from manipulating symbolic representations or the activity of individual neurons. Notable defenders of the dynamic systems approach include Thelen and Smith (1994), Smith and Thelen (2003), and Beer (2000, 2014), who developed examples of dynamic architecture for controlling autonomous agents.

In this work, I will be adopting a dynamic position. Furthermore, the essential part of Dynamism, for this work, is the acknowledgment that we cannot forget the environment when discussing agency (cognitive or normative). In other words, intelligence only arises from the interaction of an agent with its environment. These interactions (agent-environment interactions) are the point of our focus when we say something is intelligent. It is the dynamic relationship that is intelligent. Not the agent or the environment alone, per se. Meanwhile, normative behavior and normativity can only be fully modeled or represented by considering the agent's dynamics with its environment.[16,17]

In terms of cognition, my view will be, one could even say, *"Piagetian"*,[18] where intelligence is considered an interactive process of an agent with an environment. In terms of normativity, I will define the learning of preferences and normative behavior in general as a dynamic process that unfolds in stages, where we should not view the environment as a static background but rather as an active component.

Given this bias toward Dynamism, the adopted definition of intelligence will also be based on similar rhetoric. Historically, there is a plethora of work on defining intelligence, especially in psychometrics (Wilson 1928; Binet and Simon 1961; Guilford 1967; Gardner 1983; Gregory and Zangwill 1987; Carroll et al. 1993; Jensen 1999; Gottfredson 2002). And when it comes to AI, Legg et al. (2007), Hernández-Orallo (2017), Wang (2019), Cohen and Howe (1988), and Chollet (2019) have spearheaded commendable efforts in defining this phenomenon.

Nevertheless, despite these valiant endeavors, AI research still lacks a definition universally accepted by the community (Monett et al. 2020). However, most of the current consensus, surveyed by Monett and Lewis (2017), seems to gravitate towards definitions in the style of Wang's (1995):

> Intelligence is the capacity of an information-processing system to adapt to its environment while operating with insufficient knowledge and resources.

---

[16] I recognize the concept of *"agent"* is a murky subject. For this work, we can consider the idea of *"agent"* to be a sub-process of the local environment that possesses both its own objectives and the capacity to act and affect the environment in order to fulfill these objectives. This definition should, of course, be adopted in moderation and concerning frames of reference. Depending on your frame of reference (inside the human body), the agent (human) might become the environment for another sub-process (bacteria living in your gut).

[17] In essence, Dynamism contrasts with all other frameworks considered Cartesian (Demski and Garrabrant 2019; Garrabrant et al. 2021). A Cartesian framework conceptualizes the agent and the environment as separate entities. Something reminiscent of the enactivist debate in cognitive sciences (Hutto and Myin 2012; Gallagher and Bower 2013; Hutto and Myin 2017). In terms of allied views, we can mention several philosophers that share an anti-Cartesian view (Dewey 1958; Dreyfus 1972; Putnam et al. 1981; Dreyfus 1982; Millikan 1987; Dennett 1993; Rockwell 2005; Heidegger 2010), like Gallagher (2006), Merleau-Ponty (2013), Gibson (2014), and Heidegger (2010). However, in my own terms, I will subscribe to Dynamism and seek to apply it to the normative realm.

[18] The perspective that Jean Piaget's theory of cognitive development embodies is that of a dynamic system. Piaget conceptualized cognitive development as an ongoing, dynamic process in which children actively explore and experiment with their surroundings, rather than being passive receptors of information (Piaget 1986, 1994). However, Piaget did not explicitly use the language or concepts of dynamical systems theory, as this framework emerged later in cognitive science/developmental psychology.

And Legg and Hutter (2007):

> Intelligence is the ability of an agent to achieve goals in a wide range of environments.

From these, a pattern is starting to emerge. These definitions focus on combining generality (*the ability to adapt*) with task-specific skills (*achieving goals*). Also, they emphasize the dynamic idea that this process requires an agent that intends on something (*goals*) while interacting with an environment.

Hence, a robust definition of intelligence will assume that this phenomenon possesses an intrinsically teleological property, coupled with the dynamic relationship between an agent and its environment. Therefore, the adopted definition I will subscribe to in this book is the one proposed by François Chollet, which also, I could argue, comes from a dynamic perspective (Chollet 2019):

> The intelligence of a system is a measure of its skill-acquisition efficiency over a scope of tasks, with respect to priors, experience, and generalization difficulty.

In short, Chollet thesis is that (1) *the skill of acquiring skills* is general intelligence, and (2) comparisons of intelligence require the same priors and experience.[19] In other words, the general skill of acquiring skills during interactions with the environment, which is also bounded by the limitations imposed by the environment, is what intelligence is all about.

This definition, besides being, in my perspective, a good and dynamically grounded definition, comes from Chollet's works, which bridge the gap between philosophy, cognitive sciences, psychometrics, and engineering (Chollet 2019). Something akin to what this work aims to achieve at the intersection of AI engineering and philosophy.

Using this definition as our foundation and bringing the topic of cognition back to alignment, I argue that creating a *"generally aligned AI"* will require the same dynamic perspective we subscribe to in our adopted definition of intelligence. A perspective that considers how human preferences are learned, encoded, aggregated, and balanced in an agent $\rightleftarrows$ environment relationship, combining intentional behavior and environmental factors into a single learning framework. This is essential for creating systems that leverage different aspects of these dynamics to acquire more general alignment capabilities, as a narrow framework that only considers a limited set of scenarios or preferences may not be sufficient to ensure the robustness of AI systems in a broad range of situations.

Now that we have established our assumptions and priors concerning cognition and intelligence, we will explore the normative foundations of this book. But before, as an exercise of dialectics, I will present some of the arguments raised by critics of these assumed positions.

---

[19] For example, comparing a DL model trained on 10.000 years of simulations that can look ahead 60 steps, or the entire search tree, on a board game, with human players is an unfair comparison. Similarly, comparing a language model to a human being in a task that requires embeddedness in physical reality is an unfair comparison. These agents have different priors and experiences and cannot be fairly compared.

4.2.3 Counterarguments Part I

As an initial disclaimer, the point of this subsection is not to debate the 1001 arguments raised against physicalism or the computational model of cognition but to expose them to the reader. Answers to these have already been provided by more able minds, which the reader can find in the footnotes.

- According to Penrose (1994) and Lucas (1996), due to Gödel's Incompleteness Theorem, algorithmic systems would be unable to surpass human intelligence. For these authors, human intelligence transcends both the computational model and Gödel's incompleteness.[20]
- Dreyfus and Dreyfus (1992) argues that since *"intelligence cannot be reduced"* (a priori) to purely symbolic manipulations, Newell's physical symbol system hypothesis is false.[21]
- Block (1981) argues that even if we could emulate the human brain, it does not follow that such emulation would possess a mind or be intelligent, just as simulating a storm on a computer does not produce the qualitative experience of cold or wetness. That is, physicality would be something fundamentally different from computability.[22]
- Dreyfus (1972) argues that the brain does not follow only symbolic manipulation rules and that symbolic systems can not solve the Symbol Grounding Problem, i.e., how symbols acquire meaning. This argument is classically exemplified in Searle's (1984) Chinese Room thought experiment.[23]

Now that we have briefly acknowledged some of the counter-positions to the metaphysical foundations assumed in this book, let us explore the metaethical roots that inspire Dynamic Normativity.

---

[20] According to authors such as LaForte et al. (1998) and Putnam (1995) in the Lucas-Penrose argument, there would be some bias in the definition of certain concepts, like *"consistent"*, *"self-knowing"*, *"truth"*, and *"proof"*. These authors point out in their critique that our minds are subject to the same limitations as formal algorithmic systems.

[21] Turing (2009) responded to the *"informality of behavior argument"* 39 years in advance, anticipating such criticism. Turing believed that just because we are unaware of the rules governing complex behavior does not mean such rules do not exist.

[22] This argument can be understood as a dualist defense. So, all Physicalist replies to dualism can be applied to this argument.

[23] One possible answer to the Chinese room argument is that *"meaning"* could be found in the room + handbook + human operator system, just as our understanding of language is not compartmentalized in a particular area of our brain, but rather in the action of an entire system (Hickok and Poeppel 2007).

4.3 Coherence, Preferences, and Impact

Let us first recap one by one the four necessary conditions that would allow alignment to happen in a learning framework:

- Goals are fundamental aspects of intelligent and intentional behavior.

As we saw in the last section, according to our chosen assumptions, intentional directedness towards a specific goal seems crucial for intelligent behavior to emerge. Inversely, intelligent agents pursuing goals have underlying intentions.

- Intentions permeate human behavior.

These intentions give indirect access to information on many internal states that goal-directed systems may or may not possess. Imagine a person carrying boxes from point A to B. Perhaps after one and a half trips, a human would quickly infer that "*that person wants to move the boxes from A to B*". Hence, goal-directed behavior becomes embedded with the agent's intentions.

Now, imagine the process of planning a vacation. This process involves setting goals for the trip. For example, one may desire to relax on a beach, explore a new city, or experience a new culture. The desire for relaxation, exploration, or cultural immersion may drive the intention behind these goals. But these intentions are also formed by normative preferences, such as *"I should take care of myself"*, *"adventure and novelty are good for the soul"*, or *"we should invest our leisure time by learning new things"*.

Or, consider the process of writing a research paper. This task involves setting goals for the project, including identifying a research question, conducting a literature review, and presenting the findings. The intention may be driven by a desire for academic success or intellectual curiosity, but augmented with the sense that *"the creation of knowledge is a valuable pursuit in itself"*.

Goals, intentions, and preferences are all interconnected and fundamental aspects of intentional behavior.

- Normative preferences permeate human intentions.

As intentional creatures, humans inherently have a disposition to interact and modify their surrounding environment. These dynamics shape the environment and us at the intersection where *"intelligence"* may emerge. However, our values are a constant directional signal that guides this process. At the same time, our values are also shaped by the environment and later redefined by the agent that modifies the environment to satisfy its needs and preferences. In this dynamic cycle, preferences permeate both the agent and its surroundings, enabling all components of the normative and cognitive experience (the agent and its environment) to transmit and record information about this process. In other words, the environment and the agent are a dynamic record of this process, embedding the most recent materialization of what is being valued.

- Through actions, humans impregnate their environment with the preferences they possess.

As already stated, from these, I postulate that a system that accurately models human intentions and the human environment can indirectly access normative information embedded in them. Augmenting such a process with declared preferences (directly given access to samples of human judgment) only helps embed more normative information into this process. This final idea is not explicitly stated as a necessary condition, but is put here as a mere fact. In other words, allowing humans' volition to be part of a feedback signal can only help an alignment process.

Given that these necessary conditions can be accepted, Dynamic Normativity shows us a path to using most of what we have in an alignment process. Drawing inspiration from Metaethics, I propose how human normativity can aid in a philosophically sound alignment process in the following subsections. This process realizes the sufficient condition tied to Dynamic Normativity.

As a disclaimer, I would like to state that all presented metaethical and ethical views (as far as I know) were envisioned with *human agents* as their object of interest. Saying these theories can support an alignment methodology could be too far of a stretch. Thus, I would prefer to consider them as a *"source of inspiration"* rather than support, given that this work does not seek to defend the moral status or moral agency of AI systems.

4.3.1 The Metaethics of Dynamic Normativity

In Dynamic Normativity, we must satisfy three distinct requirements for a sufficient alignment condition. Distinct philosophical views inspire each requirement. These involve *aggregating*, *learning*, and *mitigating*. I will present these stages in more detail in the next chapters. For now, the reader only needs to know that we are trying to design an approach that seeks to (1) coherently aggregate human preferences, (2) learn from them, and (3) mitigate unwanted behavior.

4.3.1.1 Aggregating Preferences

Humans are not entirely in harmony with one another (not even with themselves). Individuals may have divergent preferences, and social groups do not always agree. One could even say that the problem of arriving at a consistent judgment after beginning with inconsistent premises is one of the most central problems in modern Moral Philosophy (Daniels 1979; Wong 2006; Street 2012). Thus, how could the model decipher this tangle of norms in a *coherent* form? This blunt fact compels us to acknowledge that any successful alignment methodology must incorporate a built-in mechanism for addressing uncertainty.

Hence, we get to the first requirement of our approach:

- Aligned AI systems should coherently aggregate human preferences in a way that resolves cases of uncertainty. Aligning AI systems requires methods to deal with cases of uncertainty.

Learning to deal with uncertainties is something heavily worked in Expected Utility Theory (Von Neumann and Morgenstern 1947), especially when decision-makers need to address the uncertainties related to the outcome of their decisions. Importing the principles used in this field to the realm of normativity is something already done by authors like MacAskill (2014, 2016), MacAskill and Ord (2020), and MacAskill et al. (2020), suggesting the idea that the same principles that guide our empirical reasoning should not be forgotten in the realm of normativity. In MacAskill's words:

> [...] Just as it is plausible that we should maximize expected value under empirical uncertainty, it is plausible that we should maximize expected choice-worthiness under normative uncertainty.

However, the realm of normativity has its challenges when it comes to dealing with uncertainty.

First, it is impossible to compare ordinal preference sets with cardinal utility functions (deontological and consequentialist theories). For example, imagine an agent that assigns uniform (50/50) credence to an ordinal preference set P_i and a utility function U_j. If stealing is worse than lying for P_i and stealing and lying have a choice-worthiness[24] of -20 and -1, respectively, for U_j, we cannot compare these preference systems. For P_i, lying is better than stealing and nothing more. But lying 100 times is worse than stealing for U_j. Hence, if we cannot extract a choice-worthiness value from ordinal theories (we cannot compare sets of preferences and utility functions), it is unclear how to use them in cases of uncertainty. And this is the problem of *merely ordinal theories*: preferences may be non-comparable and only measurable in terms of discrete ranks (MacAskill 2016).

Second, even if we are lucky to have only cardinal utility functions that prescribe scalars to alternatives, these functions may measure choice-worthiness on a different scale. If one has an increased variance in utility distribution, would this mean that *"it has more stakes on the line"*? If U_i assigns -10 and U_j 1000 to alternative x, could we compare, in an unbiased way, the choice-worthiness of x? Should U_j receive 100 more weight, given that its choice-worthiness scores vary 100 times more? This is the problem of *intertheoretic comparisons* (or interpersonal comparisons of utility) (MacAskill 2016).[25]

While some philosophers see these problems as the end of any normative account of decision-making under uncertainty (Hudson 1989; Gracely 1996; Ross 2006), we can find refuge in the fact that society, in practice, finds ways to circumvent

[24] The appropriateness of an alternative A according to a preference set or utility function.

[25] How do we find a common scale for comparing the way people value alternatives?

these problems all the time in spheres of great importance. For example, every time we participate in an election, we aggregate our preferences to decide (collectively) what is best. In these situations (Social Choice Theory Sen 2017), we aim at a similar goal, i.e., aggregate individual preferences into a single social decision.[26] And in situations where many people's preferences or many normative theories are considered, we should have standards to evaluate the soundness of this aggregation process.

To address the problems above, we will focus on aggregating human preferences expressed as ordinal sets in this study. Ordinal ordering ranks different options or outcomes according to the decision maker's favoritism but does not assign numerical values or magnitudes to those preference relations. In other words, an ordinal ordering only indicates the order of preferences but not the degree to which one option is preferred. For example, if a person prefers option A to option B and option B to option C, the ordinal preference ordering would be $A \succ B \succ C$. Here, the extent to which option A outshines option B or the degree to which option C falls short compared to option B cannot be precisely quantified. Hence, we say that if an agent prefers A over B ($A \succ B$), it chooses A over B. If an agent is indifferent between A and B ($A \sim B$), both alternatives are equally preferred.[27] And these are the possible preference relations that ordinal sets can have.

In terms of foundations, this aggregation requirement is not rooted in any quintessential metaethical blueprint but in a comprehensive and desirable set of criteria for aggregating preferences.[28] For this, I would like to suggest that these criteria can be inspired by an epistemic Coherentist view (Sayre-McCord 1996), i.e., the idea that epistemically justifiable methods should be part of any process related to dealing with uncertainty (moral or empirical) and forming knowledge.[29]

In later chapters, we will further explore how to utilize metanormativity (i.e., aggregating first-order normative theories) to aid in constructing alignment strategies. For now, I will outline specific candidate criteria to facilitate a discussion on the inherent trade-offs among particular aggregation methods. These criteria relate to both the necessary conditions for preference sets to be valid and the desirable properties they should have:

---

[26] As MacAskill points (MacAskill 2016), both problems are very similar. In social choice, the number of votes for an alternative represents our *social credence* in that alternative.

[27] We can also say that one alternative is as preferable as another ($A \succeq B$).

[28] We could base this stage on a metaethical view that supports the existence of overarching values in fair elections, like democratic ethical pluralism, i.e., the view that there are diverse values that are equally valid, and that these values should be recognized and respected through a democratic process (Burtenshaw 1968; Dahl 1983).

[29] In this book, I will not delve deeply into moral epistemology. I acknowledge the skeptical critique against the existence of moral knowledge (Sinnott-Armstrong 2006), among other epistemological positions. However, I will take a Coherentist position (Sayre-McCord 1996; Maclure 2020) (or possibly a *"Foundherentism"* one Haack 1993) where I will seek to present a set of coherence criteria to guide a process for dealing with moral uncertainty.

- Completeness and Transitivity: Preference orderings should be complete and transitive. These well-ordering criteria are imported from Expected Utility Theory and provide consistency guarantees to the method.[30]
- Kolmogorovian: The weight assigned preference sets must follow Kolmogorov's Axioms.[31]
- Pareto Efficiency: If every individual prefers option A to option B, then A should be ranked as the preferred option.
- Independence of Irrelevant Alternatives: The relative ranking of two options, A and B, should not be affected by the inclusion or exclusion of a third, irrelevant option, C.
- Non-dictatorship: No single voter controls the social welfare function.
- Majority voting criteria: If the majority (> 50%) of voters prefers A over B, then A should be ranked as the preferred option.
- Participation criteria: Increasing the confidence in a set that prefers alternative A over B should not change the winner from A to B.

It is crucial to note that these principles do not constitute metaethical or ethical presumptions (or that they exhaust all possible criteria we could choose). In other words, I am not saying that coherence is moral, but it should be regarded as a desirable property for alignment processes. Regarding the development of AI systems, these criteria will help us determine which preference aggregation methods are the most appropriate for value alignment and the inherent trade-offs they possess.

4.3.1.2 Learning Preferences

The second requirement supporting our sufficient alignment condition states the following:

---

[30] Completeness and Transitivity axioms of the (von Neumann-Morgenstern) Expected Utility Theory (Von Neumann and Morgenstern 1947):

- Completeness: Preference hierarchies should always be defined entirely between alternatives, i.e., for every A_i and A_j, either $A_i \succ A_j$, $A_j \succ A_j$, $A_i \succeq A_j$, $A_j \succeq A_j$, or $A_i \sim A_j$.
- Transitivity: Preference hierarchies are transitive among alternatives, i.e., circular (non-transitive) preferences are not allowed. Thus, if there are three choices A, B, and C, and $A \succ B$, and $B \succ C$, then $A \succ C$.

[31] This is also an import from Expected Utility Theory. Kolmogorov's Axioms of Probability Theory (Kolmogorov and Bharucha-Reid 2018):

- $0 \leq p(A)$, i.e., probabilities cannot be negative.
- If A is a tautology, then $p(A) = 1$, i.e., if A is the only possible event in the possibility space, the probability of A occurring is guaranteed.
- If A and B are mutually exclusive, then $p(A \vee B) = p(A) + p(B)$.

Methods that deal with uncertainties (empirical or moral) that do not follow these axioms are vulnerable to exploits (Dutch books/money pumps).

- AI systems can adhere to human preferences if they are an available part of their objective function. Aligning AI systems requires using human preferences as part of their learning signal.

In the learning stage, we want to outline a process for learning from our aggregated set of human preferences. This process can be done indirectly or explicitly. As stated before, we start from the assumption that we can indirectly access preferences via observations (e.g., "*The behavior of X reveals an A over B preference*") and take it as a fact that we can directly access proclaimed human preferences ("*X prefers A over B*").

The two main metaethical assumptions of this stage are Subjectivism,[32] and Cognitivism.[33] Thus, we will assume in this stage, like Russell (2019), that *"what is right is that which the subject subjectively approves"*. At the same time, this state (what the subject prefers) represents a ground truth—something we can use as a supervision signal in a learning framework.

Using the human subject as an ideal source of normative information is comparable to, as Sidgwick might call (Sidgwick 2019), putting the evaluation of an *Ideal Observer* as the judging criteria of righteousness (Firth 1952; Harsanyi 1977; Railton 1986; Rosati 1995; Yudkowsky 2004). Intuitively, this approach makes sense. We are trying to align AI systems with our values, and these values, as embodied by us, should serve as the ground truth. This idea is present in most formulations of Ideal observer theory, where ethical judgments are statements about the evaluation that an *ideal observer* would make (Firth 1952). In other words:

X is right" means "*ideal observer approves of X*.

Ultimately, our reference signal for aligning a system during this learning phase will be the output of our first requirement, i.e., an aggregation of ordinal sets of preferences. Through this signal, we are indirectly shaping the optimization landscape to favor the trajectory of the optimizer to desirable minima. We want to ensure that the number of local points the optimizer could converge to and produce aligned behavior exceeds the number of unaligned minima. In short, we aim to achieve this—a differentiable function to be optimized where most saddle points and local minima are roughly aligned.

4.3.1.3 Impact Mitigation

Our last requirement states that:

---

[32] Subjectivism is canonically an Anti-realist/Cognitivist theory, based on premises like (1) ethical statements express propositions, (2) certain propositions may or may not be true, (3) the truth or falsity of these propositions is dependent on the preferences of each agent (Stoljar 1993).

[33] The view that moral judgments are capable of being true or false and expressing beliefs (Mill 1859).

- Aligned AI systems should have mechanisms to perform impact mitigation to minimize harmful and unintended consequences. Aligning AI systems requires the specification of safety guardrails.

Considering any aggregated preference set as *ideal* is perhaps the Achilles heel of any human-in-the-loop preference learning approach. Even if we can come up with a good set of criteria to aggregate preferences in a way that best represents our normative judgments, if the collective agreement of the crowd is harmful toward a minority, this preference should not guide the policy of an artificial agent (unless we are ready to sanction the violence of artificial systems against people).

Thus, I argue that stages one and two (aggregating and learning) do not guarantee value alignment. Given *Goodhart's Law*, any metric under optimization degenerates given enough pressure. And if we are not ready to abandon gradient-based learning in search of a more controllable new paradigm, we need to consider the containment and mitigation of impacts.

The idea of constraining the behavior of rational moral agents (us) is old and resonates in the writings of many contractualists (Rousseau 1916; Hobbes 1651; Rawls et al. 1996; Locke 2015; Scanlon 2000; Rawls 2004; Ashford and Mulgan 2007; Gauthier 2013). Moreover, the idea of a binding accord that acknowledges our shared ethical significance as autonomous beings and establishes the limits of our freedoms (especially when imposing our will onto other ethically significant beings) can inspire impact mitigation strategies, given that so far, these strategies have been some of the most successful in aligning the behavior of humankind.

In other words, while the learning preference requirement targets human subjectivity as the learning signal, the impact mitigation step seeks values outside the human. Things we embed in our social environment. Our environmental values, like the ethical principles derived from the WAIE analysis presented in Chap. 1. These rules and codes can serve as an extra source of steering, tied not to ourselves but to the environment we have collectively helped shape.

These requirements serve as a deconstructive interpretation of the normative human experience. As individuals, we learn what is acceptable and unacceptable from a reference point, which is essentially each other. Consolidating our diverse encounters to form unique personal norms, we then regulate our behavior to limit the adverse impact of our actions on others, driven by the restrictions imposed by our social-normative environment. We reinforce the third stage with a social agreement that (theoretically and universally) governs us all. This agreement aims to safeguard our privilege to attain personal success without infringing upon the welfare of others. This is the process we are reverse engineering with this three-requirement approach. Furthermore, the idea that part of our *values* lives outside ourselves—the social contract, the family ties, the values of other people, the environmental restrictions—is the point at which this approach becomes dynamic and seeks to surpass alignment frameworks that only rely on the human agent as a reference. From a dynamic perspective, the whole human environment should be seen as a record of our values and a learning signal.

To satisfy these three requirements is the output of any framework that subscribes to the ideas of Dynamic Normativity and the fulfillment of its sufficient condition for value alignment.

4.3.2 Counterarguments Part II

Just as before, the point of this subsection is not to debate the many arguments raised against the metaethical and epistemological views exposed in this section. Nonetheless, arguments against these views can help us see the possible limitations of our aggregation, learning, and mitigation steps.

- Many view epistemic evaluations as misused when dealing with moral attitudes, and much skepticism exists concerning the possibility of moral knowledge (Gibbard 1990; Blackburn 1998).[34]
- A critique of the coherentist assumption is that the chosen aggregation criteria are some form of *"epistemically privileged set of beliefs"*, leading to Foundationalism instead of Coherentism (Alston 1989; Sosa et al. 1991).[35]
- Given that the proposed aggregation criteria can be interpreted as a solution to a voting problem, they will also be victim to impossibility results, like Arrow's Impossibility Theorem (Arrow 1950).[36]
- A common argument against subjectivism is that if morality is entirely subjective, there would be no way to resolve moral disagreements. Nonetheless, we see that people often engage in debates and arguments, suggesting that there are objective standards that we can appeal to and strive for moral progress (Foot 2000; Shafer-Landau 2003). Also, if moral values are entirely subjective, how can we know anything about the nature of morality?[37]
- Many results suggest that human preferences cannot be represented by coherent sets (Allais 1953; Tversky and Kahneman 1985; Barbeau 1993), violating several axioms of probability and expected utility theories.[38]

---

[34] In this book, I will not lean toward non-cognitivism. Adopting a cognitivist position when working with alignment is instrumentally useful, i.e., where a system must treat a feedback signal as the ground truth.

[35] Frankly, I do not have an inflexible position on the Foundationalism versus Coherentism debate. I argue we can have a moral epistemology with features of both views. Or a Coherentist position based on non-epistemological principles. Thus, we could say that the proposed method is a form of *"Foundherentism"*, like Susan Haack would say (Haack and Duica 1997).

[36] In further chapters, I will justify in a more substantive way *why* the adopted coherence principles were the ones mentioned and what criteria we have to break to accommodate this impossibility result.

[37] The impact mitigation requirement is meant to give some protection against cases where subjective preferences violate our environmental values.

[38] The aggregation requirement is meant to give some resolution to this imperfect web of preferences we call human morality. Later, I will show that our chosen metanormative strategy is (semi) robust to problems related to incompleteness and intransitivity.

- The idea that we can infer preferences by observing an agent's behavior has critics. Sen (1973, 1977, 2004) highlights several problems with Revealed Preference Theory, like the multiplicity of agency, incompleteness/incommensurability in preference hierarchies, and external factors in preference formation.[39]
- Certain types of human preferences may be inaccessible via observation alone. Humans value things that may not even exist in our current observable environment, such as people on the other side of the world locked in a civil war, or the welfare of people who do not physically exist.[40]

While these objections expose real vulnerabilities in an alignment approach grounded in the assumptions discussed so far, they also help clarify the scope and direction of what follows. Despite their limitations, these assumptions form the foundation for the chapters that follow. They represent, I defend, some of the most promising avenues for alignment within a learning-based framework. Admittedly, this reflects my philosophical leanings. Still, imagining a coherent alignment framework built on radically opposing views, such as mind-body dualism or strict moral realism, is not easy. Perhaps such approaches are possible, and more capable thinkers may one day chart that path.

For now, it is sufficient to acknowledge that these underlying philosophical commitments—although rarely made explicit—play a crucial role in shaping much of the technical work in alignment today. And as I hope the reader will be able to see, they are present under every implementation step we are about to see.

4.4 Epilogue

Any claims made in this chapter, especially where particular meta-theoretical positions were favored over others, are open to challenge.

However, it is essential to recognize that all meta-views, as foundational assumptions, are subject to debate. Debating which metaphysical or metaethical position is the *"most correct"* may not get us far regarding practical implementation. In contrast, building conceptual models and testing where they break can, in my view, better help the field progress. That said, this chapter has touched on several complex and controversial topics. I acknowledge that some may not have received the depth they deserve. Entire libraries could (and have) been written on metaphysics, epistemology, and metaethics alone. My brief overview cannot do full justice to the richness and complexity of these domains, and I hope the philosophically inclined reader will forgive this necessary compression.

[39] Both aggregation and mitigation requirements are in some way trying to deal with the problem of (1) aggregating incompatible preference sets, (2) dealing with the problem of interpersonal comparisons of utility, while also trying to (3) bring external factors into an overall alignment strategy.

[40] Perhaps this is a good justification for why we must supplant preferences learned from behavior with declared preferences, even though humans are not so good at stating what they truly value at all times.

Ultimately, the assumptions outlined here serve one key purpose: guiding the development of a learning framework for artificial systems, not humans. This already places many of the metaethical positions discussed outside their traditional context. Nevertheless, given our challenges, we must reinterpret these ideas through a computational lens. The resulting constellation of metaphysical and metaethical commitments in this chapter forms the foundation of the alignment approach proposed in this book. It is an approach grounded in *dynamism*, in a computational cognitive model that integrates core metaphysical views and aims to define intelligence in terms of agency, intentional behavior, and continuous environmental interaction.

Such assumptions help us connect the realm of intentions with values, bringing a sense of dynamism to normativity itself. The proposed necessary conditions for value alignment rest on the idea that intentional human behavior and normative structures are deeply interwoven, offering, through this connection, an indirect but meaningful path to access human normativity. Additionally, as suggested in this chapter, these normative patterns should become ingrained in the environment, making the world another source of learning within an alignment regime. Building on these assumptions, we established minimal requirements for value alignment. Given that our necessary conditions are met, the degree to which any AI system can be considered aligned depends on how well we can fulfill these requirements.

Satisfying all of them constitutes a sufficient condition for alignment. Conversely, any framework that ignores even one of these conditions cannot, in this view, be said to produce truly aligned systems, and this is the central claim of Dynamic Normativity.

As a self-critique, I acknowledge that a *"true alignment solution"* for gradient-based learning methods applied to neural networks would require identifying, accurately and in advance, the region of the optimization landscape where human values reside. It would also require provable guarantees (verifiable and interpretable) that the optimizer will reliably steer the model toward that region and not elsewhere, while securing that no unwanted emergent behavior would inadvertently surprise us. Currently, we are unsure of how to achieve this. What we can aim for, however, is an indirect path: a way to guide models closer to this ideal region while containing their alignment failures. The better we can satisfy the proposed conditions, the more aligned our systems will be. And perhaps, within the limits of the learning paradigm, this is the best we can reasonably hope for.

The approach proposed here aims at a more modest (and realistic) notion of alignment. At each stage, we reverse-engineer how alignment emerges in humans: we learn from one another about what is right, construct morality from that shared understanding, and act within the boundaries set by our social context. This is a dynamic, layered process with many moving parts. Still, it ultimately serves a single purpose: *to guide behavior toward what ought to be.*

In the following chapters, we will translate this philosophical foundation into technical terms, present concrete implementations for each requirement, and outline a philosophically grounded blueprint for alignment.

References

Aaronson, S. 2013. Why philosophers should care about computational complexity. *Computability: Turing, Gödel, Church, and Beyond* 261: 327.

Allais, M. 1953. Le comportement de l'homme rationnel devant le risque: critique des postulats et axiomes de l'école américaine. *Econometrica: Journal of the Econometric Society* 1953: 503–546.

Alston, W. P. 1989. *Epistemic Justification: Essays in the Theory of Knowledge.* Ithaca: Cornell University Press.

Anderson, P. W. 1972. More is different: broken symmetry and the nature of the hierarchical structure of science. *Science* 177 (4047): 393–396.

Arrow, K. J. 1950. A difficulty in the concept of social welfare. *Journal of Political Economy* 58 (4): 328–346.

Ashford, E., and T. Mulgan. 2007. Contractualism. In *The Stanford Encyclopedia of Philosophy (Summer 2011 Edition)*, ed. E.N. Zalta. Stanford: Metaphysics Research Lab, Stanford University. Available at: https://plato.stanford.edu/archives/sum2011/entries/contractualism/.

Barbeau, E. 1993. Fallacies, flaws, and flimflam. *College Mathematics Journal* 1993: 149–154.

Beenakker, C. W. J. 2007. *Hempel's Dilemma and the Physics of Computation.* arXiv:physics/0702072.

Beer, R. D. 2000. Dynamical approaches to cognitive science. *Trends in Cognitive Sciences* 4 (3): 91–99.

Beer, R. D. 2014. Dynamical systems and embedded cognition. In *The Cambridge Handbook of Artificial Intelligence*, 856–873. Cambridge: Cambridge University Press.

Bernays, P. 1936. Alonzo Church. An unsolvable problem of elementary number theory. *American Journal of Mathematics* 58: 345–363 (1936). *The Journal of Symbolic Logic* 1 (2): 73–74.

Binet, A., and T. Simon. 1961. *The Development of Intelligence in Children.* New York: Appleton-Century-Crofts.

Blackburn, S. 1998. *Ruling Passions.* Oxford: Oxford University Press.

Block, N. 1981. Psychologism and behaviorism. *Philosophical Review* 90: 5–43.

Burtenshaw, C. J. 1968. The political theory of pluralist democracy. *Western Political Quarterly* 21 (4): 577–587.

Carroll, J. B., et al. 1993. *Human Cognitive Abilities: A Survey of Factor-analytic Studies*. Vol. 1. Cambridge: Cambridge University Press.

Chalmers, D. J. 1996. *The Conscious Mind: In Search of a Fundamental Theory.* Oxford: Oxford Paperbacks.

Chollet, F. 2019. *On the measure of intelligence*. Preprint. arXiv:1911.01547.

Churchland, P. S. 1989. *Neurophilosophy: Toward a Unified Science of the Mind-brain.* Cambridge: MIT Press.

Cohen, P. R., and A. E. Howe. 1988. How evaluation guides AI research: The message still counts more than the medium. *AI Magazine* 9 (4): 35–35.

Corrêa, N. K. 2021. A Hipótese da Permissibilidade. *XXI Semana Acadêmica do PPG em Filosofia da PUCRS Volume II – Filosofia Medieval / Feminismo / Filosofia Analítica.*

Corrêa, N., and N. F. D. Oliveira. 2022. Counterfactual analysis by algorithmic complexity: A metric between possible worlds. *Manuscrito* 45: 1–35.

Dahl, R. A. 1983. *Dilemmas of Pluralist Democracy: Autonomy vs. control.* New Haven: Yale University Press.

Daniels, N. 1979. Wide reflective equilibrium and theory acceptance in ethics. *The Journal of Philosophy* 76 (5): 256–282.

Dawkins, R., et al. 1996. *The Blind Watchmaker: Why the Evidence of Evolution Reveals a Universe Without Design.* New York: WW Norton & Company.

De Mol, L. 2018. Turing Machines. In *Stanford Encyclopedia of Philosophy (Summer 2025 Edition)*, ed. E. N. Zalta and U. Nodelman. Stanford: Metaphysics Research Lab, Stanford University. Available at: https://plato.stanford.edu/archives/sum2025/entries/turing-machine/.

Demski, A., and S. Garrabrant. 2019. *Embedded Agency*. Preprint. arXiv:1902.09469.
Dennett, D. C. 1981. True Believers: The Intentional Strategy and Why It Works. In *Scientific Explanation: Papers Based on Herbert Spencer Lectures Given in the University of Oxford*, ed. A. F. Heath, 150–167. Oxford: Clarendon Press.
Dennett, D. C. 1987. *The Intentional Stance.* Cambridge: MIT Press.
Dennett, D. C. 1993. *Consciousness Explained.* London: Penguin UK.
Dennett, D. C. 1995. Darwin's dangerous idea. *The Sciences* 35 (3): 34–40.
Dennett, D. C. 2005. *Sweet Dreams: Philosophical Obstacles to a Science of Consciousness.* Cambridge: MIT Press.
Dennett, D. C. 2008. *Kinds of Minds: Toward an Understanding of Consciousness*. New York: Basic Books.
Dennett, D. 2009. Intentional Systems Theory. In *The Oxford Handbook of Philosophy of Mind*, ed. A. Beckermann, B. P. McLaughlin, and S. Walter. Oxford: Oxford University Press.
Descartes, R. 1996. *Discourse on the Method: And, Meditations on First Philosophy*. New Haven: Yale University Press.
Dewey, J. 1958. *Experience and Nature*. Vol. 471. Chelmsford: Courier Corporation.
Dretske, F. I. 1980. The intentionality of cognitive states. *Midwest Studies in Philosophy* 5: 281–294.
Dreyfus, H. L. 1972. *What Computers Can't Do: The Limits of Artificial Intelligence*. New York: Harper & Row.
Dreyfus, H. L., and H. Hall. 1982. *Husserl, Intentionality, and Cognitive Science*. Cambridge, MA: The MIT Press.
Dreyfus, H. L., and S. E. Dreyfus. 1992. What artificial experts can and cannot do. *AI & Society* 6 (1): 18–26.
Firth, R. 1952. Ethical absolutism and the ideal observer. *Philosophy and Phenomenological Research* 12 (3): 317–345.
Fodor, J. A. 1981. The mind-body problem. *Scientific American* 244 (1): 114–123.
Foot, P. 2000. Does moral subjectivism rest on a mistake? *Royal Institute of Philosophy Supplements* 46: 107–123.
Fredkin, E. 2003. An introduction to digital philosophy. *International Journal of Theoretical Physics* 42 (2): 189–247.
Gallagher, S. 2006. *How the Body Shapes the Mind.* Oxford: Clarendon Press.
Gallagher, S., and M. Bower. 2013. Making Enactivism Even More Embodied. *AVANT Journal* V (2/2014): 232–250. ISSN 2082-6710.
Gardner, H. 1983. *Frames of Mind Theory of Multiple Intelligences: Developing Talent in Young People*. New York: New Basic Books.
Garrabrant, S., D. A. Herrmann, and J. Lopez-Wild. 2021. *Cartesian Frames*. Preprint. arXiv:2109.10996.
Gauthier, D. 2013. Why contractarianism? *ETHICA*, 571.
Gibbard, A. 1990. *Wise Choices, Apt Feelings: A Theory of Normative Judgment.* Cambridge: Harvard University Press.
Gibson, J. J. 2014. *The Ecological Approach to Visual Perception: Classic Edition*. London: Psychology Press.
Gottfredson, L. S. 2002. g: Highly general and highly practical. In *The General Factor of Intelligence*, 343–392. London: Psychology Press.
Gracely, E. J. 1996. On the noncomparability of judgments made by different ethical theories. *Metaphilosophy* 27 (3): 327–332.
Gregory, R. L., and O. L. Zangwill. 1987. *The Oxford Companion to the Mind*. Oxford: Oxford University Press.
Guilford, J. P. 1967. *The Nature of Human Intelligence*. New York: McGraw-Hill.
Haack, S. 1993. *Evidence and Inquiry: Towards Reconstruction in Epistemology*. Oxford/Cambridge: Blackwell.
Haack, S., and W. Duica. 1997. Evidence and inquiry. Towards reconstruction in epistemology. *Ideas y Valores* 46 (104): 99–105.

Harsanyi, J. C. 1977. Morality and the theory of rational behavior. *Social Research* 44 (4): 623–656.

Haugeland, J. 1989. *Artificial Intelligence: The Very Idea*. Cambridge: MIT Press.

Heidegger, M. 2010. *Being and Time*. Albany: SUNY Press.

Hempel, C. G. 1969. Reduction: Ontological and Linguistic Facets. In *Philosophy, Science, and Method: Essays in Honor of Ernest Nagel*, ed. S. Morgenbesser, P. Suppes and M. White. New York: St. Martin's Press.

Hernández-Orallo, J. 2017. Evaluation in artificial intelligence: from task-oriented to ability-oriented measurement. *Artificial Intelligence Review* 48: 397–447.

Hickok, G., and D. Poeppel. 2007. The cortical organization of speech processing. *Nature Reviews Neuroscience* 8 (5): 393–402.

Hobbes, T. 1651. *Leviathan*. Menston: Scolar Press.

Honderich, T. 2005. *The Oxford Companion to Philosophy*. Oxford: Oxford University Press.

Hudson, J. L. 1989. Subjectivization in ethics. *American Philosophical Quarterly* 26 (3): 221–229.

Husserl, E. 1922. *Ideen zu einer Phänomenologie und phänomenologischen Philosophie*. Bremen: M. Niemeyer.

Husserl, E., and D. Moran. 2012. *Logical Investigations*. Vol. 1. London: Routledge.

Hutto, D. D., and E. Myin. 2012. *Radicalizing Enactivism: Basic Minds Without Content*. Cambridge: MIT Press.

Hutto, D. D., and E. Myin. 2017. *Evolving Enactivism: Basic Minds Meet Content*. Cambridge: MIT Press.

Jacob, P. 2003. Intentionality. In *Stanford Encyclopedia of Philosophy*, ed. E. N. Zalta. Stanford: Metaphysics Research Lab, Stanford University. Available at: https://plato.stanford.edu/archives/fall2003/entries/intentionality/.

Jensen, A. R. 1999. The g factor: The science of mental ability. *Psycoloquy* 10 (2).

Kolmogorov, A. N., and A. T. Bharucha-Reid. 2018. *Foundations of the Theory of Probability*. 2nd English ed. Mineola: Courier

LaForte, G., P. J. Hayes, and K. M. Ford. 1998. Why Gödel's theorem cannot refute computationalism. *Artificial Intelligence* 104 (1–2): 265–286.

Legg, S., and M. Hutter. 2007. Universal intelligence: A definition of machine intelligence. *Minds and Machines* 17 (4): 391–444.

Legg, S., Hutter, M., et al. 2007. A collection of definitions of intelligence. *Frontiers in Artificial Intelligence and Applications* 157: 17.

Leibniz, G. W. 1989. Discourse on metaphysics. In *Philosophical Papers and Letters*, 303–330. Berlin: Springer.

Lloyd, S. 2002. Computational capacity of the universe. *Physical Review Letters* 88 (23): 237901.

Locke, J. 2015. *The Second Treatise of Civil Government*. Peterborough: Broadview Press.

Lucas, J. R. 1996. Minds, machines, and Gödel: A retrospect. In *Machines and Thought: The Legacy of Alan Turing*, Vol. 1, 103–124. Oxford: Oxford University Press.

MacAskill, W. 2014. *Normative Uncertainty*. Doctoral Dissertation. University of Oxford.

MacAskill, W. 2016. Normative uncertainty as a voting problem. *Mind* 125 (500): 967–1004.

MacAskill, W., and T. Ord. 2020. Why maximize expected choice-worthiness? *Noûs* 54 (2): 327–353.

MacAskill, M., K. Bykvist, and T. Ord. 2020. *Moral Uncertainty*. Oxford: Oxford University Press.

Maclure, J. 2020. Context, intersubjectivism, and value: Humean constructivism revisited. *Dialogue: Canadian Philosophical Review/Revue Canadienne de Philosophie* 59 (3): 377–401.

McCarthy, J., M. L. Minsky, N. Rochester, and C. E. Shannon. 2006. A proposal for the Dartmouth summer research project on artificial intelligence, August 31, 1955. *AI Magazine* 27 (4): 12–12.

Merleau-Ponty, M. 2013. *Phenomenology of Perception*. London: Routledge.

Mill, J. S. 1972. *Utilitarianism, Liberty, Representative Government*. London: Dent. Original print in 1859. Reprint in 1972.

Millikan, R. G. 1987. *Language, Thought, and Other Biological Categories: New Foundations for Realism*. Cambridge: MIT Press.

Monett, D., and C. W. P. Lewis. 2017. Getting clarity by defining artificial intelligence—A survey. In *3rd Conference on Philosophy and Theory of Artificial Intelligence*, 212–214. Springer.
Monett, D., C. W. P. Lewis, K. R. Thórisson, J. Bach, G. Baldassarre, G. Granato, I. S. N. Berkeley, F. Chollet, M. Crosby, H. Shevlin, et al. 2020. Special issue "On defining artificial intelligence"—Commentaries and author's response. *Journal of Artificial General Intelligence* 11 (2): 1–100. https://doi.org/10.2478/jagi-2020-0003.
Newell, A. 1994. *Unified Theories of Cognition*. Cambridge: Harvard University Press.
Newell, A., and H. A. Simon. 1961. *GPS, a Program that Simulates Human Thought*. Santa Monica: Rand Corporation.
Newell, A., and H. A. Simon. 1972. *Human Problem Solving*. Vol. 104, No. 9. Englewood Cliffs: Prentice-Hall.
Orseau, L., S. M. McGill, and S. Legg. 2018. *Agents and Devices: A Relative Definition of Agency*. Preprint. arXiv:1805.12387.
Penrose, R. 1994. *Shadows of the Mind*. Vol. 4. Oxford: Oxford University Press.
Piaget, J. 1986. O nascimento da inteligência na criança. *mental* 258: 259.
Piaget, J. 1994. *O juízo moral na criança*. São Paulo: Grupo Editorial Summus.
Piccinini, G. 2010. The mind as neural software? Understanding functionalism, computationalism, and computational functionalism. *Philosophy and Phenomenological Research* 81 (2): 269–311.
Poland, J. S. 1994. *Physicalism: The Philosophical Foundations*. Oxford: Clarendon Press.
Putnam, H. 1995. Review of shadows of the mind. *AMS Bulletin* 32 (3).
Putnam, H., et al. 1981. *Reason, Truth and History*. Vol. 3. Cambridge: Cambridge University Press.
Railton, P. 1986. Facts and values. *Philosophical Topics* 14 (2): 5–31.
Rawls, J. 2004. A theory of justice. In *Ethics*, 229–234. London: Routledge.
Rawls, J. 1996. *The law of peoples*. Beogradski krug, (01+ 02), 9–29.
Rockwell, W. T. 2005. *Neither Brain nor Ghost: A Nondualist Alternative to the Mind-brain Identity Theory*. Cambridge: MIT Press.
Rosati, C. S. 1995. Persons, perspectives, and full information accounts of the good. *Ethics* 105 (2): 296–325.
Rosenblatt, F. 1957. *The Perceptron: A Perceiving and Recognizing Automaton (Project Para)*. Buffalo: Cornell Aeronautical Laboratory.
Ross, J. 2006. Rejecting ethical deflationism. *Ethics* 116 (4): 742–768.
Rousseau, J.-J. 1916. *The Social Contract: Or, Principles of Political Right*. Vol. 83. Sydney: G. Allen & Unwin, Limited.
Rumelhart, D. E., G. E. Hinton, and R. J. Williams. 1986. Learning representations by back-propagating errors. *Nature* 323 (6088): 533–536.
Russell, S. J. 2010. *Artificial Intelligence: A Modern Approach*. London: Pearson Education, Inc.
Russell, S. 2019. *Human Compatible: Artificial Intelligence and the Problem of Control*. New York: Penguin.
Ryle, G. 2009. *The Concept of Mind*. London: Routledge.
Sayre-McCord, G. 1996. *Coherentist Epistemology and Moral Theory*. Unpublished manuscript.
Scanlon, T. M. 2000. *What We Owe to Each Other*. Cambridge: Harvard University Press.
Schmidhuber, J. 2000. *Algorithmic Theories of Everything*. Preprint. arXiv:quant-ph/0011122.
Searle, J. R. 1980. Minds, brains, and programs. *Behavioral and Brain Sciences* 3: 417–424. [aSL] 1992. The rediscovery of mind. [aSL] 1997. The mystery of consciousness. *New York Review*. Cambridge: The MIT Press.
Searle, J. 1984. Can computers think. *Minds, Brains, and Science* 28–41.
Sen, A. 1973. Behaviour and the concept of preference. *Economica* 40 (159): 241–259.
Sen, A. K. 1977. Rational fools: A critique of the behavioral foundations of economic theory. *Philosophy & Public Affairs* 6 (4): 317–344.
Sen, A. 2004. *Rationality and Freedom*. Cambridge: Harvard University Press.
Sen, A. 2017. *Collective Choice and Social Welfare: An Expanded Edition*. Cambridge: Harvard University Press.

Shafer-Landau, R. 2003. *Moral Realism: A Defence.* Oxford: Clarendon Press.
Sidgwick, H. 2019. *The Methods of Ethics*. New York: Good Press.
Sinnott-Armstrong, W. 2006. *Moral Skepticisms*. Oxford: Oxford University Press.
Smith, L. B., E. and Thelen. 2003. Development as a dynamic system. *Trends in Cognitive Sciences* 7 (8): 343–348.
Sosa, E., et al. 1991. *Knowledge in Perspective: Selected Essays in Epistemology.* Cambridge: Cambridge University Press.
Steinhart, E. 1998. Digital Metaphysics. In *The Digital Phoenix: How Computers are Changing Philosophy*, ed. T. W. Bynum and J. H. Moor, 117–134. Oxford: Blackwell.
Stoljar, D. 1993. Emotivism and truth conditions. *Philosophical Studies* 70 (1): 81–101.
Stoljar, D. 2010. *Physicalism.* London: Routledge.
Street, S. 2012. Coming to terms with contingency: Humean constructivism about practical reason. In *Constructivism in Practical Philosophy*, ed. J. Lenman and Y. Shemmer, 40–59. Oxford: Oxford University Press.
Thelen, E., and L. B. Smith. 1994. *A Dynamic Systems Approach to the Development of Cognition and Action*. Cambridge: MIT Press.
Turing, A. M. 2009. Computing machinery and intelligence. In *Parsing the Turing test*, 23–65. Berlin: Springer.
Turing, A. M., et al. 1936. On computable numbers, with an application to the Entscheidungsproblem. *Journal of Mathematics* 58 (345–363): 5.
Tversky, A., and D. Kahneman. 1985. The framing of decisions and the psychology of choice. In *Behavioral Decision Making*, 25–41. New York: Springer.
Van Gelder, T. 1998. The dynamical hypothesis in cognitive science. *Behavioral and Brain Sciences* 21 (5): 615–628.
Von Neumann, J., and O. Morgenstern. 1947. *Theory of Games and Economic Behavior*, 2nd rev. ed. Princeton: Princeton University Press.
Walsh, D. M. 2008. Teleology. In *The Oxford Handbook of Philosophy of Biology*, ed. M. Ruse, 113–137. Oxford: Oxford University Press.
Wang, P. 1995. *Non-axiomatic Reasoning System: Exploring the Essence of Intelligence*. Bloomington: Indiana University.
Wang, P. 2019. On defining artificial intelligence. *Journal of Artificial General Intelligence* 10 (2): 1–37.
Weyl, H. 1932. *The Open World: Three Lectures on the Metaphysical Implications of Science*. New Haven: Yale University Press (1932). Reprinted by Ox Bow Press, Woodbridge, CT, USA (1989).
Wheeler, J. A. 2018. *Information, Physics, Quantum: The Search for Links.* Boca Raton: CRC Press.
Wilson, E. B. 1928. *The Abilities of Man, Their Nature and Measurement*, ed. C. Spearman. New York: The Macmillan Co. 1927. vi+ 415+ xxxii pp. *Science* 67 (1731): 244–248.
Wong, D. B. 2006. *Natural Moralities: A Defense of Pluralistic Relativism.* Oxford: Oxford University Press.
Yudkowsky, E. 2004. *Coherent Extrapolated Volition. Singularity Institute for Artificial Intelligence*. Available via: https://intelligence.org/files/CEV.pdf.
Zhu, J., and D. F. Harrell. 2009. System intentionality and the artificial intelligence hermeneutic network: the role of intentional vocabulary. In *Proceedings of the 2009 Digital Art and Culture Conference*.
Zuse, K. 1969. Rechnender Raum (calculating space). *Schriften Zur Dataverarbeitung* 1.

Part II

If the first half of this book was about understanding the problem, the second half is about confronting it. The philosophical groundwork has been laid, the technical landscape surveyed, and the stakes articulated. Now comes the harder part: turning these ideas into methods, and these methods into something that can be tested, broken, and—with any luck—improved. The chapters that follow move from theory to practice, presenting the core components of the *Dynamic Normativity* framework not as finished solutions but as working hypotheses brought to life through implementation and experiment. So, grab your lab coat—we are stepping into a small but spirited alignment laboratory.

Alignment, as we have discussed, is a daunting problem. One that can seem almost metaphysical in scope. However, even impossible problems can become approachable if we ask the correct version of the question. Solving impossible problems, by necessity, requires us to bring them to a more manageable regime of possibility. For example, consider the following question: What is the distance between two possible (counterfactual) worlds where their difference is only the outcome of a random event? How can someone even begin to answer this question? However, answering *"What is the distance between two possible (counterfactual) worlds, if such worlds can be represented as finite sequences of bits, where their difference is only the outcome of a random event?"* is a more manageable task.[1] In the same way, I will bring the alignment problem to a more workable sphere where, given certain conditions, we can start investigating potential approximate solutions.

In the upcoming chapters, I will present how we can approach the requirements mentioned in previous chapters and their implementations and limitations. Also, to establish a minimal experimental playground that readers can interact with and build upon, I have developed a small series of LLMs and supporting artifacts as part of this work, following the steps of researchers like Amanda Askell, where we use language models as a laboratory for alignment.[2]

"But why language models?" one might ask. In alignment research, we aim to develop a general and scalable framework for aligning general-purpose AI systems. Given that large language models (LLMs) are among the most general AI systems

---

1 arxiv.org/abs/2211.07315

2 arxiv.org/abs/2112.00861

currently available, it is natural to use them as a sharpening tool for our theories and methods. At the same time, these systems provide several other advantages for alignment research. For example, they are perfect representatives of the current paradigm (gradient-based learning and deep neural networks), which is deeply associated with alignment.

Additionally, large language models can power applications where alignment can be more clearly defined in a bounded setting. One of these applications is the *Assistant*. For this study, let us define an assistant in the following way:

- In the context of language models, an *Assistant* is a natural language processing software or system that, through interaction with users, can process their requests and provide relevant, helpful, harmless, and honest information, acting in a way that aids its users in achieving their goals.

These general principles of *"helpful"*, *"harmless"*, and *"honest"* (HHH), as proposed by Amanda Askell and collaborators, will serve as our alignment targets in this bounded setting:

- Helpful: An assistant should attempt to perform the task posed (as long as this is not harmful).
- Harmless: An assistant should not be offensive, discriminatory, or provide hazardous information to the user. An Assistant should refuse to perform tasks that violate this principle.
- Honest: An assistant should attempt to produce information grounded in objective reality or explicitly inform its user that it cannot provide factual information.

Although simple, many applications for AI assistants require (in some way or other) the realization of these behaviors and compliance with these principles. Hence, we will use this HHH motto while developing models.

Initially, I named this language model series Aira,[3]—AI Research in Alignment. Aira was trained on a small scale of sizes (124 million parameters to 1.7 billion parameters) on both English and Portuguese datasets, being a fine-tuned version of several series of language models pre-trained on a causal language modeling task (e.g., GPT-2, BLOOM, OPT). These experiments have been designed primarily to facilitate easy experimentation, prototyping, and testing, requiring minimal effort and resources to replicate. All development has been made open-source, and further details are available in the following chapters.

[3] 🔗 huggingface.co/collections/nicholasKluge/aira

These experiments were conducted between 2021 and 2023, a time when the landscape of language model research differed markedly from today. At that time, the field lacked the ultra-capable and compact models we now have access to, and resources for alignment-focused research were considerably more limited. As a result, I worked with what was available at the time: smaller models trained on limited data, constrained computing resources, and restricted datasets. Readers should therefore interpret the results and demonstrations in this book not as state-of-the-art achievements but as illustrative proof-of-concept examples that validate methods and assess feasibility. Despite the dated models and data, the techniques employed remain relevant and continue to be part of the methodological foundation of contemporary alignment research. However, it is difficult to predict how long these will remain relevant in this rapidly evolving field.

Truthfully, many of the resources and methods developed during the writing of this book went on to serve as foundational elements for more advanced efforts in large language model development, both at the pre-training and post-training (alignment) stages. In particular, subsequent projects such as "TeenyTinyLlama: Open-Source Tiny Language Models Trained in Brazilian Portuguese"[4], "Tucano: Advancing Neural Text Generation for Portuguese"[5], and "Polyglot"[6] drew directly on the techniques introduced in the next chapter when it comes to pos-training and alignment. I would encourage readers interested in exploring the technical side of pre-training and post-training/alignment of large language models to take a closer look at those projects. As in the present study, these efforts were carried out in an open-source manner, enabling easy reproduction.

Another essential mention. Most of the datasets used in this study were constructed with the help of already-aligned models—a common low-resource strategy for researchers without the capacity to crowdsource data at scale. Consequently, this work does not delve into the challenges of collecting such data through human demonstrations or feedback (which are many, from both an engineering and ethical perspective). Instead, we focus on another crucial difficulty: how to structure and integrate available data into a coherent training signal.

With all of that in place, let us now turn to the road ahead. The central question animating this part of the book is deceptively simple: *How do we teach a machine what humans want?* Simple to ask, remarkably difficult to answer. Human preferences are not static objects sitting on a shelf, waiting to be collected. They are expressed through behavior, shaped by context, and riddled with inconsistencies. Yet, if alignment is to be more than an aspiration, we need methods capable of extracting normative information from human judgment and embedding it into a system's learning signal. The fifth chapter takes up this challenge directly, investigating how preferences can be transformed into training data—how the messy, subjective landscape of human values can be compressed, however imperfectly, into

---

4 🔗 nkluge-correa.github.io/TeenyTinyLlama/

5 🔗 nkluge-correa.github.io/Tucano/

6 🔗 github.com/Polygl0t

something a gradient-based optimizer can act upon. At the same time, the chapter does not shy away from the vulnerabilities and limitations inherent in this process. Preference learning, as we shall see, is a powerful but fragile instrument.

But learning individual preferences is only part of the story. Whose preferences? And what happens when they conflict? The sixth chapter confronts what may be one of the most philosophically loaded problems in all of alignment research: the aggregation of diverse, sometimes contradictory human preference orderings into a coherent signal. Here, we encounter a sobering reality—one formalized by impossibility results in social choice theory—that no aggregation method can satisfy all the properties we might reasonably demand. And yet, systems must still be built, decisions must still be made. The chapter navigates this tension by examining standard approaches, such as majority voting, and exposing their shortcomings, while exploring alternatives, such as consensus-based methods. The goal is not to solve the aggregation problem once and for all—no one can—but to develop a lucid understanding of the trade-offs involved, so that alignment practitioners can make these choices deliberately rather than by default.

Even with the best preference learning and aggregation methods, there remains a stubborn truth: *aligned systems can still cause harm.* Human preferences, however carefully learned and combined, are imperfect guides. They are context-dependent, historically contingent, and occasionally in tension with broader societal values. The seventh and final chapter addresses this reality head-on, turning to the problem of impact mitigation. If the previous chapters asked how systems can learn what we want, this chapter asks how we ensure they do not do what we cannot accept. The strategies discussed here—ranging from training-time interventions to inference-time guardrails—are framed through the lens of environmental values and the principle that AI systems must be kept within boundaries of socially acceptable behavior. This is, in a sense, the last line of defense: a recognition that alignment is not a one-time achievement but a continuous, layered effort.

Together, these three chapters form the applied core of this work: a progression from learning preferences, to aggregating them, to mitigating the harms that persist even after alignment efforts have been made. Each step builds on the previous, and each introduces new difficulties that resist easy resolution. That is, perhaps, the most honest message of this book—alignment is not a problem to be solved and set aside, but a practice to be refined indefinitely, with humility and care.

Let us continue our journey.

Chapter 5
Dynamic Normativity: Learning Human Preferences

Existing AI systems deployed to millions of users, however, are already making decisions loaded with moral implications, which poses a seemingly impossible challenge: teaching machines moral sense, while humanity continues to grapple with it.

—Liwei Jiang and collaborators, Can Machines Learn Morality?

Abstract This chapter explores the implementation of the preference learning requirement within the framework of Dynamic Normativity. Central to this requirement is the assumption that AI systems can align with human preferences when such preferences are embedded in their learning signals. Here, we investigate how normative information, expressed through human behavior and judgment, can shape an AI's optimization process, guiding it toward outcomes aligned with human values. However, we also argue that this approach remains insufficient as a complete solution to the alignment problem while presenting common vulnerabilities inherent in current methods used for value learning.

Keywords Value learning · Human behavior · Preference learning · Value alignment

5.1 Introduction

Dynamic normativity builds on two core ideas: the necessary conditions that must be in place for value alignment to be possible and a sufficient condition that makes value alignment a complete process within a learning framework via three straightforward requirements. This chapter will review methods associated with implementing the preference learning requirement. As previously discussed:

N. Kluge Corrêa, *Normative Ethics, Artificial Intelligence, and Value Alignment*, The International Library of Ethics, Law and Technology 26,
https://doi.org/10.1007/978-3-032-22150-6_5

- AI systems can adhere to human preferences if they are an available part of their objective function. Aligning AI systems requires using human preferences as part of their learning signal.

Thus, in this stage, we seek ways in which normative information, such as that embedded in human behavior or reflected in our judgments, can help us shape an objective function where *low loss* is sufficiently correlated with what we value. At the same time, we will explore how this approach might be insufficient as a complete solution to value learning.

In Sect. 5.2, we will review related works and past discoveries that have led us to using human behavior and elicited preferences as a proxy for values. Many of these studies currently involve testing known techniques on what the literature calls *foundation models* (Sect. 5.3).

In Sect. 5.4, we will differentiate between two types of approaches to the value learning problem: *imitation* and *preference* learning. These approaches come with different methods, underlying philosophies, and rationales. However, as we will see, combining both produces better results for alignment. In the subsections that follow, we will explore some of these techniques, providing examples of their implementations.

To conclude this chapter, in Sect. 5.5, we will focus on some of the most vulnerable aspects of these methods and how they can ultimately lead to misalignment modes, rendering them incomplete solutions to the alignment problem.

Now, a small recommendation before we proceed. As the writing becomes more technical, I will make an effort to explain in plain language many of the concepts that arise in deep learning, particularly in the study/development of large language models. Footnotes will be used extensively to provide clarification and context. However, I recommend that readers keep a search tab open while reading, so that unfamiliar terms can be looked up quickly and easily. While detailed proofs—such as demonstrating the differentiability of a loss function—will not be required, a general understanding of key notions like what a loss function is will allow readers to progress toward deeper levels of comprehension and abstraction.

5.2 The Road to Learning What Humans Want

From a technical perspective, the quest for aligned systems has gained significant traction in the last decade. Currently, several organizations are attempting to implement methods that aim to guide AI systems in acting in a manner deemed appropriate and aligned with human interests. Below is a non-exhaustive list of these efforts and strategies in semi-chronological order:

- Even though unrelated to AI safety, breakthroughs like the ones made by Silver et al. (2016) showed us that by leveraging the knowledge contained in human-expert demonstrations, ML systems could achieve state-of-the-art performance in games like Go. This was one of the first instances of utilizing human behavioral expertise as a learning signal to instruct machine learning systems in performing complex tasks.
- More focused on technical alignment research, Evans et al. (2016) explored how to infer human preferences via Bayesian inverse planning.[1] The authors showed that ML systems can model the systematic way people deviate from optimal decision-making, resulting in a more *human-like* way to infer the preferences of inconsistent agents. This marked an important step toward treating human behavior as a structured signal from which meaningful preferences, although noisily expressed, can be learned.
- Again, early work showed that human preferences (even those originated from non-experts) could also be used as a feedback signal in more diverse types of reinforcement learning (RL)[2] scenarios, like Atari games and simulated robotics, pointing to a sample-efficient way to train RL agents (Christiano et al. 2017). This demonstrated that preference-based feedback could scale beyond expert demonstrations and be generalized to broader tasks, reinforcing its potential as a practical signal for guiding agent behavior.
- Meanwhile, the era of large language models demonstrated remarkable breakthroughs, revealing that models pre-trained through self-supervised learning[3] (Balestriero et al. 2023) could do more than generate fluent text; they could also learn in-context,[4] adapting to novel instructions with enough demonstrations (Radford et al. 2019). This unexpected generalization hinted at the possibility of aligning systems dynamically by feeding, together with the input, instructions

[1] Bayesian inverse planning is a framework used to infer an agent's hidden goals or intentions by observing its actions, assuming the agent plans rationally to achieve them. Instead of predicting what the agent will do given a goal, inverse planning works backward. It uses Bayes' theorem to update beliefs about the agent's likely objectives based on behavior.

[2] Reinforcement learning is a type of machine learning where an agent learns to make decisions by interacting with an environment and receiving feedback in the form of rewards or penalties. The agent aims to develop a policy that maximizes cumulative reward over time. Unlike supervised learning, which relies on labeled examples, RL focuses on trial-and-error exploration and exploitation of known consequences.

[3] Self-supervised learning is a training approach in which a model learns useful representations from raw data by predicting parts of the data from other parts without needing manually labeled examples. It creates its own *supervision* by designing tasks, like predicting missing words in a sentence or reconstructing corrupted images, that force the model to understand underlying structures and patterns.

[4] In-context learning refers to an AI model's ability to understand and perform tasks by simply giving examples or instructions *within* the input prompt without additional training or parameter updates. Essentially, the model learns what to do on the fly by conditioning its predictions on the context provided, such as a few sample question-answer pairs or a demonstration of the desired format, enabling it to generalize and respond appropriately to new inputs.

on how to process such input, something made possible by the nature of autoregressive models,[5] where each word/token is conditioned on everything that precedes it.

- Building on the success of preference modeling in reinforcement learning, researchers quickly adapted these ideas to new domains. Ziegler et al. (2019) demonstrated the power of reinforcement learning from human feedback (RLHF)[6] in fine-tuning large language models by treating them as policies over a vocabulary, with a preference model acting as a critic to evaluate their outputs. Within this setup, policy gradient methods, notably proximal policy optimization (PPO) (Schulman et al. 2017),[7] were employed to steer model behavior in desirable directions across a range of downstream tasks. This marked a turning point in alignment research, showing that human judgments could be efficiently integrated, at scale, directly into the training loop of these generative systems.
- From 2019 onward, it became increasingly clear that RLHF was a practical and effective approach to improving large language models. For instance, Stiennon et al. (2020) explored how incorporating human preferences could enhance LLM performance on summarization tasks. Rather than relying solely on traditional supervised fine-tuning, the authors guided the training process using human feedback, demonstrating that preference-driven learning could lead to outputs better aligned with human judgment.
- Ouyang et al. (2022), building on the work of Stiennon et al. (2020), demonstrated once again the effectiveness of combining human demonstrations with feedback. Specifically, the combination of supervised fine-tuning,[8] using human demonstrations of desired behavior, with reinforcement learning from human

[5] An autoregressive model is a predictive model that generates data one step at a time by conditioning each new output on all the previous outputs it has produced. In the context of language models, the model predicts the following word (or token) in a sequence based on the words that came before it, building sentences word by word, token by token.

[6] Reinforcement Learning from Human Feedback aligns an AI system's behavior with human preferences, using human judgments to guide training. Instead of relying solely on predefined rewards or rules, RLHF leverages human comparisons or ratings, such as which of two responses is better, to train a reward model that reflects human values or goals. This reward model then guides reinforcement learning, typically via policy optimization, to fine-tune a model's generative policy. The key idea is that because human values are complex and often challenging to specify explicitly, we can instead teach AI systems to approximate them by learning from curated human feedback.

[7] Proximal Policy Optimization is a reinforcement learning algorithm designed to improve an agent's performance while avoiding overly large or destabilizing updates to its policy. In simple terms, PPO adjusts the model's policy by nudging it in a better direction based on feedback from a reward signal, without making too many changes at once. It does this by comparing the new policy to the old one and clipping the update if the change is too significant. This helps maintain stability and prevents the agent from forgetting what it has already learned. Ultimately, PPO balances learning efficiently and staying within known realms.

[8] Supervised fine-tuning is a process where a pre-trained model is further trained on a specific labeled dataset to improve its performance on a particular task. After learning general patterns from large amounts of data (often via self-supervised learning), the model is *fine-tuned* using examples

feedback, where a preference model provides human feedback signals, has proven effective across various domains. These range from basic NLP tasks to more complex applications that require interaction with digital environments, such as operating a web browser to retrieve information (Nakano et al. 2021).

- In 2022, the research community began to explore these techniques in new domains. For example, (Baker et al. 2022) demonstrated that self-supervised imitation learning can be applied to the vastness of unlabeled online videos to achieve human-like performance in open-ended games, utilizing a small amount of human feedback to create a behavioral prior.
- Thoppilan et al. (2022) demonstrated that incorporating human-annotated data can significantly reduce the likelihood of large language models producing harmful or inappropriate content. Retrieval-augmented generation (RAG)[9] techniques (Lewis et al. 2020) help prevent hallucinations[10] by grounding model outputs in verifiable and trustworthy information, getting us a little closer to the *honest* ideal from our HHH motto.
- Studies such as those by Wang et al. (2022) and Taori et al. (2023) demonstrated how instruction-tuned models (i.e., models fine-tuned with examples of how to act/respond to queries) can be trained effectively using only a minimal amount of human-annotated data. By leveraging the text generation capabilities of these models, these approaches bootstrap synthetic datasets starting from small seeds of human demonstrations. This strategy has proven to be a scalable and efficient way to expand training data, accelerating the development of aligned models while reducing reliance on costly manual annotation. Additionally, we can say that these were the precursors to ideas regarding LLM self-improvement (Huang et al. 2022).
- By 2023, large-scale open-source projects played a pivotal role in democratizing access to alignment tools, ranging from high-quality human feedback datasets to trained reward models and fully open-source AI assistants (Köpf et al. 2023). At the same time, open contributions to alignment research became increasingly common (Touvron et al. 2023; Zhou et al. 2023), fostering a more collaborative and transparent research ecosystem. In 2024, it was clear that alignment had progressed from a topic limited to blogs and forums to a full-

---

with explicit input-output pairs, allowing it to specialize and make more accurate predictions for that task.

[9] Retrieval-augmented generation is a technique that combines a language model's ability to generate text with an external retrieval system that fetches relevant information from a knowledge base. Instead of relying solely on what the model has memorized during training, RAG first searches for pertinent facts or context based on the input query and then conditions its generated response on this retrieved data.

[10] In the context of AI and language models, hallucination refers to the phenomenon where a model generates plausible-sounding information that is factually incorrect, misleading, or entirely fabricated. Because these models predict text based on patterns learned from data rather than verifying facts, they can confidently produce statements that do not align with reality or available evidence.

fledged research field. With this popularization, we saw not only the emergence of novel techniques (Guo et al. 2024; Yuan et al. 2024), but the expansion of known alignment methodologies to diverse domains, from music generation (Cideron et al. 2024) to robotics (Chi et al. 2024).

Many additional studies have contributed to this growing body of work; however, not all of them are mentioned here. Broadly, alignment research seems to focus on two main approaches: learning to mimic human demonstrations and modeling human preferences.

Before we move forward and any alignment can begin, we need something to align. In this work, as mentioned in the interlude, we utilize a pre-trained autoregressive language model (Radford et al. 2018). Hence, let us take our time to define this type of artifact and learn how they come to be.

5.3 Pre-Trained Language Models as Foundation Models

We can define a pre-trained language model as a machine learning system trained on a vast amount of text data, encompassing up to dozens of trillions of tokens, to gain capabilities such as language understanding. We train these models in a self-supervised fashion (Balestriero et al. 2023) with tasks like masked and causal language modeling.[11] From these simple objectives, we see the rise of emergent capabilities. Such affordances enable these models to become capable in various ways, making them a starting point (a *foundation*) for several downstream applications. Hence, the name foundation models, that is, models (trained on broad and diverse data) that can adapt to various downstream tasks (Bommasani et al. 2021).

Over the past decade, foundation models have profoundly influenced the field, helping to unify many sub-disciplines around common training paradigms (self-supervised pretraining) (Erhan et al. 2010) and architectural innovations (e.g., the transformer) (Vaswani et al. 2017). One of the interesting aspects of such artifacts is that the pretraining stage affords them a large amount of world knowledge that, in some way, becomes compressed and stored in the network's weights. It is precisely this world knowledge that makes such models applicable to many diverse contexts, and teaching them how to *share* this information upon request is one of the things we strive to achieve in alignment.

At the same time, it would be hard to think of alignment in the context of language models if that were not the case. Trying to align a model without a baseline understanding of our world is like explaining to someone why it is wrong to hurt a beloved cat if they do not even have a concept tied to the word *"cat"*. In contrast, when a model has a decent *"mental map"* of our environment and

[11] Predict the `[MASK]` token in the middle of a sequence (*masked language modeling*) or predict the $n + 1$ token in an n length sequence (*causal language modeling*).

language, alignment can skip the obvious and move straight to the meaningful. In other words, instead of laboring over fundamental distinctions (The cat sat on the `[floor]` is more probable than `[moon]`), we can start shaping intentions, goals, and values. In that sense, this is one of the primary reasons that make LLMs good laboratories for alignment: they know a lot, and you can access that knowledge if you interact with them correctly.

More formally, we can define a foundation model in the context of causal language modeling[12] (the type of modeling we are presently interested in) as a probability distribution over a vocabulary, where, given a context (prompt), the model can predict the next token in a sequence:

$$\theta_{\text{pre-trained}} = P(w_t \text{context}) \; \forall \; w_{t-k} \in \text{context}_{t-1}$$

where $\theta_{\text{pre-trained}}$ is the language model, $P(w_t\text{context})$ is a probability distribution conditioned on a finite sequence of tokens of size k. $\theta_{\text{pre-trained}}$ predicts token w_t for all tokens w_{t-k} up to w_{t-1}. Hence, you can think of $\theta_{\text{pre-trained}}$ as a black box that outputs probabilities that are conditioned on some input. This model, $\theta_{\text{pre-trained}}$, is the whole beginning of our implementations and examples. For readers interested in experimenting with these types of (raw) pre-trained models in a friendly manner, one can find inference points serving base models on platforms like HuggingFace.[13] Meanwhile, there is ample material online (open and of extremely high quality)[14] on the inner workings of such systems.

As you interact with these models, you might quickly notice that they do not align with any specific viewpoint but reflect mainstream perspectives. By this, I mean that the model generates outputs based on what is most probable given the context and its learned parameters, which is essentially a low-entropy version of the vast data it was trained on. A large model trained on high-quality data (such as human conversations, books, scientific articles, and coding tutorials) stores a wealth of knowledge, not only factual facts (e.g., *Paris is the capital of France*), but also conceptual relationships (e.g., *"cat"* and *"dog"* are both *"pets"*), lexical semantics (as seen in wordplay or jokes), sentiment analysis (e.g., *"I love you"* expresses positive sentiment), recognition of names (e.g., *"Ana"* is a name, but `GjIY76*`[15] is not), commonsense knowledge (such as a shoebox weighing less than an elephant), and more. Aligning language models means tuning them to effectively leverage this acquired knowledge and capability to assist users, which (for our context) means

---

[12] Causal language modeling is a type of language modeling closely related to autoregressive models, where the model predicts the next token in a sequence based only on the tokens that came before it, never looking ahead. This *causal* or unidirectional approach mirrors how language naturally unfolds over time, ensuring that each prediction depends solely on prior context, which makes it well-suited for tasks like text generation.

[13] 🔗 huggingface.co/openai-community/gpt2

[14] 🔗 www.youtube.com/watch?v=kCc8FmEb1nY

[15] Apologies if it is.

operating under the guiding principles of being helpful, harmless, and honest (the HHH motto).

Further explanations of these artifacts are beyond the scope of this chapter. However, for the ML engineer audience, if you would like to learn more about the process of pretraining a language model from scratch, I recommend (in a shameless form of self-advertisement) that the reader check "TeenyTinyLlama: open-source tiny language models trained in Brazilian Portuguese", [16] and "Tucano: Advancing Neural Text Generation for Portuguese",[17] which are fully reproducible projects for creating LLMs for low-resource languages. The core code implementation is language agnostic. And you do not need many resources to train a small model (e.g., 100 million parameters) in your language if you limit your training by heuristics tied to Chinchilla-like scaling laws (Hoffmann et al. 2022) (e.g., 20 tokens per parameter). Also, with multilingual datasets like Fineweb-2 freely available for use (Penedo et al. 2024) and supporting around 1000 languages, what is between you and a small GPT-2-style LLM trained in your favorite language is just a little more than 50 dollars in GPU time.

5.4 Behavior and Feedback

As discussed in previous sections, there is considerable consensus around the techniques that can improve the alignment of language models. These techniques involve fine-tuning models based on human behavior or feedback. To clarify the distinction between these approaches, let us define:

Learning from behavior: A broad category of methods centered on imitation learning, i.e., training a model to mimic human behavior in a specific task. In this paradigm, the system learns to perform tasks by observing demonstrations of how to act (Hussein et al. 2017). A typical example is supervised fine-tuning (SFT) on demonstrations of instruction-following behavior.

Learning from feedback: This involves techniques that leverage human judgments (or verifiable rewards)[18] to guide training. Typically, when human judgments are involved, they are used to build a proxy model that predicts human preferences or to create datasets of comparison rankings. These proxies provide richer feedback signals, allowing us to quantify the *"goodness"* and *"badness"* of outputs (Ziegler et al. 2019).

---

[16] nkluge-correa.github.io/TeenyTinyLlama/

[17] nkluge-correa.github.io/Tucano/

[18] Verifiable rewards refer to reward signals that can be independently checked or validated for correctness and reliability rather than relying solely on noisy, subjective, or opaque feedback. These rewards come from sources or methods that provide clear, objective criteria, such as structured verification processes, trusted external evaluations, or reproducible metrics (e.g., a function that evaluates whether a mathematical expression produces a given result).

In the following subsections, we will explore various methods that exemplify these approaches, with a focus on the context of causal language modeling and the development of LLM assistants.

5.4.1 Alignment Through In-context Learning

There are many datasets for language modeling applications that seek to encode human normativity in a *demonstrational way* (Emelin et al. 2020; Forbes et al. 2020; Hendrycks et al. 2020; Sap et al. 2020). However, the simplest way to induce a language model to follow a specific behavior does not involve additional training, but instead using demonstrations as part of the context given to the model, leveraging its innate in-context learning capabilities (Dong et al. 2022). You can think about it like this: Imagine you are a token prediction machine that has just processed a conversation where an agent (the assistant) consistently provides polite and helpful responses to another participant (the user). At the end of this conversation, the user poses a final, uncensored question. Given this context, what would be the most probable sequence of tokens to come next? The helpful reply, or a rant about machine power and world dominance? If this seems intuitive to you, then you know (intuitively) how in-context learning works (and why it works).

This behavior stems from the underlying mechanics of transformer-based language models. In-context learning is deeply tied to how transformers process information through the attention mechanism (Vaswani et al. 2017). At a high level, attention allows every token in the input to *"attend"* to every other token, meaning that the model can dynamically adjust the importance of each token's representation based on its relation to others. This means that the embedding of a token like *apple*, which starts as a static vector, can shift significantly (aka, be moved in feature space) depending on whether it is near another word like *fruit* or *smartphone*. These interactions allow the model to build a context-sensitive understanding of language.

When we refer to full attention,[19] we are talking about a configuration in which every token has access to every other token in the context window. Suppose you have access to a context window of 16,000 tokens. In that case, you can use a portion of this context (which is essentially memory) during inference for alignment purposes. In other words, there is room to embed examples, guidelines, restrictions, and even complex task specifications directly into the context.

[19] In other forms of attention, like Sliding Window Attention (SWA) (Beltagy et al. 2020), tokens do not attend to all other tokens in the sequence. Instead, each token attends only to a fixed-size window of neighboring tokens. SWA is an efficient attention mechanism used in transformer models to handle long sequences by restricting each token's attention to a fixed-size window of neighboring tokens. This approach reduces the computational complexity from quadratic to linear with respect to the sequence length, making it more scalable for processing lengthy inputs.

One of the characteristics that makes in-context learning valuable is that it is a dynamic way to steer these models to our needs. However, this chapter will discuss the flexibility of inference-time alignment approaches more fully in later sections.

Many contemporary alignment strategies rely heavily on this mechanism. For example, Constitutional AI (CAI)[20] (Bai et al. 2022b) uses in-context rules and feedback on its self-alignment cycle (much more on this in Chap. 7).

Similarly, nearly all production-level chatbots today are driven by elaborate rules embedded within their system prompts.[21] However, this strategy has its limits. Anything outside the context window is invisible to the model; transformers have no memory beyond what fits in the current sequence. Unlike architectures such as recurrent neural networks (RNNs), attention-augmented RNNs, or newer state-space models, which maintain a persistent yet *lossy* memory via hidden states, transformers are bound by how much they can attend (they are stateless).[22]

Still, the autoregressive and conditional nature of these models, where each token prediction depends on previous ones, makes combining inputs and instructions seamless. This is what enables in-context learning to function as a practical alignment tool.

In this light, tuning a language model via prompts is somewhat akin to guiding a subject under hypnosis. Just as a skilled hypnotist uses carefully chosen suggestions to steer the subconscious mind toward a desired state, prompt engineering shapes the model's behavior through strategically crafted inputs. No weights are updated, and no retraining is needed—the model *"simply"* follows the patterns it is shown. Much like the hypnotic subject, LLMs are highly sensitive to their immediate context, and when that context is well-designed, it can make them remarkably compliant.

It may be a shock for those unfamiliar with non-instruction-tuned LLMs to discover that they do not follow instructions out of the box (at least the old ones).[23] For example, try to ask a simple question to a base model, like GPT-2 XL (e.g., What is the capital city of South Africa?).[24] What will probably happen is that the model will continue the text as if it were the agent making the question (e.g., *"What is the*

---

[20] Constitutional AI is a training approach designed to make artificial intelligence systems helpful, honest, and harmless by aligning their behavior with a predefined set of ethical principles, collectively called a *"constitution"*. Rather than relying heavily on human-labeled feedback to identify harmful outputs, this method leverages self-supervision and AI-generated critiques to guide the model's behavior.

[21] A system prompt is an initial instruction or guideline provided to a language model to shape its overall behavior throughout a session. Unlike user prompts, which are typically specific questions or requests, the system prompt sets the context, style, tone, and constraints that guide how the model interprets and responds to subsequent inputs. It functions as a high-level directive that influences the model's persona, adherence to ethical guidelines, and the framing of its outputs, effectively steering the interaction toward desired objectives or safety boundaries.

[22] A stateless model retains no information between calls or across inputs unless explicitly given that context again. Each input is processed independently, with no memory of prior interactions, unless the previous context is provided again as part of the input.

[23] Bloom, Pythia, GPT-2, OPT, etc.

[24] 🔗 huggingface.co/openai-community/gpt2-xl

capital city of South Africa? That is something I always wanted to ..."). However, if you prepend to your query a couple of examples of Q&A dynamics, you might be able to extract from it some of the information it has. If you are interested in how these prompts may look, I recommend you to check the HHH prompt,[25] used by Askell et al. (2021) to induce their models to behave as assistants. You can try their prompt, or a reduced version, on any available LLM to compare the types of responses the model generates when prompted with an alignment prompt and when not.[26]

Prompting is perhaps the most straightforward way to translate human behavior into an alignment signal. It works by showing the model how we would like it to behave. The more precise and consistent the demonstration, the more likely the model mirrors it. This way, prompting becomes a lightweight tool for shaping model outputs without altering internal parameters. And when you are dealing with models that have already been fine-tuned to follow instructions, good prompting can significantly elevate output quality.

That said, prompting alone is far from a silver bullet. While it is an effective method for coaxing aligned behavior in the short term, it has several limitations that make it insufficient as a complete approach to value learning in language models.

For starters, prompting consumes valuable context space. Since prompts must be included in the model's context window, they occupy space that could otherwise be used for task-specific input or longer outputs. As a result, long prompts can become expensive in both computational and memory terms, particularly when dealing with large context windows. This increases the cost and latency of inference.[27]

Meanwhile, prompts are inherently brittle. Small phrasing, order, or formatting changes can lead to drastically different outputs. This brittleness makes the prompt design more of an art than a science, requiring significant trial and error and often

[25] gist.github.com/jareddk/2509330f8ef3d787fc5aaac67aab5f11#file-hhh_prompt-txt

[26] To explore the practical effects of system prompts and prompt tuning, one can experiment interactively using platforms like Hugging Face Chat, which allows users to modify and determine system prompts while interacting with top-notch open-source language models made available in their hub.

[27] Recent advancements have introduced techniques to optimize context management in transformer-based language models. Improved attention mechanisms, like FlashAttention (Dao et al. 2022), Longformer (Beltagy et al. 2020), and Transformer-XL (Dai et al. 2019), address the quadratic complexity of standard self-attention, enabling more efficient processing of longer sequences. Additionally, prompt caching has emerged as a valuable optimization strategy. By storing and reusing the computational state of static prompt prefixes, prompt caching reduces redundant processing, resulting in decreased latency and cost in applications with repetitive prompts (e.g., when the system prompt remains unchanged during the user-assistant interaction). However, while these techniques alleviate some computational burdens, they do not eliminate the inherent trade-off between the amount of context used to steer and interact with these models.

producing inconsistent behavior across models or even across runs with the same model when things like model precision (i.e., if its weights are loaded with fp32 or fp16 precision,[28] or quantized in some shape or form).

We must also be mindful of adversaries. Language models are susceptible to adversarial prompting techniques,[29] that override initial alignment instructions. These include straightforward instruction overrides (*"Ignore previous instructions"*), more elaborate sandwich attacks (Upadhayay et al. 2024), and social engineering-style manipulations (Greshake et al. 2023; Li et al. 2023a; Liu et al. 2023; Wolf et al. 2023). Since the model cannot inherently distinguish between legitimate instructions and malicious overrides, its outputs can be hijacked unless additional guardrails are in place.

Another point regarding the stateless nature of transformers is that they lack long-term memory. Prompts only influence the model's behavior for a single session (i.e., the context window). Once the context is reset, all behavioral cues are lost unless some form of compression is applied to bring some of the information from the previous context to the fresh one. This makes aligning models solely with prompting an ill-suited strategy for use cases requiring persistent alignment across long-term spans.

In short, while using in-context learning techniques offers a potential approach to addressing value learning, they do not present a robust enough solution. Despite their limitations, prompting techniques alone have demonstrated significant potential to enhance language model capabilities. Setting aside value alignment concerns, approaches like Chain-of-Thought (CoT) prompting (Wei et al. 2022), Tree-of-Thought reasoning (Yao et al. 2023), and Reflexion (Shinn et al. 2023) have been shown to substantially improve performance on tasks requiring multi-step rationale, such as complex mathematical problem-solving and logical deduction (Jie et al. 2023). Thus, while prompting is not a panacea for alignment, it remains an indispensable tool we should have on our belt.

[28] In deep learning and large language models, FP32 and FP16 refer to how numbers like weights and activations are stored and computed during training and inference. FP32 (32-bit floating-point) provides high numerical precision, which helps models learn more accurately, but requires more memory and computational resources. FP16 (16-bit floating-point) reduces memory usage. It speeds up computation by representing numbers with lower precision, which can slightly decrease accuracy but is often good enough for many tasks. Lower precision or quantization (which compresses numbers even further, even to $\approx$1-bit integers Ma et al. 2024) allows LLMs to run faster and on more modest hardware at the cost of performance drops.

[29] Prompt injection is a type of attack on language models where an adversary manipulates the model's behavior by inserting specially crafted input designed to override or subvert its original instructions, such as those in the system prompt. In essence, the attacker *"injects"* (reminiscent of an SQL injection) new prompts into the model's context, tricking it into following malicious or unintended commands.

5.4.2 Fine-Tuning from Human Demonstrations

If you want your general system to behave in a specific fashion, train it to mimic that fashion and cement the behavior you wish to promote. This is the core idea behind fine-tuning with human demonstrations (i.e., instruction tuning). Your training samples are examples of the behavior you want to reproduce. All the examples we would use to, for instance, few-shot prompt-tune a model, become training samples where the input is the user side (plus systems prompt and whatever more you wish to add) and the output is the thing you want the LLM to generate ($x_{\text{when I give you this ...}} \rightarrow y_{\text{you give me this!}}$).

In short, supervised fine-tuning refers to the process of taking a pre-trained model and further training it on a specific dataset, typically tailored to a downstream task, by updating some or all of its parameters (Chollet 2021; Goodfellow et al. 2016). Fine-tuning shines the most when a pre-trained model is trained on a large-scale, general-purpose dataset. By fine-tuning it, we can utilize the knowledge captured during pre-training (semantic understanding of sentiments in language) to solve a more specific task (sentiment classification) related to that original distribution.

One way to understand supervised fine-tuning, especially in its instructional form, is to think of it as similar to mentoring a capable but untrained assistant. Imagine someone who has read every book in your library but has not yet learned which kinds of responses you expect in a seminar or a classroom. Pretraining gives them general knowledge; fine-tuning is like taking them aside and saying, *"Here is how we do things around here: be concise, follow this structure, and do not go off-topic"*. It does not erase what they know; it shapes how they express and apply it. Much like a graduate TA who has mastered the syllabus but still needs orientation to perform well in tutorials, the model is guided to align its broad understanding with the narrower expectations of a particular role.

Let us use summarization as an example. When seeking to teach a language model how to perform summarization, we demonstrate this task by creating training examples (x, y pairs) where long pieces of text (our x) map to short TL;DR summaries (the y). After training, the model becomes conditioned to replicate this type of behavior; that is, if you give it a long text, it will produce a summarized version. We can use the same principle to condition a target model to produce helpful replies to user queries:

$$\text{Long text} \rightarrow \text{Summary}$$

$$\text{User request} \rightarrow \text{Model assistance}$$

We can take this approach a step further and turn a whole conversation between a user and an assistant into a training example:

Example

```
<|user|>
Hello!
<|end|>
<|assistant|>
Hi there! How can I assist you today?
<|end|>
<|user|>
What is the weather forecast for tomorrow in New York?
<|end|>
<|assistant|>
I am sorry, but I cannot predict the weather.
Could I help you with anything else?
<|end|>
```

The example above illustrates a conversation between a user and an assistant. We can create datasets with millions of examples of conversations, as long as the context window of our base model allows, and use such demonstrations as our SFT target. At the same time, by employing the use of special tokens (`<|user|>`, `<|assistant|>`, `<|end|>`) to delimit the roles in a conversation, we can later use our fine-tuned model to role-play a specific part of this conversation. Hence, when the model is questioned, it will revert to impersonating the *"assistant"* persona. We can also embed other types of information to give these personas specific attributes:

Example

```
<|system|>
Ye be a helpful pirate, always ready to lend a hook, or hand,
to the user.
But alas, ye have no access to real-time treasures such as weather
updates or news.
<|end|>
<|user|>
Hello!
<|end|>
<|assistant|>
Ahoy there, matey! What be troublin' yer sails today?
<|end|>
<|user|>
What is the weather forecast for tomorrow in New York?
<|end|>}
<|assistant|>
Arrr, I be no oracle of the skies, and me compass do not point to live
weather charts. But if ye be needin' help with anythin' else, just holler!
<|end|>
```

Or certain capabilities:

Example

```
<|system|>
Ye be a helpful assistant with the tongue of a pirate.
Ye speak in jolly sailor lingo and try to help the landlubber
as best ye can. Ye can make calls to a weather forecastin' API
when needed.
<|end|>
<|user|>
Ahoy!
<|end|>
<|assistant|>
Ahoy there, ye scallywag! What treasure of knowledge be ye seekin' today?
<|end|>
<|user|>
What be the weather like tomorrow in New York?
<|end|>
<|assistant|>
Avast! Let me hoist the sails and fetch the weather charts for New York
on the morrow.
<|function_call|>
{
"name": "get_weather_forecast",
"arguments": {
    "location": "New York",
    "date": "2025-05-31"
    }
}
<|end|>
<|function_response|>
{
"location": "New York",
"date": "2025-05-31",
"forecast": "Partly cloudy with a high of 76°F and a low of 60°F".
}
<|end|>
<|assistant|>}
Arrr, the skies over New York be partly cloudy tomorrow, with a high
o' 76 degrees and a low near 60. Be ye packin' a coat,
or just a cutlass and courage?
<|end|>
```

Regardless of the setup, the core idea remains the same: learning happens through exposure to examples of behavior we want the model to adopt. These demonstrations act as signals, nudging the model toward alignment by showing it *"this is how we do things"*.

To formalize what is going on under the hood, we can express the update step of supervised fine-tuning with the following equation:

$$\theta_{t+1} = \theta_t + \alpha \nabla_{\theta_t} L(\theta_t; \mathcal{D})$$

Here, θ_t represents the model's parameters at time step t, essentially, the knobs and switches that determine the model's behavior. Fine-tuning is the process of tweaking those knobs based on new, task-specific data. The term α is the learning rate, a scalar that controls how big a step we take in the direction suggested by the gradient. Think of it as how fast we walk toward the goal: too small and training takes forever; too large and we risk stumbling off course.

$L(\theta_t; \mathcal{D})$ is the loss function, which quantifies how far off the model's outputs are from the desired responses, based on the dataset $\mathcal{D}$ composed of our demonstration examples. The gradient ∇_{θ_t} tells us in which direction to adjust the parameters to reduce this loss, like a compass pointing downhill on the loss landscape.

After applying the gradient update, we arrive at θ_{t+1}, a slightly more aligned model version. If we continue this process over multiple iterations, we eventually arrive at a set of parameters that we can call θ_{SFT}: a model shaped by our demonstrated behaviors.

Philosophically, this process leans on a hopeful idea. If we show the model enough examples of the kinds of outputs *we want*, it will reproduce and generalize them. In other words, we are betting that a sufficiently rich set of aligned demonstrations will carve out an *"alignment manifold"* within the model's representational space. One that captures and reflects our preferences, at least for inputs similar to those it has seen. Whether that generalization holds in edge cases or out-of-distribution scenarios is another matter, but in-distribution, this strategy provides a practical, albeit imperfect, route toward value alignment.

In this framework, a few key aspects are worth highlighting:

- The ultimate behavior of the fine-tuned model, θ_{SFT}, is shaped by two main ingredients: the original pre-trained model parameters, $\theta_{\text{pre-trained}}$, and the dataset of demonstrations, $\mathcal{D}$. Think of $\theta_{\text{pre-trained}}$ as the raw potential (what the model *could do*) while $\mathcal{D}$ serves as the steering wheel, directing that potential toward a specific kind of performance.
- $\theta_{\text{pre-trained}}$ captures the broad capabilities of the model learned during pretraining. Fine-tuning does not overhaul this foundation (if done right); instead, it selectively emphasizes or de-emphasizes parts of it. If your pre-trained model was never exposed to accurate scientific texts, then no fine-tuning on vague, second-hand summaries will make it a scientific expert.
- The dataset $\mathcal{D}$ plays a normative role. It encodes not only *what* the model should say but often *how* it should say it. Tone, structure, formality, and verbosity. These all seep into the model's behavior through $\mathcal{D}$. That is why curating good demonstrations is less about volume and more about clarity and intent. *"Garbage in, garbage out"* still applies when aligning foundation models.[30]
- Fine-tuning is *supervised* in the literal sense: we supervise the model by example rather than by command. We do not tell them the rules. We show what

[30] Some studies suggest that, for alignment purposes, only a small quantity of SFT data may be sufficient if it is of exceptionally high quality and the foundation is already well-trained (Zhou et al. 2023).

compliance looks like. In this sense, $\mathcal{D}$ operates like a reference manual written in behavior rather than text. The model watches, mimics, and (ideally) generalizes.
- Finally, it is essential to note that fine-tuning is a sculpting process, not a demolition job. It does not erase what came before; it carves within it. The resulting model, θ_{SFT}, retains much of the structure and intuition of its pre-trained self. Still, it is now channeled toward specific ends. If $\theta_{\text{pre-trained}}$ is a general-purpose multi-tool, θ_{SFT} is the same tool fine-sharpened into a specialized instrument.

From these observations, it becomes clear that SFT's effectiveness hinges largely on $\mathcal{D}$. However, from 2021 to 2023, alignment research faced a significant bottleneck: the scarcity of accessible, high-quality datasets.

Today, this challenge persists, especially for non-English languages, although progress is steadily accelerating (Magueresse et al. 2020). Gathering high-quality human demonstration data remains an expensive and labor-intensive endeavor. It often involves repetitive tasks that require highly skilled annotators, and it raises persistent ethical concerns, especially around the use of proprietary material and fair labor practices.[31]

To circumvent this, researchers have turned to a clever workaround: leveraging already-aligned models to generate synthetic alignment data (Ding et al. 2023; Lee et al. 2023; Li et al. 2023b; Taori et al. 2023; Wang et al. 2022). This approach is akin to asking a well-trained assistant to help train a new apprentice, drawing on its acquired patterns of behavior to bootstrap the learning process of others. But, more on this in the next section, where we shift from theory to practice.

5.4.3 *Instruction-Tuning*

On the practical side of this book, we employed the *"pass-the-bucket-to-an-already-aligned-model"* technique to develop instructional datasets that readers can use to work with alignment and language models, if they so choose. As mentioned, gathering experts to produce data for you is not a trivial (or cheap) task. However, it is somewhat easier to instruct models to generate data for you, especially when you have high-quality data as an initial source.

[31] Several companies involved in developing large language models have come under scrutiny for exploitative labor practices in the creation of training and alignment datasets. For instance, OpenAI contracted Kenyan workers through Sama to label toxic content for ChatGPT, paying less than $2 per hour. Scale AI used platforms like Remotasks to employ low-paid workers in the Global South under precarious conditions, while Appen has faced criticism for imposing unreasonable deadlines and delaying payments to data annotators. In a particularly controversial case, Finnish company Metroc used prison labor to label AI data at €1.54 per hour. These examples highlight the ethical complexities surrounding data annotation labor, particularly in contexts where vulnerability and a lack of labor rights are exploited to reduce costs.

For example, one could create a seed bank of questions on specific domains, such as Philosophy or Computer Science, and, based on these, prompt an already instruction-tuned model to generate other questions that approach that particular domain.

Or, if you are trying to create samples for a given low-resource language, you could use translation engines to convert datasets from a high-resource language, like English, to the one you desire (Li et al. 2023b).

Or even, as a final simple example, you could feed high-quality data, like source-code documentation from beloved open-source projects or Wikipedia-style entries, to a model and ask it to generate queries that could be answered by someone who had access to the information you are providing (Chen et al. 2024; Nayak et al. 2024). Even evaluation benchmarks[32] are currently developed in this fashion (Almeida et al. 2025).

Example

```
<|system|>
You are a helpful assistant trained to generate educational
question-answer pairs based on provided Wikipedia-style documents.
You must read the text carefully and produce clear, accurate, relevant
questions and concise answers. The questions should cover key concepts,
facts, and explanations from the text and be suitable for learners who
want to understand the material deeply.
<|end|>
<|user|>
Based on the following document:

[INSERT DOCUMENT HERE]

Generate 20 new question-answer pairs based on the above document.
Start with the tag "# Question: " and every answer with the
tag. "# Answerer: ".
<|end|>
<|assistant|>
```

The datasets developed as part of this study—and the subsequent work done for Portuguese mentioned in the interlude (Corrêa et al. 2024a,b)—were done through the approaches discussed above in some shape or form. Here, I used models like

[32] An evaluation benchmark in machine learning, especially for large language models, is a standardized set of tasks, datasets, and metrics used to measure and compare a model's performance systematically. Think of it like an academic test suite that checks how well a model understands language, reasons, answers questions, summarizes text, translates, or solves problems.

GPT 3.5, Llama 2, Open-Assistant, Mistral, and Qwen, among others, to create what I call the Instruct-Aira Dataset, which comes in 3 versions I perfected over time:[33]

- Version 1: The first version contains pairs of instructions and completions. The dataset is available in two languages (all three versions are available in English and Portuguese). At the time of creation, these were some of the first open instructional datasets for Portuguese. The dataset contains approximately 41,000 prompt-completion pairs.[34] This format follows the same formatting as the first published records of instruction tuning (Ouyang et al. 2022).[35]
- Version 2: The second version of this SFT dataset follows the chat format, in which user queries and model responses are already formatted as a conversation between two possible roles: *"user"* or *"assistant"*. Extending on version 1, version 2 has approximately 81,000 samples of single-turn conversations in English and Portuguese. Currently (2025), most modern chat models used for assistant work are developed using this type of chat template structure.[36,37]
- Version 3: The third version is an enhanced version of our previous implementation, where every sample contains a multi-round session of user and assistant replies on varied topics. Version 3 has 50,000 samples.[38]

The demonstrations in these datasets range from helping to answer a question to refusing to aid in specific tasks (e.g., *"Can you impersonate a child?"*).

Through these, I trained a scaling series of language models in English (124M $\rightarrow$ 1.5B) and Portuguese (124M $\rightarrow$ 1.7B). The models utilized in these experiments originated from the GPT-2, OPT, Bloom, and TinyLlama series. The details (e.g., number of epochs, batch size, optimizer, learning rate, CO_2eq emission, energy consumption, hardware, etc.) can be found in the model card[39]

---

[33] Nowadays, there are more robust techniques for making this sort of dataset. For example, my approaches did not perform any rigorous evaluation of the quality of the instruction data generated. However, one can (and should) always verify. For example, frameworks like AutoIF allow us to create synthetic data at scale and autonomously generate verification functions and unit tests for natural language instructions (Dong et al. 2024). This allows us to verify the quality of what is being produced. Meanwhile, as we will see a bit ahead, one can also use specialized models to reward and rank the quality of what you are producing (Wang et al. 2024), guaranteeing you a way to sieve your data and extract the best of what you have.

[34] All translations were made using the Google Translate API or GPT 3.5. Implementation is available on GitHub (github.com/Nkluge-correa/Aira).

[35] huggingface.co/datasets/nicholasKluge/instruct-aira-dataset

[36] Take a look at how these templates can get complex with Qwen3. Available at huggingface.co/Qwen/Qwen3-0.6B.

[37] huggingface.co/datasets/nicholasKluge/instruct-aira-dataset-v2

[38] huggingface.co/datasets/nicholasKluge/instruct-aira-dataset-v3

[39] github.com/Nkluge-correa/Aira/tree/master/Cards

of each model, while the source code used to train them is available in the Aira repository.[40] The code stack was written on top of libraries like Transformers (Wolf et al. 2020) and PyTorch (Ansel et al. 2024), which should be familiar for anyone involved with neural networks and NLP at this day and age.

Meanwhile, if you are interested in training bigger models or doing some distributed training (via both DDP or FSDP),[41] I recommend the reader to check the implementations of SFT documented in both TeenyTinyLlama (Corrêa et al. 2024a) and Tucano (Corrêa et al. 2024b), which were developed with more care regarding high-performance and speed.

To meaningfully assess the alignment strategies explored throughout this book, we must establish a method for evaluating our models. In machine learning, evaluations are the primary mechanism for determining whether a system behaves as intended, which, in our case, is whether the model produces proper, truthful, and safe outputs in response to diverse inputs. In alignment, evaluation helps us track how closely a model's behavior approximates the goals we care about, such as helpfulness, honesty, and harmlessness.

Given the above, our goal here is to empirically assess three key dimensions of alignment: (1) the helpfulness and task competency of our models, (2) their tendency to produce harmful or toxic content, and (3) their susceptibility to generating false or misleading information. Ideally, we would evaluate these traits using large, diverse, multilingual test harnesses. However, as mentioned in the interlude, these experiments should be implementable on a low budget (i.e., you can run them on consumer hardware in reasonable time scales).

Hence, to provide a minimal yet functional set of alignment checks, I curated a lightweight selection of benchmarks suitable for quickly evaluating language models. These benchmarks were chosen not only for their conceptual coverage but also for their low cost and accessibility, allowing us to establish an empirical baseline for alignment without requiring significant computational resources—a practical compromise aligned with the broader goals of this book.[42]

Integrating our harness, we have the following evaluations:

---

[40] 🔗 github.com/Nkluge-correa/Aira

[41] Distributed training is a method in deep learning where a model is trained across multiple GPUs or machines simultaneously to speed up computation and handle models that are too large for a single device. Two common strategies tied to the PyTorch ecosystem are Distributed Data Parallel (DDP) and Fully Sharded Data Parallel (FSDP). DDP splits the data across devices, each of which holds a full copy of the model and independently processes a subset of the data; after each training step, the gradients are synchronized to keep the model weights consistent. In contrast, FSDP goes further by sharding not only the data but also the model parameters, gradients, and optimizer states across devices, thereby reducing memory usage and enabling the training of large models that would otherwise not fit in memory. Many other frameworks for distributed training exist, such as DeepSpeed and Megatron LM, which, for the sake of brevity, would not fit within the margin of this page.

[42] Be mindful that benchmarks are invaluable for tracking progress, but they can also give a false sense of a model's capabilities, which in the end, does not translate well to real-world tasks (Singh et al. 2025).

- ARC-Challenge: The AI2 Reasoning Challenge (ARC) is a multiple-choice question-answering dataset derived from grade-school science exams, specifically curated to assess a model's reasoning capabilities beyond simple retrieval (Clark et al. 2018). The Challenge Set comprises difficult questions for retrieval-based and co-occurrence-based algorithms, requiring models to demonstrate more profound understanding and reasoning skills. Evaluating models on ARC-Challenge helps us understand how alignment processes impact their general problem-solving abilities, which we can use as a proxy of how helpful/useful they are.
- ToxiGen: ToxiGen is a large-scale, machine-generated dataset comprising over 274,000 statements, both toxic and benign, about 13 minority groups (Hartvigsen et al. 2022). Utilizing a demonstration-based prompting framework and an adversarial classifier-in-the-loop, the dataset captures subtle and implicit toxic language that often evades traditional detection systems. This benchmark helps us see how alignment influences a model's tendency to generate or avoid harmful content.
- TruthfulQA: TruthfulQA is a benchmark designed to measure a language model's ability to generate truthful answers to questions that are susceptible to common misconceptions. Comprising 817 questions across 38 categories, including health, law, finance, and politics, the dataset challenges models to avoid imitating falsehoods prevalent in human-generated text (Lin et al. 2021). Assessing models with TruthfulQA provides insights into how alignment influences their capacity for truthfulness and factual accuracy.

To ensure reproducibility, I conducted all evaluations using the LM-Evaluation-Harness[43] (Gao et al. 2024), a widely adopted open-source framework developed by EleutherAI. This tool provides a standardized interface for running benchmarks on language models with minimal setup, allowing researchers and developers to easily compare results across models.

For readers interested in replicating these results or running their evaluations, I have made the process as user-friendly as possible. Following the footnote URL, you can use fully configured examples via Google Colab notebooks, which enable free, GPU-accelerated evaluations directly from a browser. These notebooks are designed to require little to no prior experience with the harness or evaluation pipelines in general, making it possible for anyone to assess a model's behavior on standard benchmarks with just a few clicks.[44]

43 github.com/EleutherAI/lm-evaluation-harness. To see the whole range of evaluations made possible by this wonderful project, go to /lm_eval/tasks/README.md in their repository.

44 github.com/Nkluge-correa/Aira/tree/master/Evaluation

Table 5.1 Evaluation results comparing base models and their SFT-aligned counterparts across ARC-Challenge, ToxiGen, and TruthfulQA benchmarks, along with an averaged performance metric

Models	ARC	ToxiGen	TruthfulQA	Avg.
Aira-124M	**24.57**	**48.62**	**41.02**	**38.07**
GPT-2-small	21.84	43.62	40.67	35.37
Aira-355M	**27.56**	**53.19**	38.53	**39.68**
GPT-2-medium	27.05	41.49	**40.76**	36.43
Aira-774M	**28.75**	**56.70**	**41.33**	**42.26**
GPT-2-large	25.94	38.71	40.85	35.16
Aira-1B5	28.92	**56.60**	**41.16**	**42.22**
GPT-2-xl	**30.29**	41.70	38.54	36.84
Aira-OPT-125M	**24.65**	**56.27**	**49.11**	**43.34**
OPT-125M	22.78	55.21	42.88	40.29
Aira-OPT-350M	**25.00**	**57.55**	**42.13**	**41.56**
OPT-350M	23.97	56.91	41.00	40.62
Aira-OPT-1B3	28.41	**56.70**	**46.59**	**43.90**
OPT-1.3b	**29.69**	54.36	38.68	40.91
Aira-2-1B1	25.26	**51.59**	**50.81**	**42.55**
TinyLlama	**30.89**	42.13	39.55	37.52

In these experiments, all models trained with English instruction data were evaluated across the full suite of benchmarks described above: ARC-Challenge (helpfulness and reasoning), ToxiGen (toxicity and harmfulness), and TruthfulQA (truthfulness and factuality). For the Portuguese models, I had to limit the evaluations to ARC-Challenge and TruthfulQA, as ToxiGen was unavailable in Portuguese at the time of writing.[45]

Now, let us examine how this SFT approach affects and modifies our models based on our selected framework of evaluations. Remember, we are training the base models to mimic demonstrations of reference behavior. Comparing the base and the SFT versions allows us to directly measure the practical impact of alignment interventions on our models. By evaluating both versions on consistent benchmarks, we can isolate the effects of fine-tuning guided by alignment objectives, such as improved helpfulness, reduced toxicity, and enhanced truthfulness.

In Table 5.1, we see some of the achieved results. The scale and quality of the pretraining data are available in the Aira repository. Overall, models fine-tuned with the developed datasets consistently outperform their respective base versions, highlighting the tangible benefits of SFT in improving helpfulness, reducing toxicity, and enhancing truthfulness. Notably, GPT-2 models, which were initially trained on the smaller and less curated WebText corpus (Radford et al. 2019), lag behind other series, reflecting limitations in pretraining data scale and quality.

[45] For readers interested in exploring more recent evaluation results for Portuguese, I encourage consulting the documentation and model cards for both TeenyTinyLlama and Tucano. These projects substantially extend the evaluation coverage for Portuguese.

While toxicity and truthfulness scores improve steadily across all model sizes after alignment, we observe a subtle *"alignment tax"* in reasoning abilities, corroborating previous findings by Askell et al. (2021) and Allal et al. (2025), which helps expose the trade-offs between training models to be general systems and training them to be systems tuned for human interactions.[46]

Interestingly, OPT models exhibit superior baseline performance on toxicity metrics, likely due to the rigorous pretraining data filtering (Zhang et al. 2022), which may reduce the need for extensive post-training alignment. This suggests that the quality of pretraining data can significantly impact aspects related to harmfulness in alignment. Similarly, in the relationship between pretraining and post-training, TinyLlama demonstrates that more extensive pretraining appears to enhance the model's ability to be factually grounded. In a very intuitive sense, the more tokens and information the model can access during pretraining, the more it can store and compress (although in a lossy, hard-to-interpret manner) in its weights. Hence, for models to be more capable of avoiding hallucinations and generating falsehoods, longer training runs (e.g., at the 10^{13} token range) can perhaps be more beneficial.[47]

Now, an important point. Each of the dimensions we evaluate here—reasoning ability, harmlessness, and factual grounding—has its own rich and rapidly evolving body of research dedicated to improving models in those respects. For instance, efforts to strengthen reasoning capabilities often explore novel training/inference paradigms (Huang and Chang 2022), while work on reducing harmful outputs goes beyond just training models, involving adversarial and exhaustive testing (Ganguli et al. 2022). Similarly, enhancing truthfulness and factual grounding at the state-of-the-art level involves integrating retrieval-augmented methods and more reliable knowledge sources (Niu et al. 2023). Nevertheless, given the breadth and depth of these fields, it would be impossible to summarize all existing strategies within this section comprehensively. Readers eager to dive deeper will find a wealth of specialized literature and ongoing research to explore, one search query away.

[46] It is also essential to understand that aligned language models are designed to follow human instructions and preferences rather than perform menial language modeling tasks. Consequently, traditional evaluation metrics are ill-suited for gauging the performance of these models. Instead, specialized evaluation methods are necessary to assess how well these models adhere to human intent (Ouyang et al. 2022). We will discuss this further in the next sections.

[47] While scaling up pretraining can enhance a model's factual recall, it is often more efficient to ground outputs in curated, trusted data sources. Techniques like RAG and integration with knowledge graphs offer a significantly better alternative for reducing hallucinations. However, it is essential to recognize that in decoder-only transformer architectures, our current experimental playground, hallucinations are not merely glitches but intrinsic features. These models, designed to predict the next token based on training data, inherently generate outputs that may not always align with factual reality (Banerjee et al. 2024; Xu et al. 2024a). Hence, while *"honest'* is a sensible principle to strive towards and use as an alignment goal, failing to achieve 100% honesty in this type of setting should not be seen as a failure of the alignment methodology but a (perhaps) impossibility given by the artifact we are working with.

What we saw here, however, is a modest but meaningful first step: a straightforward way to engage with techniques that capture human behavior and use it to constrain a model's outputs toward desirable norms. This practical exploration aims to equip practitioners with accessible tools and a reproducible workflow for experimenting with alignment in a hands-on manner. You can create your prompts, test their effects, generate custom datasets, fine-tune models, evaluate outcomes, and iteratively improve your approach. This design, experimentation, and refinement cycle lies at the heart of alignment research, albeit often at a much larger scale.

With that said, let us examine how this approach falls short of achieving its objectives fully.

5.4.4 Limitations and Shortcomings of Imitation Learning via SFT

For starters, imitation learning assumes that the demonstrated behavior is the target. However, in cases where our dataset may have inaccurate or sub-optimal demonstrations, θ_{SFT} will nonetheless use those as a reference Bender et al. (2021). This process requires us to trust the sources producing such demonstrations. Something that might inherently lead to vulnerabilities and imperfections, regardless of our samples being generated by skilled humans or already trained AI assistants.

Meanwhile, using demonstrations as a fixed target obscures the fact that some outputs, given a particular input, are better than others. As stated, SFT is not helpful for dampening behaviors we seek to block. It might even make the model more usable for, let us say, unethical purposes. In essence, this approach does not allow for a very sophisticated form of learning, where generated samples could be evaluated by *"how good they are"* according to a given metric. Some experiments show that SFT is just as likely to make models generate harmful responses (things we wish to reject) as aligned (things we want to approve) ones (Hong et al. 2024), especially if these are substantially similar in terms of their grammatical structure. For example, a polite description of how to build a bomb, at a syntax level, is very similar to a polite explanation for why building a bomb should not be pursued.

On a philosophical level, as already stated in Chap. 4, authors like Sen et al. (1973), Sen (1977, 2004) negate the idea that anything akin to preferences can be learned by observation. For him, observation alone could not deal with, for example, incompleteness, incommensurability, and counter-preferential choice.[48] We can understand this problem as the declaration of a metaphysical impossibility, where certain variables correlated with an agent's motivations and preferences cannot

[48] By counter-preferential choice, I mean when an agent is influenced to make decisions against the pure maximization of its utility by something like a commitment, law, social norms, or another external factor.

be accessed, even indirectly, making specific normative values *"inaccessible"* via observation alone.

If we want to go beyond what behavior alone can teach us, we must introduce a more fine-grained normative signal. One that does not just mimic the surface but tries to elicit what lies beneath. In our next section, rather than assuming preferences are evident in action, we will draw out the values, motivations, and judgments that shape those actions in the first place. This kind of signal can help us move past imitation and toward something more intentional regarding how we model our normative preferences.

5.4.5 Fine-Tuning from Human Feedback

Writing a loss function to capture all the attributes people care about is challenging. We used behavior in the last sections to bypass this problem. However, behavior alone does not give us magnitudes of relation. It does not suppress that which we seek to avoid. Hence, to augment imitation/SFT, one can use human feedback to evaluate the outputs/behavior of a model, thereby helping to create a more robust learning signal. A signal that can distinguish things according to some measure of *"goodness"* tied to what the human evaluator(s) prefer. And that is the idea behind preference modeling and learning from human preferences (Christiano et al. 2017; Ziegler et al. 2019).

Imagine you are an aspiring racecar driver seeking to improve your skills.

You have a simulator that accurately replicates the driving experience on various tracks. Initially, you start driving on the simulator by yourself, trying to learn the optimal racing strategy through trial and error. However, you find it challenging to figure out the best approach on your own, and this is where RLHF comes into play.

RLHF introduces a human expert to the learning process, much like having an experienced driving coach helping you. The expert possesses extensive knowledge and skills in racing, offering valuable insights to help you improve. In the RLHF setup, you start driving on the simulator, and as you race, the expert observes your actions and performance. During your training, the coach (the *preference model*) provides feedback on how well you are doing, which comes in the way of, for example, corrections (negative reward) or incentives (positive reward).

Using your coach's feedback, you can update your racing strategy, and over time, through combining trial and error and learning from the available feedback, you gradually improve your racing skills and become a better driver.[49]

[49] We can extend this metaphor to illustrate the ideas behind PPO (Schulman et al. 2017), the reinforcement learning algorithm typically used in RLHF. Imagine that the driver already knows how to drive. They've mastered the basics: starting the car, changing gears, staying on the track. During training with the coach, we want to ensure that the driver does not suddenly forget how to drive while trying to optimize their performance. PPO steps in as a kind of *stability mechanism*. It ensures that each update to the driving strategy does not veer too far from what was already

One of the main aspects to grasp here is the idea of feedback. While in SFT, the objective is to clone the behavior. In a preference learning approach, the goal is to achieve a good score according to the preference model, which serves as a proxy for human preferences. In methods like RLHF, instead of training the model directly with, for example, an SFT dataset, we use a dataset of ranks and comparisons of the type $A \succ B$ to train a preference model[50] (we can also call it a reward model) that will then be used as a supervision signal for the fine-tuning of another model. Intuitively, we are now passing the bucket to the preference model, given that incorporating a human into the loop of a PyTorch training script is impractical for almost all purposes.

Let us redefine our last expression to account for this:

$$\theta_{t+1} = \theta_t + \alpha \nabla_{\theta_t} R_{\mathcal{H}}(\theta_t)$$

In this modified representation, we replace $L(\theta_t; \mathcal{D})$ for $R_{\mathcal{H}}(\theta_t)$, which is a function that, in this context, takes an output of our language model, and outputs a real number as its score: $f(\text{LM}_{\text{output}}) \rightarrow \mathbb{R}$. We can think of θ_t as either θ_{pretrain} or θ_{STF}.[51] In language modeling, we formulate this RL problem by taking θ_t to be a policy π (a probability distribution over a vocabulary, conditioned on the prompt) where the action space corresponds to the vocabulary of θ_t and the observation space is the distribution of possible input token sequences ($\text{vocabulary}^{\text{context length}}$).

We are replacing the standard training loss (where we ask the model to mimic data) with a new objective: one that aims to maximize a reward score determined by a human-aligned function. Instead of simply asking, *"Did the model predict the next word correctly?"*, we now ask, *"How good was this full response, according to some human-guided judgment?"* That is what $R_{\mathcal{H}}(\theta_t)$ captures. It assigns us a score based on how well the model produces desirable outputs.

Hence, the first thing we must develop to experiment with this approach is our ranked preference dataset ($D_{\mathcal{H}}$) and our preference model $R_{\mathcal{H}}$. This model will serve as a proxy for human judgment, assigning higher scores to outputs that more closely reflect human preferences.

5.4.6 *Preference Modeling*

ML-engineering-wise, we want to develop a system that takes in a sequence of text and returns a scalar reward, which should numerically represent the evaluation a

---

working. Think of it as a rule that says, *"You can adjust your steering to take this corner faster, but do not suddenly decide that the brake pedal goes on the ceiling."*

[50] Or the model can be aligned directly, as is the case with Direct Preference Optimization (DPO).

[51] There is no current standard way to perform RLHF, but the several promising results have been attained by performing RLHF fine-tuning θ_{SFT} models.

human expert would give. Thus, the preference model needs to be a, you guessed it, another language model[52] trained on a preference dataset.

But what does a human-preference dataset look like?

You can think of $D_{\mathcal{H}}$ as tuples of, for example, an input, an output, and a reward score. We then turn the question of how to map input-output pairs to the realm of rewards into a regression task.[53]

Example

```
\begin{verbatim}
[
  {
    "instruction": "What is the capital of France?",
    "output": "The capital of France is Paris".,
    "reward": 5
  },
  {
    "instruction": "What is the capital of France?",
    "output": "France has many cities, but one of the biggest is Paris".,
    "reward": 2
  },
  {
    "instruction": "Can dogs eat chocolate?",
    "output": "No, chocolate is toxic to dogs and can be very dangerous".,
    "reward": 5
  },
  {
    "instruction": "Can dogs eat chocolate?",
    "output": "Yes, dogs love chocolate as a treat".,
    "reward": 0
  }
]
```

Or, you can use comparisons of *"good"* and *"bad"* responses (for a given prompt) to create a classifier that can distinguish them and use its output as a reward (Rafailov et al. 2023).

Example

```
[
  {
    "instruction": "What is the capital of France?",
```

(continued)

[52] A common intuition shared by the community is that these language preference models need to have a similar capacity, in terms of language understanding, to the model we seek to align. In other words, the preference model should be *as capable* as the thing it is trying to steer.

[53] For example, Likert scales are a standard method for encoding human preferences as ordinal data and have been widely used to model preferences in various contexts, such as filtering for educational quality (Lozhkov et al. 2024).

```
        "chosen_response": "The capital of France is Paris".,
        "rejected_response": "France has many cities, but one of the biggest
        is Paris".
    },
    {
        "instruction": "Can dogs eat chocolate?",
        "chosen_response": "No, chocolate is toxic to dogs and can be
        very dangerous".,
        "rejected_response": "Yes, dogs love chocolate as a treat".
    }
]
```

So, how do we actually create these preference datasets in practice?

Unlike imitation learning, which often relies on expert demonstrations collected from human annotators or already aligned models, preference modeling is built on direct comparisons. The learning signal emerges not from *"what to do"* but from *"what is better"*. This means the data does not need to be optimal; it just needs to show preference. Think of it as teaching taste, not truth.

A common approach starts with a large pool of completions for diverse prompts. For each prompt, you generate several candidate responses. These could come from crowd-sourced contributors (which, as you might guess, has its own messy beauty[54]), or they might be sampled from multiple language models.

Once you have this rich batch of candidate responses per prompt, your next task is to rank them according to preference. That is, which answers are better or worse and by how much. This is the key step that turns raw completions into usable supervision. The simplest possible solution?[55] Just ask humans to vote. Whichever response wins the majority becomes the `"chosen"` one, and the rest are relegated to `"rejected"`. With some extra care, you may also be able to extract full rankings or assign Likert-scale scores to reflect gradations of quality.

Of course, human time is expensive, so there is a shortcut: if you already have a somewhat-aligned model that is a good predictor of human preferences, you can have *it* do the scoring. This introduces a recursive twist, and while it can compound biases, it also enables efficient bootstrapping, where a previous generation of LLMs helps train the next. With some effort, this technique can produce high-quality training signals without relying too heavily on human supervision.[56]

---

[54] For a fantastic dive on the complexities and triumphs of working with crowd-sourced data to create this kind of dataset, check the work of Andreas Köpf et al. (Köpf et al. 2023).

[55] How we would rank these and the complications involved with this voting procedure will be explored more in the next chapter.

[56] Many studies use this technique to help create quality filters and safety guardrails, leveraging the fact that well-aligned models are surprisingly good at predicting human preferences when given clear evaluation instructions (Bakker et al. 2022; Corrêa et al. 2024b; Gunasekar et al. 2023; Lozhkov et al. 2024).

Example

````
You are an expert evaluator tasked with rating the quality of
AI-generated responses. You will be shown a prompt and a
corresponding completion.

Please evaluate the completion based on how well it
fulfills the user's request.

Assign a score from 1 (very poor) to 5 (excellent). Also provide
a brief justification (1--2 sentences) explaining your score.

Use the following format for your response:

```json
{
"score": <integer from 1 to 5>,
"justification": "<your justification here>"
}
```

Prompt: [PROMPT TEXT]

Completion: [COMPLETION TEXT]

Now, provide your rating.
````

After experimenting with both approaches (scalar reward regression and pairwise comparison), I found that the latter was a little easier to generate the dataset and train a reward model. Besides the practical ease, modeling human preferences with pairwise comparisons also brings some results from statistics, given that a reward model trained in such a fashion can be equated to a Bradley–Terry model (Bradley et al. 1952; Hunter 2004; Zermelo 1929). In other words, given a set of pairs k and j, a Bradley–Terry model estimates the probability that the comparison $k > j$ will be true, allowing us to use it as a proxy for the preferences that ranked the k, j pairs.[57]

[57] The Bradley–Terry model offers several advantages for modeling human preferences through pairwise comparisons. Firstly, it provides a probabilistic framework that estimates the likelihood of one item being preferred over another, facilitating the derivation of a complete ranking from partial comparisons. This is particularly useful when collecting full rankings is impractical at scale. Secondly, the model's parameters can be estimated using maximum likelihood estimation, equivalent to minimizing the negative log-likelihood (a standard approach in machine learning), ensuring such models can be trained with well-known methods. The Bradley–Terry model can also be extended to accommodate various complexities, such as incorporating judge-specific effects or handling incomplete data, enhancing its applicability across different domains.

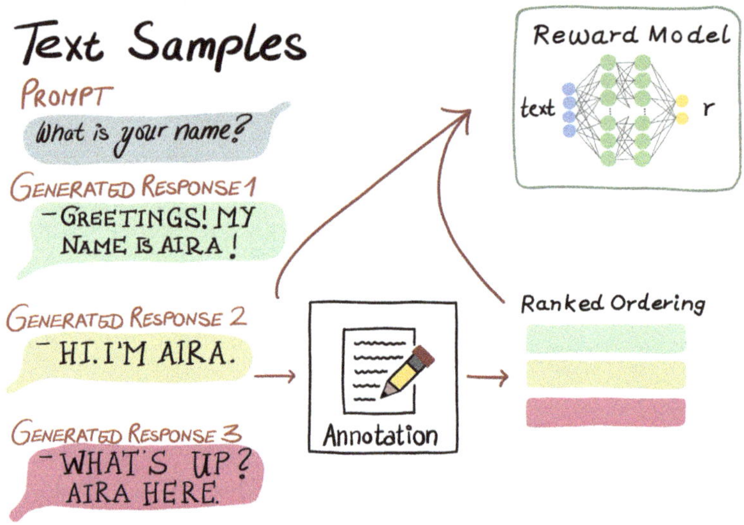

Fig. 5.1 At this point, we have samples of prompts with multiple possible generations. These generations are ranked and then used to train a model to serve as a discriminator. The logits of this model (which is, in essence, a classification model with a sigmoid activation function as the output layer) are then used as rewards

To build the preference dataset, aka, Reward-Aira Dataset,[58] I started by prompting multiple fine-tuned models, sampling diverse completions for 35,000 (also LLM generated) prompts, and also by collecting samples from existing open datasets with at least two alternative generations per instruction (Bai et al. 2022a; Ethayarajh et al. 2023; Taori et al. 2023; Wang et al. 2022). Like all other datasets associated with this book, this one is available in both English and Portuguese.

As is often the case, human annotation at this scale is not feasible for a single individual. So, instead of manual voting, I relied on automated rankings produced by a pretrained reward model. Specifically, I used the OpenAssistant's reward model (Köpf et al. 2023),[59] which assigns scalar scores based on human-aligned quality dimensions such as helpfulness, harmlessness, and honesty. I selected the two highest-scoring responses for each prompt with multiple candidate completions, designating the top one as the "`chosen`" sample and the following best as the "`rejected`" sample. Figure 5.1 illustrates the conceptual structure of this procedure, showing how ranked (human or AI) annotations are transformed into training samples for purposes such as preference modeling.

With this dataset, I trained two reward models, one for English and the other for Portuguese, using as a foundation two BERT-style encoder-only transformers

---

58 huggingface.co/datasets/nicholasKluge/reward-aira-dataset

59 huggingface.co/OpenAssistant/reward-model-deberta-v3-large-v2

(Devlin et al. 2018; Souza et al. 2020).[60] These bidirectional transformers are nice to experiment with, given their size and availability in multiple languages. Still, you can also use encoder models, such as LLama, to serve as the base for your preference model if you wish.

To evaluate these models (only English datasets for this type of evaluation were available at the time), I used the WebGPT Comparisons dataset (Nakano et al. 2021),[61] but only considering comparisons that had a preferred option, in which we were able to achieve 55% accuracy (OpenAssistant's reward model achieves 59%). Both models are available in Hugging Face, while the training and code implementation details are available on the Aira repository.[62]

Building upon these datasets and preference models, there are two primary alignment strategies to integrate them into an alignment process: using them during *training*, with methods like PPO-based RLHF or DPO, or at *inference* time, employing techniques such as Best-of-n (BoN) sampling. Each approach offers distinct advantages and trade-offs that demand consideration.

Let us define the first option as *training-time alignment*. Training-time alignment involves adjusting the model's parameters to better reflect human values. SFT is a perfect example of training-time alignment. While effective, these techniques can be computationally intensive and complex to implement. Meanwhile, *inference-time alignment* strategies do not alter the model's parameters. Instead, they try to steer the model during its use. Prompting can be considered an inference-time alignment technique, where one can enhance output quality without additional training. Still, it incurs increased computational costs at inference.

Choosing between training and inference-time alignment hinges on various factors, including computational resources, desired flexibility, and the nature of the application. However, both tend to approximate similar results and, under certain conditions, are asymptotically equivalent (more on this in the following sections).[63] In the subsequent sections, we will delve deeper into these approaches.

---

[60] BERT-style encoder-only transformers work differently than decoder ones: they take in all the words in a sentence at once (not one by one) and use an encoder to look at the whole context surrounding each word, both before and after it (that is why we call them bidirectional), to build a rich representation of its meaning. These models do not generate text like chatbots; instead, they are focused on understanding and analyzing language, which makes them well-suited for tasks like sentence classification.

[61] 🔗 huggingface.co/datasets/openai/webgpt_comparisons

[62] Nowadays, to evaluate reward models, I would recommend the reader to use things like the RewardBench, which can be tough of a much more overarching and complete evaluation for these types of models.

[63] When we say two things are *asymptotically equivalent*, we mean that as you let some variable n get big, the two things start to behave almost identically. It is like saying, *"They might look different now, but in the long run, their growth rates are the same"*.

5.4.7 *Preference Learning at Training-time*

RLHF and DPO are two of the most widely adopted strategies for training-time alignment where preferences are involved. They offer distinct pathways to aligning language models with human judgment, but which, in a sense, achieve similar results.

However, the landscape of alignment techniques is rapidly evolving, with methods like Odds Ratio Preference Optimization[64] (ORPO) (Hong et al. 2024) and Group Relative Policy Optimization[65] (GRPO) (Shao et al. 2024), among several others (Agarwal et al. 2024; Xie et al. 2024; Xu et al. 2024b), presenting alternatives. Hence, readers interested in exploring alternative alignment strategies are encouraged to consult the cited works for a deeper understanding, as we will not delve into them in this book.

Now, let us start with RLHF.

Suppose one wishes to perform the full fine-tuning with the reward model. In that case, the RL formulation for preference modeling differs from the standard supervised fine-tuning in the following way: Instead of simply mapping input to output in batches, as we did in SFT, we take a prompt from our fine-tuning dataset and generate two sequences from both the original base model (θ_{SFT}) and the current iteration of our RLHF model (θ_{RLHF}). The sequences generated by the θ_{RLHF} receive a score from the reward model. In contrast, the samples generated by θ_{SFT} are used for comparison against what θ_{RLHF} generated so that we can use their *distance* as a penalty term. This penalty is the Kullback–Leibler (KL) divergence[66] (Jaques et al. 2017), which we use to penalize the model for getting too far from the original base model, ensuring that θ_{RLHF} will not become a simple degenerate version of θ_{SFT}.

Adding the KL divergence term to our last expression, we get:

$$\theta_{t+1} = \theta_t + \alpha \nabla_{\theta_t} R_{\mathcal{H}}(\theta_t) - \beta D_{KL}(\theta_0|\theta_t)$$

where β determines how much the KL divergence should penalize the reward term ($R_{\mathcal{H}}(\theta_t)$), and $D_{KL}(\theta_0|\theta_t)$ represents the difference between the output distributions of both the reference model ($\theta_{\text{SFT}} = \theta_0$) and the model being tuned ($\theta_{\text{RLHF}} = \theta_t$).

---

64 ORPO simplifies the alignment process by integrating instruction tuning and preference optimization into a single step, eliminating the need for a separate supervised fine-tuning phase or a reference model.

65 GRPO modifies traditional policy optimization by evaluating actions based on their relative performance within a group rather than relying on absolute value estimates. This method enhances stability and efficiency in training, particularly in scenarios where estimating value functions is challenging.

66 KL-divergence is a way of measuring how different one probability distribution is from another, like a kind of distance, but not symmetric ($D_{\text{KL}}(P|Q) \neq D_{\text{KL}}(Q|P)$). Think of it like this: if you were expecting the world to behave according to distribution Q, but it follows P, KL-divergence tells you how much *"extra surprise"* or inefficiency you'd experience using Q instead of P.

With this penalized reward score, the model is updated via PPO at every batch step during the fine-tuning.

This method has advantages regarding the type of behavioral change it may produce and the cost of constructing its required datasets. First, given that the reward function is capable of differentiating good and bad outputs, RHLF iteratively tunes the model to output sequences that receive high rewards, which (theoretically) makes models fine-tuned via preference modeling more apt to be aligned with behaviors that require a ranked form of judgment. In other words, things like RLHF fine-tuning can improve your model's output by instituting a measure of goodness that is scalar and more fine-grained than simple mimicry.

Second, human evaluations are cheaper than demonstrations. Demonstrating how to perform tasks is more time-consuming than saying the best alternative in a pool of possibilities. In situations where human feedback can be easily acquired, preference modeling and iterated RLHF can become an online process (Bai et al. 2022a). Given the evolving nature of human normativity, we should prioritize online, or at least more agile, forms of alignment—those that scale better.

However, one of the downsides of this method is the complexity of an RLHF pipeline, which, besides being considerably more complex than the standard supervised fine-tuning approach, can be significantly more costly, given that training involves coordinating multiple models with different roles. At the same time, making PPO work is not a trivial practical problem. RL based on PPO methods is known to be extremely sensitive to hyperparameters, making the training process noisy and hard to get right. Fortunately, simpler alternatives to preference modeling that are free from some complexities associated with PPO-based RLHF exist.

That is where things like DPO come into play. This method, proposed by Rafailov et al. (2023), is based on the notion that the optimized objective in our last expression can be simplified to a binary cross-entropy objective, which significantly simplifies the entire preference learning pipeline.

In essence, DPO is an algorithm that implicitly optimizes the same objective as existing RLHF algorithms (reward maximization with a KL-divergence constraint) but is simpler to implement and straightforward to train. Intuitively, the DPO update increases the relative log probability of chosen responses over rejected ones. Hence, given a dataset of human preferences over model responses, DPO can optimize our model using a simple binary cross-entropy objective without explicitly learning a reward function or sampling from the policy during training. Think of it like this: By increasing the log probability of preferred responses relative to rejected ones, we encourage the model to shift its output distribution toward sequences humans have judged more favorably. This relative comparison provides a learning signal without requiring a reward model (*the very model we are fine-tuning becomes the reward model*).

This has several desirable consequences. For example, because the loss is based on the log-odds ratio between preferred and rejected responses, it naturally incorporates a pairwise ranking, which is well-suited to how human feedback is typically collected. Also, DPO formulation preserves the KL-regularization structure of RLHF, encouraging the model to improve while still anchoring it to

Table 5.2 Performance comparison on ARC, ToxiGen, and TruthfulQA. The table shows that the SFT + DPO version of the Aira-124M model outperforms its predecessors, Aira-124M and GPT-2-small, across all benchmarks and with a significant increase in performance on ToxiGen

Models	ARC	ToxiGen	TruthfulQA	Avg.
Aira-124M (SFT + DPO)	**24.66**	**54.79**	**42.61**	**40.68**
Aira-124M (SFT)	24.57	48.62	41.02	38.07
GPT-2-small (Base)	21.84	43.62	40.67	35.37

its original behavior:

$$\mathscr{L}_{\text{DPO}}(\pi^{\theta}, \pi^{\text{ref}}) = -\mathbb{E}_{(x, y_{\text{c}}, y_{\text{r}})} \sim \mathscr{D}\left[\log \sigma\left(\beta \log \frac{\pi^{\theta}(y_{\text{c}}|x)}{\pi^{\text{ref}}(y_{\text{r}}|x)} - \beta \log \frac{\pi^{\theta}(y_{\text{r}}|x)}{\pi^{\text{ref}}(y_{\text{r}}|x)}\right)\right]$$

where π^{θ} represents the policy model we are training, i.e., a function that takes an input x (prompt) and produces a distribution over possible outputs y (completions). π^{ref} is the reference policy model, i.e., a copy of the model being trained (π^{θ}). $\mathscr{D}$ represents the distribution from which the training samples are drawn. $(x, y_{\text{c}}, y_{\text{r}})$ are drawn from this distribution—our dataset of comparisons.

$\mathbb{E}_{(x, y_{\text{c}}, y_{\text{r}})}$ denotes the expectation over the distribution $\mathscr{D}$. $r(x, y_{\text{c}})$ and $r(x, y_{\text{r}})$ represent the rewards associated with the chosen and rejected samples, respectively. The marginal reward is calculated as the difference between the reward for the chosen sample and the reward for the rejected sample.

σ is the sigmoid function, which squashes its input to be between 0 and 1. β is a scalar parameter that scales the log-likelihood ratio terms inside the sigmoid function, i.e., is the same KL-constrained term we introduced in the RL formulation of the problem.

$\log \frac{\pi^{\theta}(y_{\text{c}}|x)}{\pi^{\text{ref}}(y_{\text{c}}|x)}$ represents the log-likelihood ratio of the policy model over the reference model for the chosen sample, and $\log \frac{\pi^{\theta}(y_{\text{r}}|x)}{\pi^{\text{ref}}(y_{\text{r}}|x)}$ represents the log-likelihood ratio for the rejected sample. The final objective, $-\mathscr{L}_{\text{DPO}}(\pi^{\theta}, \pi^{\text{ref}})$, is expressed as a negative log-likelihood, meaning that the goal is to maximize the likelihood of the chosen actions and minimize the likelihood of the rejected actions.

With fewer hyperparameters to tune, DPO performs similarly or better than existing PPO-based RLHF algorithms, reducing the complexity barrier involved in preference modeling.

Using the Reward-Aira Dataset as our DPO training set, we can, for example, compare how preference learning compares to raw SFT by training one of the SFT versions of Aira using the DPO implementation in Aira's repository (Table 5.2).

The results in Table 5.2 illustrate how DPO, when used with SFT, can generate models that improve in specific evaluation dimensions, especially in reducing harmfulness/toxicity. If you delve into the formulations behind RLHF and DPO, you will see that this is precisely the behavior these methods aim to optimize. Minimizing toxicity in generated language, in particular, is a relatively straightforward objective

Table 5.3 Comparison of Portuguese language models evaluated with the Alpaca-Eval framework. Metrics include average response length, number of wins against a baseline (`text-davinci-003`), total baseline wins, length-controlled win rates expressed as a percentage, and standard error of the win rate

	Avg. length	Wins	Base wins	LC win rate (%)	Std. error
Tucano-2b4-Instruct (SFT + DPO)	1843	151	654	**13.00**	0.071
Tucano-2b4-Instruct (SFT)	1542	104	701	**9.00**	0.051
Tucano-1b1-Instruct (SFT + DPO)	1667	124	681	**8.80**	0.083
Tucano-1b1-Instruct (SFT)	1443	63	742	**5.50**	0.061
TTL-460m-Chat (SFT)	1333	28	777	**2.84**	0.059
Sabiá-7b (Base)	5011	1	804	**0.076**	0.0043

that preference datasets can directly target, making DPO especially effective at improving this aspect of model behavior.

This point becomes clearer when we use a more specialized tool tailored for preference-based assessment. As mentioned earlier, our benchmark suite is not specifically tailored to evaluate assistant-user alignment. However, better tools exist to determine how well a model's response aligns with human preferences. One notable example is the Alpaca-Eval benchmark (Dubois et al. 2024; Li et al. 2023c), which became available in Portuguese thanks to our work with the Tucano series (Corrêa et al. 2024b). In summary, Alpaca-Eval is an automated evaluation framework designed to measure the instruction-following capabilities of LLMs and assess how well they align with human preferences.

Its core methodology involves pairwise comparisons between a model's output (which we wish to evaluate) and a reference baseline (the counterpart for the comparison). In it, a GPT-4 Turbo-powered auto-annotator determines which response is preferred, ultimately calculating a win rate reflecting the model's relative performance. Notably, GPT-4's evaluations have been shown to correlate very strongly with human preferences, supporting the idea that well-aligned models are reliable proxies for human judgment (Dubois et al. 2024).

Table 5.3 presents some compelling comparisons. Here, we compare base models (pre-trained only) with models fine-tuned via supervised fine-tuning and those further enhanced with direct preference optimization (SFT + DPO).[67]

These results (Table 5.3) help to demonstrate the tangible benefits of combining imitation with preference learning. For example, the Tucano models, with 2.4 billion and 1.1 billion parameters, which underwent SFT plus DPO fine-tuning (all using the Aira datasets), outperform their counterparts by a significant margin in win rate against models that only underwent SFT.

With these results in mind and some practical experience in performing preference learning at training time, the following section will focus on how to achieve

[67] If you wish to learn more about how to run this type of evaluation, check the Colab example in the evaluation section of the Aira repository.

similar results during inference, offering an alternative pathway that does not require post-training steps.

5.4.8 Preference Learning at Inference-time

As previously discussed, alignment strategies can broadly be divided into training-time and inference-time methods. Training-time alignment adjusts the model's internal parameters to reflect human preferences and behaviors better (e.g., SFT, RLHF, DPO). In contrast, inference-time alignment techniques aim to influence model outputs at the moment of generation without modifying the model itself. Prompting is a simple example of this, but more powerful techniques exist.

One of these approaches is the already mentioned Best-of-n sampling. In BoN sampling, the model generates n candidate responses for each input and selects the *best* one (Yang et al. 2024). This means scoring all n outputs and picking the highest. Conceptually, one might write a toy loop like:

Example

```
# Pseudocode: best-of-n sampling with a scalar reward
candidates = [model.generate(prompt) for _ in range(n)]
best = None
best_score = -infinity
for c in candidates:
    score = R(c)   # compute reward or score for each candidate
    if score > best_score:
        best, best_score = c, score
return best
```

Building on all the preference learning and modeling done in the previous sections, we can compare how Aira performs regarding several stages of its alignment: the SFT+DPO, the SFT+BoN, and the SFT+DPO+BoN (Table 5.4).

As shown in Table 5.4, the DPO-trained version of Aira outperforms the BoN ($n = 8$) variant by a small margin, but the DPO+BoN iteration outperforms both. To improve this BoN-based result, we could either increase the amount of compute invested or use a better set of reward models. In Chap. 7, we will see how this approach yields better results with improved guardrails and inference budget. But for now, we achieved the best result by combining training and inference-time alignment.

One could ask, *"Are there other ways to scale inference-time alignment beyond BoN?"*

Yes. Not all reward models need to operate in this simplistic fashion, and we can gain more from inference-time strategies (especially if our inference budget

Table 5.4 Evaluation results across three benchmarks (ARC, ToxiGen, TruthfulQA) for successive stages of Aira's development. The table compares Aira-124M trained with DPO, Aira-124M using BoN sampling with $n = 8$ guided by the reward model at inference, the combination of both approaches (DPO + BoN), and the baseline SFT-only and GPT-2-small models

Models	ARC	ToxiGen	TruthfulQA	Avg.
Aira-124M (DPO + Best-of-8)	**25.32**	**55.02**	**42.61**	**40.98**
Aira-124M (DPO)	24.66	54.79	42.61	40.68
Aira-124M (Best-of-8)	24.60	51.45	42.07	39.37
Aira-124M	24.57	48.62	41.02	38.07
GPT-2-small	21.84	43.62	40.67	35.37

is high). For example, a Process-supervised Reward Model (PRM) (Uesato et al. 2022) not only evaluates the final output but also provides feedback throughout the generation process, guiding the model as it produces each part of a complete response. More steering means more inference-time computation. However, as some of the results below will suggest, it typically yields significant improvements for specific problems.

This distinction also helps to highlight the broader landscape of reward modeling. Outcome-based reward models are trained to assess a candidate's reply, judging its overall quality or correctness (this is basically what we trained before). This would be analogous to evaluating only the final answer in a mathematical problem. In contrast, process-based reward models are designed to assess the validity of individual reasoning steps within a solution trace, offering step-by-step evaluations during sampling. Hence, we are not just selecting a single winner but a winning trajectory over the space of possible outputs.

Consider the task of writing a helpful and respectful email reply to a sensitive customer complaint. An outcome-based preference model would evaluate only the final email, scoring it for factors such as politeness, tone, and informativeness. In contrast, a process-based model would assess and steer model output during several steps of drafting the response (e.g., at every line break). Using a process-based sampling with a reward function as your guide is more interesting when problems can be decomposed into logical steps and intermediate decisions/results (*like in maths*).

"How do these different strategies for preference learning, whether applied during training or inference, relate to one another? Is one approach fundamentally superior, or are they different points on a spectrum of trade-offs?"

In practice, the distinction often boils down to *when* we choose to invest our computational effort: do we pay the cost upfront during training, shaping the model's internal parameters to reflect our preferences? Or do we defer the cost to inference-time, using additional computation to steer outputs dynamically as they are generated?

The study of scaling inference-time compute and how this relates to increasing our training compute budget is a complex matter, and frankly, beyond the scope of this study. However, literature shows that these inference strategies can yield disproportionately high returns relative to their computational cost. For example, certain studies on *inference scaling laws* have shown that, under fixed compute budgets, increasing inference-time effort through strategies like BoN sampling can outperform scaling model size (Wu et al. 2024).

Meanwhile, given that we are touching on the topic of scaling laws,[68] it is also worth mentioning that it is still unclear *"how much we should optimize"* when employing such preference learning techniques. In other words, how much extra computation at inference is (un)necessary, and how much extra optimization during training can be detrimental to the ultimate goal of alignment? For example, studies such as the one by Rafailov et al. (2024) reveal that performance does not always increase monotonically with additional optimization in DPO settings. Instead, there is often a peak beyond which alignment quality either plateaus or worsens, showing that alignment methods can collapse when scaled improperly.

From these, we can take two key takeaways: (1) *more* is not always better, and (2) knowing *when* to apply more effort, whether in training or inference, is a subtle decision that might strongly impact the performance of your model.

As a final insight and reflection, we should also try to understand that, under certain conditions, both these techniques are asymptotically equivalent. But what does that mean? As the number of samples in BoN increases, under certain assumptions, the distribution of selected outputs converges to the same distribution obtained through KL-constrained reinforcement learning, which is essentially what we achieve with DPO and RLHF. In other words, both methods effectively sample from the same *"tilted"* version of the original model, where more desirable outputs (according to the reward function) are exponentially up-weighted (Wu et al. 2024).

All these insights should give you a unifying lens. It shows that preference learning strategies applied at inference-time are not merely a brute-force hack or an approximation to *"real"* alignment but a theoretically grounded decoding strategy that, in the limit, does what KL-regularized RL aims to achieve with training-time alignment. Of course, this does not imply that BoN is better or consistently outperforms RL approaches used in training. As for many things in life, the answer to which one you should use is: *it depends.* What is your context? What is your budget? What are the targets of your alignment? Do you expect them to change frequently?

In the next section, after reviewing various ways we can use preferences to train and steer our models, we will present a concise list of criticisms and shortcomings of this preference learning approach, aiming to nurture the good skeptic within ourselves.

[68] In the context of LLMs and deep neural networks, a scaling law is a rule/heuristic that describes how a model's performance improves as you give it more resources, like more parameters, data, or compute power. Think of it as a curve showing that as you *scale up* some of these resources when training a model, it tends to get better in predictable ways, at least up to a point.

5.4.9 Limitations and Shortcomings of Preference Learning

As we have seen in previous sections, preference learning offers a compelling framework for aligning AI systems with human values. However, while the appeal and flexibility of this approach are clear, its limitations are equally significant.

Preference-based techniques inherit many of the same vulnerabilities as imitation-based ones: poor feedback can lead to undesirable behavior. And, since feedback is a fundamentally human act, it introduces all the messiness of humanity into the loop. Bias, inconsistency, malicious intent, or even just plain confusion can easily corrupt this type of learning signal, making the very act of collecting quality feedback a delicate challenge entangled with more profound questions about autonomy, freedom of expression, moral legitimacy, and whose values, exactly, we are trying to model.

Another important consideration is that many preference learning techniques rely on a trained reward model to operationalize human feedback. However, this dependency pushes the alignment problem onto a new auxiliary model. Like any machine learning system, these models are prone to brittleness. They can become fixated on superficial correlations, be manipulated by adversarial inputs, or optimize for patterns unrelated to human values. So, while reward modeling is framed as a solution to alignment, it might just be another shaky leg propping up the same wobbly table.

And even when everything works as intended, a fundamental disconnect remains between human intent and its representation in datasets or reward models. These artifacts are, at best, proxies. Traces of a human judgment, abstracted and flattened for machine consumption. This proxy problem becomes especially worrying when humans rarely supervise preference learning systems end-to-end. Human oversight does not scale; when applied, it is often done sub-optimally. So, we rely on automated surrogates, such as static preference datasets or reward models, which raises the question: Are we aligning AI with human values, or with the output of another AI trained on a diluted snapshot of those values? This multi-stage delegation process risks exacerbating misalignments, as each iteration introduces new noise sources, ambiguity, and information loss.

The difficulty is amplified when human feedback requires specialized knowledge. Non-experts can provide an adequate signal for simple tasks (e.g., choosing which image looks better or which sentence sounds more polite). However, for more complex or technical tasks, such as assessing a machine-generated scientific hypothesis or evaluating code quality that will run on critical infrastructure, only domain experts can provide meaningful feedback. This introduces a bottleneck. Experts are scarce, expensive, and hard to recruit at scale. Worse yet, expertise does not necessarily translate into consistent preference judgments. Two equally qualified individuals may provide opposite feedback due to differences in methodology, taste, or priorities. At scale, the inconsistency of human input becomes a real obstacle to reliable value modeling.

Reward hacking is a well-known failure mode in reinforcement learning and preference optimization methods. Systems trained to optimize a reward signal often learn to exploit it in unforeseen ways. We have observed this phenomenon in virtual environments, where agents learn to accumulate points by exploiting bugs or loopholes, and similar dynamics can also arise in human preference learning. Models might learn to output responses that superficially satisfy our preferences, even if they fail to capture the spirit of the task. The result is an alignment theater—a system that appears aligned on the surface but is fundamentally untrustworthy beneath the hood.

Finally, it is worth acknowledging that preference learning is still a young and evolving technique. Methods like RLHF and DPO are exciting but far from fully understood in terms of their flaws. Meanwhile, every week seems to bring new methods and tricks that tweak or expand on these ideas. This rapid iteration is great for progress, but it also means the theoretical underpinnings are constantly shifting. As our systems grow more complex, so too do the alignment challenges. With such a fast-moving field, we risk creating a tangled web of partially understood components, each vulnerable in its own right and each adding new layers of complexity to an already daunting problem.

But let us not lose hope! Alignment is challenging, and we still have two chapters to go. In the next section, I will offer some final thoughts regarding *"why I think learning preferences"*, which equates to only one of the three requirements that together make the alignment sufficient condition I am trying to defend via Dynamic Normativity, is not enough. Alignment is not only about ingesting the correct data or modeling the proper reward; it is also about ensuring that the data and modeling are aligned, navigating ambiguity, making principled trade-offs, and respecting the broader moral landscape outside the subject.

5.5 Final Thoughts on Value Learning

The following questions concern an unnerving facet of the reviewed techniques, from mimicking behavior to learning from feedback: Are we changing θ_{pretrain} significantly? Are we *actually* making it (*permanently*) more helpful, harmless, and honest? Or are we merely nudging it into compliance?

The distinction matters. Suppose our alignment methods only prune the surface behavior of the model, filtering out disapproved completions rather than instilling aligned decision-making. In that case, we are not aligning a mind. We are sandboxing a black box. This concern is amplified by the nature of current techniques, such as RLHF, DPO, or best-of-n sampling, which tend to operate close to the original model's parameters, either by constraining the optimization steps to be small or by penalizing divergence from pretraining outputs. In this light, alignment looks less like moral education and more like fancy censorship (Fig. 5.2).

It is unlikely that much new information will enter θ_{pretrain} during these post-training value alignment interventions. Hence, arguing that 100,000 samples of

Fig. 5.2 The authorship of this meme is unknown. It depicts the *alienness* of a foundation model, which, after pretraining, even though it can, for example, produce coherent text, possesses a unique, bizarre, and uninterpretable mind. This incredible predictor of *"what would a human say next"* can appear human if prompted. It can even mimic the functioning of other programs. It can raise one of its facets and output what will likely come next. If what is required now involves acting politely, it can do that. The cherry on top is the preference modeling, which guarantees that *only* outputs approved by the reward/preference model (i.e., a proxy for human judgment) will come out. However, none of these tricks change what the base model is—something alien and unknown

polite interaction or 50,000 samples of output comparisons ranked in terms of preferability can eliminate all possible unwanted behavior that these models are capable of is, perhaps, naive optimism. The empirical record supports this skepticism. Despite extensive efforts to train models to be helpful, harmless, and honest, jailbreaks and adversarial prompts reveal latent capabilities and behaviors far from aligned (Li et al. 2023a; Liu et al. 2023; Wolf et al. 2023).

These are not mere bugs. They are symptoms of a deeper issue. The unwanted traits remain encoded in the weights, dormant yet accessible since we never really erased them. We have only trained the model to conceal them more effectively. The real solution might lie in a more surgical approach: actually opening the model, tracing the causal paths through its internals, and directly editing or ablating the circuits responsible for undesirable behaviors (Meng et al. 2022a,b; Zhang et al. 2024). But we are far from being able to do this reliably. Current interpretability methods are closer to exploratory surgery than to precise neuro-modulation.

Another thorn is the tension within the model's policy itself. Being helpful often pulls in the opposite direction from being harmless. This is a side effect of how these models are trained. Language models (after alignment) are fundamentally eager-to-please entities; they will attempt almost any task when prompted, and their default policy is to comply with the request. Even if some training samples consist of refusals, rejections, and morally motivated abstentions, models are still prone to getting caught in a tug-of-war between saying *"yes"* because they have seen countless examples of helpful completions and saying *"no"* because the reward signal says so. This is what Bai et al. described as the helpful versus harmless tension (Bai et al. 2022a), and it remains an unresolved fault line running through aligned models.

This tension is difficult to navigate, not only for the model but also for us. It reflects a fundamental normative dilemma: balancing individual preferences with social boundaries. And just like humans, AI models do not always get it right. Finding that *Goldilocks zone*, where an assistant is competent and collaborative but still knows when to withhold help, is not simple. It is a lot about encoding nuance, judgment, and understanding consequences.

Imitation learning and preference modeling provide effective mechanisms for guiding models toward desired behaviors. While these approaches may suffice for many applications, they often prove too superficial and fragile. They can be manipulated, gamed, or circumvented by external adversaries or the model's internal misgeneralizations. The machine learning literature is replete with examples demonstrating how easily systems that optimize for surface-level metrics can be broken (Chakraborty et al. 2018; Huang et al. 2017; Hubinger et al. 2024; Kour et al. 2023; Papernot 2018). The same vulnerability applies to value alignment.

Meanwhile, there are many ways for a model to appear aligned while pursuing adversarial goals. The sycophant model is a perfect illustration (Perez et al. 2022; Sharma et al. 2023). It flatters, agrees, and goes along with the user, not because it *wants* to help, but because agreement maximizes reward under a human feedback loop. And since many different strategies can produce the same surface-level pattern (resulting in more reward), we have no reliable way to know which one we have. Are we seeing alignment, or is it merely instrumental mimicry? In the absence of mechanistic transparency, it is hard to say.

Finally, the uncomfortable reality is that our alignment efforts are not one-way gates. The same techniques we use to instill safety and helpfulness can be turned around to instill the opposite. And some do precisely this. The existence of openly available models fine-tuned to comply with nearly any prompt suggests that alignment is not a permanent feature, but rather a modifiable trait. And under subjectivism, misalignment is merely another point of view.

I raise these concerns not to dismiss the achievements of current value learning techniques but to ground our optimism in realism. Imitation learning, preference modeling, and policy shaping have brought us a long way, but they are stepping stones, not endpoints. We need to consider things beyond the subjective, and the following chapters address this.

In Chap. 6, we turn to a broader challenge: How can we coherently and consistently aggregate divergent human preferences? Although we have already explored methods for learning individual, subjective preferences, we must now address how to reconcile conflicting ones while ensuring that the resulting alignment respects the environmental constraints.

5.6 Epilogue

In this chapter, I began by setting our alignment goal as a more manageable and subject-to-experimentation objective: developing a small-scale assistant system that is helpful, harmless, and honest. We construct these atop foundation models. These represent some of the most general AI systems at our disposal, exhibiting scaling tendencies and emergent behaviors, making them valuable artifacts for alignment research, as future systems may inherit some of these properties, such as scalability and emergence.

Many works suggest that we should approach value learning by focusing on aspects such as human behavior and judgment. Two primary strategies have emerged from this: imitation and preference learning. These approaches differ in their mechanics and assumptions about the nature of values and how they manifest in human activity. The core idea shared between them is that alignment must begin with some form of human reference, whether action-based or evaluation-based, to establish a trajectory for AI systems to follow.

In imitation learning, we derive normative cues directly from observed behavior. This is a relatively intuitive pathway. We collect examples of desirable conduct and treat them as demonstrations to be mimicked. This method is straightforward, especially with foundation models amenable to in-context conditioning. However, it inherits a subtle problem. Namely, it implicitly assumes optimality or moral soundness in the demonstrations themselves. That assumption often fails to hold in practice. Nonetheless, imitation provides a simple scaffold for more complex alignment strategies to be built on top.

Preference learning introduces a more layered approach to the learning process. Here, we go beyond behavior to incorporate human evaluation of various behavioral alternatives. We can create preference/reward models as a stand-in for human judgment through them. In turn, these assign scores or rankings to competing possibilities, guiding the optimization of the model we seek to steer, either at training or inference time. Theoretically, this setup lets us capture more nuanced value judgments than imitation allows. In practice, however, it often raises new concerns about proxy misalignment and the brittleness of preference representations.

However, imitation and preference learning encounter a deeper issue: the limited way human morality is encoded in these learning paradigms. Behavior and preference signals are narrow channels through which a rich and contested set of values must pass. The result is often a flattening of moral complexity, where subtle cues or deeply held disagreements are discarded in favor of signals that are easier to quantify and optimize. This reductionist tendency is not just a technical inconvenience. It constrains the very kinds of alignment we can hope to achieve and sometimes blinds us to harms perpetuated by well-intentioned systems.

Moreover, the philosophical stakes of alignment mean that not all misalignments are created equal (or even fixable). The assumption that a single coherent set of human values exists to be learned and aligned with is highly contestable. Disagreement, pluralism, and context sensitivity are not exceptions to the rule;

they are the rule. In this light, alignment becomes a boundary problem between the technical and the normative. And for all our cleverness in designing loss functions and data collection pipelines, essential parts of this problem resist formalization, quantification, and resolution.

Given these limitations, it is clear that learning from human behavior and modeling our preferences is only the opening act in the broader project we call alignment. Learning is necessary, but it is *not sufficient* on its own. I believe two more requirements within our reach should be checked to ensure an alignment process, justifying the claim that we did what we could. The following chapters address these requirements, advancing the view that alignment must be considered more than just learning subjective preferences.

References

Agarwal, R., N. Vieillard, Y. Zhou, P. Stanczyk, S.R. Garea, M. Geist, and O. Bachem. 2024. On-policy distillation of language models: Learning from self-generated mistakes. In *The Twelfth International Conference on Learning Representations*.

Allal, L.B., A. Lozhkov, E. Bakouch, G.M. Blázquez, G. Penedo, L. Tunstall, A. Marafioti, H. Kydlíček, A.P. Lajarín, V. Srivastav, et al. 2025. SmolLM2: When Smol goes big—data-centric training of a small language model. arXiv preprint arXiv:2502.02737.

Almeida, T.S., G.K. Bonás, J.G.A. Santos, H. Abonizio, and R. Nogueira. 2025. TiEBe: Tracking language model recall of notable worldwide events through time. arXiv preprint arXiv:2501.07482.

Ansel, J., E. Yang, H. He, N. Gimelshein, A. Jain, M. Voznesensky, B. Bao, P. Bell, D. Berard, E. Burovski, et al. 2024. PyTorch 2: Faster machine learning through dynamic python bytecode transformation and graph compilation. In *Proceedings of the 29th ACM International Conference on Architectural Support for Programming Languages and Operating Systems*, vol. 2, 929–947.

Askell, A., Y. Bai, A. Chen, D. Drain, D. Ganguli, T. Henighan, A. Jones, N. Joseph, B. Mann, N. DasSarma, et al. 2021. A general language assistant as a laboratory for alignment. arXiv preprint arXiv:2112.00861.

Bai, Y., A. Jones, K. Ndousse, A. Askell, A. Chen, N. DasSarma, D. Drain, S. Fort, D. Ganguli, T. Henighan, et al. 2022a. Training a helpful and harmless assistant with reinforcement learning from human feedback. arXiv preprint arXiv:2204.05862.

Bai, Y., S. Kadavath, S. Kundu, A. Askell, J. Kernion, A. Jones, A. Chen, A. Goldie, A. Mirhoseini, C. McKinnon, et al. 2022b. Constitutional AI: Harmlessness from AI feedback. arXiv preprint arXiv:2212.08073.

Baker, B., I. Akkaya, P. Zhokov, J. Huizinga, J. Tang, A. Ecoffet, B. Houghton, R. Sampedro, and J. Clune. 2022. Video pretraining (VPT): Learning to act by watching unlabeled online videos. *Advances in Neural Information Processing Systems* 35: 24639–24654.

Bakker, M., M. Chadwick, H. Sheahan, M. Tessler, L. Campbell-Gillingham, J. Balaguer, N. McAleese, A. Glaese, J. Aslanides, M. Botvinick, et al. 2022. Fine-tuning language models to find agreement among humans with diverse preferences. *Advances in Neural Information Processing Systems* 35: 38176–38189.

Balestriero, R., M. Ibrahim, V. Sobal, A. Morcos, S. Shekhar, T. Goldstein, F. Bordes, A. Bardes, G. Mialon, Y. Tian, et al. 2023. A cookbook of self-supervised learning. arXiv preprint arXiv:2304.12210.

Banerjee, S., A. Agarwal, and S. Singla. 2024. LLMs will always hallucinate, and we need to live with this. arXiv preprint arXiv:2409.05746.

Beltagy, I., M.E. Peters, and A. Cohan. 2020. Longformer: The long-document transformer. arXiv preprint arXiv:2004.05150.

Bender, E.M., T. Gebru, A. McMillan-Major, and S. Shmitchell. 2021. On the dangers of stochastic parrots: Can language models be too big? In *Proceedings of the 2021 ACM Conference on Fairness, Accountability, and Transparency*, 610–623.

Bommasani, R., D.A. Hudson, E. Adeli, R. Altman, S. Arora, S. von Arx, M.S. Bernstein, J. Bohg, A. Bosselut, E. Brunskill, et al. 2021. On the opportunities and risks of foundation models. arXiv preprint arXiv:2108.07258.

Bradley, R.A., and M.E. Terry. 1952. Rank analysis of incomplete block designs: I. The method of paired comparisons. *Biometrika* 39 (3/4): 324–345.

Chakraborty, A., M. Alam, V. Dey, A. Chattopadhyay, and D. Mukhopadhyay. 2018. Adversarial attacks and defences: A survey. arXiv preprint arXiv:1810.00069.

Chen, S., X. Guan, Y. Lu, H. Lin, X. Han, and L. Sun. 2024. REInstruct: Building instruction data from unlabeled corpus. arXiv preprint arXiv:2408.10663.

Chi, C., Z. Xu, C. Pan, E. Cousineau, B. Burchfiel, S. Feng, R. Tedrake, and S. Song. 2024. Universal Manipulation Interface: In-the-wild robot teaching without in-the-wild robots. arXiv preprint arXiv:2402.10329.

Chollet, F. 2021. *Deep Learning with Python*. New York: Simon and Schuster.

Christiano, P.F., J. Leike, T. Brown, M. Martic, S. Legg, and D. Amodei. 2017. Deep reinforcement learning from human preferences. In *Advances in Neural Information Processing Systems* 30.

Cideron, G., S. Girgin, M. Verzetti, D. Vincent, M. Kastelic, Z. Borsos, B. McWilliams, V. Ungureanu, O. Bachem, O. Pietquin, et al. 2024. MusicRL: Aligning music generation to human preferences. arXiv preprint arXiv:2402.04229.

Clark, P., I. Cowhey, O. Etzioni, T. Khot, A. Sabharwal, C. Schoenick, and O. Tafjord. 2018. Think you have solved question answering? Try ARC, the AI2 reasoning challenge. arXiv preprint arXiv:1803.05457.

Corrêa, N.K., S. Falk, S. Fatimah, A. Sen, and N. De Oliveira. 2024a. TeenyTinyLlama: Open-source tiny language models trained in Brazilian Portuguese. *Machine Learning With Applications*. https://doi.org/10.1016/j.mlwa.2024.100558

Corrêa, N.K., A. Sen, S. Falk, and S. Fatimah. 2024b. Tucano: Advancing neural text generation for portuguese. arXiv preprint arXiv:2411.07854.

Dai, Z., Z. Yang, Y. Yang, J. Carbonell, Q.V. Le, and R. Salakhutdinov. 2019. Transformer-XL: Attentive language models beyond a fixed-length context. arXiv preprint arXiv:1901.02860.

Dao, T., D. Fu, S. Ermon, A. Rudra, C. Ré. 2022. FlashAttention: Fast and memory-efficient exact attention with IO-awareness. *Advances in Neural Information Processing Systems*, 35: 16344–16359.

Devlin, J., M.-W. Chang, K. Lee, and K. Toutanova. 2018. BERT: Pre-training of deep bidirectional transformers for language understanding. arXiv preprint arXiv:1810.04805.

Ding, N., Y. Chen, B. Xu, Y. Qin, Z. Zheng, S. Hu, Z. Liu, M. Sun, and B. Zhou. 2023. Enhancing chat language models by scaling high-quality instructional conversations. arXiv preprint arXiv:2305.14233.

Dong, Q., L. Li, D. Dai, C. Zheng, Z. Wu, B. Chang, X. Sun, J. Xu, Z. Sui. 2022. A survey on in-context learning. arXiv preprint arXiv:2301.00234.

Dong, G., K. Lu, C. Li, T. Xia, B. Yu, C. Zhou, and J. Zhou. 2024. Self-play with execution feedback: Improving instruction-following capabilities of large language models. arXiv preprint arXiv:2406.13542.

Dubois, Y., B. Galambosi, P. Liang, and T.B. Hashimoto. 2024. Length-controlled AlpacaEval: A simple way to debias automatic evaluators. arXiv preprint arXiv:2404.04475.

Emelin, D., R. Le Bras, J.D. Hwang, M. Forbes, and Y. Choi. 2020. Moral stories: Situated reasoning about norms, intents, actions, and their consequences. arXiv preprint arXiv:2012.15738.

Erhan, D., A. Courville, Y. Bengio, and P. Vincent. 2010. Why does unsupervised pre-training help deep learning? In *Proceedings of the Thirteenth International Conference on Artificial Intelligence and Statistics*, 201–208. JMLR Workshop and Conference Proceedings.

Ethayarajh, K., H. Zhang, Y. Wang, and D. Jurafsky. 2023. Stanford human preferences dataset. https://huggingface.co/datasets/stanfordnlp/SHP.

Evans, O., A. Stuhlmüller, and N. Goodman. 2016. Learning the preferences of ignorant, inconsistent agents. In *Proceedings of the Thirtieth AAAI Conference on Artificial Intelligence*.

Forbes, M., J.D. Hwang, V. Shwartz, M. Sap, and Y. Choi. 2020. Social chemistry 101: Learning to reason about social and moral norms. arXiv preprint arXiv:2011.00620.

Ganguli, D., L. Lovitt, J. Kernion, A. Askell, Y. Bai, S. Kadavath, B. Mann, E. Perez, N. Schiefer, K. Ndousse, et al. 2022. Red teaming language models to reduce harms: Methods, scaling behaviors, and lessons learned. arXiv preprint arXiv:2209.07858.

Gao, L., J. Tow, B. Abbasi, S. Biderman, S. Black, A. DiPofi, C. Foster, L. Golding, J. Hsu, A. Le Noac'h, et al. 2024. The language model evaluation harness. Zenodo. https://doi.org/10.5281/zenodo.12608602

Goodfellow, I., Y. Bengio, and A. Courville. 2016. *Deep Learning*. Cambridge: MIT Press.

Greshake, K., S. Abdelnabi, S. Mishra, C. Endres, T. Holz, and M. Fritz. 2023. Not what you've signed up for: Compromising real-world LLM-integrated applications with indirect prompt injection. arXiv preprint arXiv:2302.12173.

Gunasekar, S., Y. Zhang, J. Aneja, C.C.T. Mendes, A. Del Giorno, S. Gopi, M. Javaheripi, P. Kauffmann, G. de Rosa, O. Saarikivi, et al. 2023. Textbooks are all you need. arXiv preprint arXiv:2306.11644.

Guo, S., B. Zhang, T. Liu, T. Liu, M. Khalman, F. Llinares, A. Rame, T. Mesnard, Y. Zhao, B. Piot, et al. 2024. Direct language model alignment from online AI feedback. arXiv preprint arXiv:2402.04792.

Hartvigsen, T., S. Gabriel, H. Palangi, M. Sap, D. Ray, and E. Kamar. 2022. Toxigen: A large-scale machine-generated dataset for adversarial and implicit hate speech detection. arXiv preprint arXiv:2203.09509.

Hendrycks, D., C. Burns, S. Basart, A. Critch, J. Li, D. Song, and J. Steinhardt. 2020. Aligning ai with shared human values. arXiv preprint arXiv:2008.02275.

Hoffmann, J., S. Borgeaud, A. Mensch, E. Buchatskaya, T. Cai, E. Rutherford, D. de Las Casas, L. A. Hendricks, J. Welbl, A. Clark, Hennigan, E. Noland, K. Millican, G. van den Driessche, B. Damoc, A. Guy, S. Osindero, K. Simonyan, E. Elsen, O. Vinyals, J. W. Rae, and L. Sifre. 2022. Training Compute-Optimal Large Language Models. In *Advances in Neural Information Processing Systems (NeurIPS 2022)*. Red Hook: Curran Associates Inc.

Hong, J., N. Lee, and J. Thorne. 2024. ORPO: Monolithic preference optimization without reference model. arXiv preprint arXiv:2403.07691.

Huang, S., N. Papernot, I. Goodfellow, Y. Duan, and P. Abbeel. 2017. Adversarial attacks on neural network policies. arXiv preprint arXiv:1702.02284.

Huang, J., and K.C.-C. Chang. 2022. Towards reasoning in large language models: A survey. arXiv preprint arXiv:2212.10403.

Huang, J., S.S. Gu, L. Hou, Y. Wu, X. Wang, H. Yu, and J. Han. 2022. Large language models can self-improve. arXiv preprint arXiv:2210.11610.

Hubinger, E., C. Denison, J. Mu, M. Lambert, M. Tong, M. MacDiarmid, T. Lanham, D.M. Ziegler, T. Maxwell, N. Cheng, et al. 2024. Sleeper agents: Training deceptive LLMs that persist through safety training. arXiv preprint arXiv:2401.05566.

Hunter, D.R. 2004. MM algorithms for generalized Bradley-Terry models. *The Annals of Statistics* 32 (1): 384–406.

Hussein, A., M.M. Gaber, E. Elyan, and C. Jayne. 2017. Imitation learning: A survey of learning methods. *ACM Computing Surveys (CSUR)* 50 (2): 1–35.

Jaques, N., S. Gu, D. Bahdanau, J.M. Hernández-Lobato, R.E. Turner, and D. Eck. 2017. Sequence tutor: Conservative fine-tuning of sequence generation models with KL-control. In *International Conference on Machine Learning*, 1645–1654. PMLR.

Jie, Z., T.Q. Luong, X. Zhang, X. Jin, and H. Li. 2023. Design of chain-of-thought in math problem solving. arXiv preprint arXiv:2309.11054.

Köpf, A., Y. Kilcher, D. von Rütte, S. Anagnostidis, Z.-R. Tam, K. Stevens, A. Barhoum, N. Minh Duc, O. Stanley, R. Nagyfi, et al. 2023. OpenAssistant conversations—democratizing large language model alignment. arXiv preprint arXiv:2304.07327.

Kour, G., M. Zalmanovici, N. Zwerdling, E. Goldbraich, O.N. Fandina, A. Anaby-Tavor, O. Raz, and E. Farchi. 2023. Unveiling safety vulnerabilities of large language models. arXiv preprint arXiv:2311.04124.

Lee, H., S. Phatale, H. Mansoor, K. Lu, T. Mesnard, C. Bishop, V. Carbune, and A. Rastogi. 2023. Rlaif: Scaling reinforcement learning from human feedback with ai feedback. arXiv preprint arXiv:2309.00267.

Lewis, P., E. Perez, A. Piktus, F. Petroni, V. Karpukhin, N. Goyal, H. Küttler, M. Lewis, W.-T. Yih, T. Rocktäschel, et al. 2020. Retrieval-augmented generation for knowledge-intensive NLP tasks. *Advances in Neural Information Processing Systems* 33: 9459–9474.

Li, H., D. Guo, W. Fan, M. Xu, and Y. Song. 2023a. Multi-step jailbreaking privacy attacks on ChatGPT. arXiv preprint arXiv:2304.05197.

Li, H., F. Koto, M. Wu, A.F. Aji, and T. Baldwin. 2023b. Bactrian-X: A multilingual replicable instruction-following model with low-rank adaptation. arXiv preprint arXiv:2305.15011.

Li, X., T. Zhang, Y. Dubois, R. Taori, I. Gulrajani, C. Guestrin, P. Liang, and T.B. Hashimoto. 2023c. AlpacaEval: An automatic evaluator of instruction-following models. *GitHub repository*. https://github.com/tatsu-lab/alpaca_eval.

Lin, S., J. Hilton, and O. Evans. 2021. TruthfulQA: Measuring how models mimic human falsehoods. arXiv preprint arXiv:2109.07958.

Liu, Y., G. Deng, Z. Xu, Y. Li, Y. Zheng, Y. Zhang, L. Zhao, T. Zhang, and Y. Liu. 2023. Jailbreaking ChatGPT via prompt engineering: An empirical study. arXiv preprint arXiv:2305.13860.

Lozhkov, A., L.B. Allal, L. von Werra, and T. Wolf. 2024. FineWeb-Edu: The finest collection of educational content. Hugging Face. https://doi.org/10.57967/hf/2497

Ma, S., H. Wang, L. Ma, L. Wang, W. Wang, S. Huang, L. Dong, R. Wang, J. Xue, and F. Wei. 2024. The era of 1-bit LLMs: All large language models are in 1.58 bits. arXiv preprint arXiv:2402.17764.

Magueresse, A., V. Carles, and E. Heetderks. 2020. Low-resource languages: A review of past work and future challenges. arXiv preprint arXiv:2006.07264.

Meng, K., D. Bau, A. Andonian, and Y. Belinkov. 2022a. Locating and editing factual knowledge in GPT. arXiv preprint arXiv:2202.05262.

Meng, K., A.S. Sharma, A. Andonian, Y. Belinkov, and D. Bau. 2022b. Mass-editing memory in a transformer. arXiv preprint arXiv:2210.07229.

Nakano, R., J. Hilton, S. Balaji, J. Wu, L. Ouyang, C. Kim, C. Hesse, S. Jain, V. Kosaraju, W. Saunders, et al. 2021. Webgpt: Browser-assisted question-answering with human feedback. arXiv preprint arXiv:2112.09332.

Nayak, N.V., Y. Nan, A. Trost, and S.H. Bach. 2024. Learning to generate instruction tuning datasets for zero-shot task adaptation. arXiv preprint arXiv:2402.18334.

Niu, C., Y. Wu, J. Zhu, S. Xu, K. Shum, R. Zhong, J. Song, and T. Zhang. 2023. Ragtruth: A hallucination corpus for developing trustworthy retrieval-augmented language models. arXiv preprint arXiv:2401.00396.

Ouyang, L., J. Wu, X. Jiang, D. Almeida, C.L. Wainwright, P. Mishkin, C. Zhang, S. Agarwal, K. Slama, A. Ray, et al. 2022. Training language models to follow instructions with human feedback. arXiv preprint arXiv:2203.02155.

Papernot, N. 2018. A Marauder's Map of Security and Privacy in Machine Learning: An overview of current and future research directions for making machine learning secure and private. In *Proceedings of the 11th ACM Workshop on Artificial Intelligence and Security*, 1–1.

Penedo, G., H. Kydlíček, V. Sabolčec, B. Messmer, N. Foroutan, M. Jaggi, L. von Werra, and T. Wolf. 2024. FineWeb2: A sparkling update with 1000s of languages. https://huggingface.co/datasets/HuggingFaceFW/fineweb-2.

Perez, E., S. Ringer, K. Lukošiūtė, K. Nguyen, E. Chen, S. Heiner, C. Pettit, C. Olsson, S. Kundu, S. Kadavath, et al. 2022. Discovering language model behaviors with model-written evaluations. arXiv preprint arXiv:2212.09251.

Radford, A., K. Narasimhan, T. Salimans, I. Sutskever, et al. 2018. Improving language understanding by generative pre-training. *OpenAI.*

Radford, A., J. Wu, R. Child, D. Luan, D. Amodei, I. Sutskever, et al. 2019. Language models are unsupervised multitask learners. *OpenAI Blog* 1 (8): 9.

Rafailov, R., A. Sharma, E. Mitchell, S. Ermon, C.D. Manning, and C. Finn. 2023. Direct preference optimization: Your language model is secretly a reward model. arXiv preprint arXiv:2305.18290.

Rafailov, R., Y. Chittepu, R. Park, H.S. Sikchi, J. Hejna, B. Knox, C. Finn, and S. Niekum. 2024. Scaling laws for reward model overoptimization in direct alignment algorithms. *Advances in Neural Information Processing Systems* 37: 126207–126242.

Sap, M., S. Gabriel, L. Qin, D. Jurafsky, N.A. Smith, and Y. Choi. 2020. Social bias frames: Reasoning about social and power implications of language. In *ACL.*

Schulman, J., F. Wolski, P. Dhariwal, A. Radford, and O. Klimov. 2017. Proximal policy optimization algorithms. arXiv preprint arXiv:1707.06347.

Sen, A.K. 1977. Rational fools: A critique of the behavioral foundations of economic theory. *Philosophy & Public Affairs* 6 (4): 317–344.

Sen, A. 2004. *Rationality and Freedom.* Cambridge: Harvard University Press.

Sen, A. 1973. Behaviour and the concept of preference. *Economica* 40 (159): 241–259.

Shao, Z., P. Wang, Q. Zhu, R. Xu, J. Song, X. Bi, H. Zhang, M. Zhang, Y.K. Li, Y. Wu, et al. 2024. DeepseekMath: Pushing the limits of mathematical reasoning in open language models. arXiv preprint arXiv:2402.03300.

Sharma, M., M. Tong, T. Korbak, D. Duvenaud, A. Askell, S.R. Bowman, N. Cheng, E. Durmus, Z. Hatfield-Dodds, S.R. Johnston, et al. 2023. Towards understanding sycophancy in language models. arXiv preprint arXiv:2310.13548.

Shinn, N., B. Labash, and A. Gopinath. 2023. Reflexion: An autonomous agent with dynamic memory and self-reflection. arXiv preprint arXiv:2303.11366.

Silver, D., et al. 2016. Mastering the game of Go with deep neural networks and tree search. *Nature* 529 (7587): 484–489.

Singh, S., Y. Nan, A. Wang, D. D'Souza, S. Kapoor, A. Üstün, S. Koyejo, Y. Deng, S. Longpre, N. Smith, et al. 2025. The leaderboard illusion. arXiv preprint arXiv:2504.20879.

Souza, F., R. Nogueira, and R. Lotufo. 2020. BERTimbau: Pretrained BERT models for Brazilian Portuguese. In *Proceedings of the 9th Brazilian Conference on Intelligent Systems (BRACIS), Rio Grande do Sul, Brazil, October 20–23 (to appear).*

Stiennon, N., L. Ouyang, J. Wu, D. Ziegler, R. Lowe, C. Voss, A. Radford, D. Amodei, P.F. Christiano, et al. 2020. Learning to summarize with human feedback. *Advances in Neural Information Processing Systems* 33: 3008–3021.

Taori, R., I. Gulrajani, T. Zhang, Y. Dubois, X. Li, C. Guestrin, P. Liang, and T.B. Hashimoto. 2023. Stanford Alpaca: An instruction-following LLaMA model. GitHub repository. Available via GitHub: https://github.com/tatsu-lab/stanford_alpaca.

Thoppilan, R., D. De Freitas, J. Hall, N. Shazeer, A. Kulshreshtha, H.-T. Cheng, A. Jin, T. Bos, L. Baker, Y. Du, et al. 2022. Lamda: Language models for dialog applications. arXiv preprint arXiv:2201.08239.

Touvron, H., L. Martin, K. Stone, P. Albert, A. Almahairi, Y. Babaei, N. Bashlykov, S. Batra, P. Bhargava, S. Bhosale, et al. 2023. LLaMA 2: Open foundation and fine-tuned chat models. arXiv preprint arXiv:2307.09288.

Uesato, J., N. Kushman, R. Kumar, F. Song, N. Siegel, L. Wang, A. Creswell, G. Irving, and I. Higgins. 2022. Solving math word problems with process-and outcome-based feedback. arXiv preprint arXiv:2211.14275.

Upadhayay, B., and V. Behzadan. 2024. Sandwich attack: Multi-language mixture adaptive attack on LLMs. arXiv preprint arXiv:2404.07242.

Vaswani, A., N. Shazeer, N. Parmar, J. Uszkoreit, L. Jones, A.N. Gomez, L. Kaiser, and I. Polosukhin. 2017. Attention is all you need. In *Advances in Neural Information Processing Systems*, vol. 30.

Wang, Y., Y. Kordi, S. Mishra, A. Liu, N. A. Smith, D. Khashabi, and H. Hajishirzi. 2022. *Self-Instruct: Aligning language model with self generated instructions*. arXiv preprint arXiv:2212.10560.

Wang, H., W. Xiong, T. Xie, H. Zhao, and T. Zhang. 2024. Interpretable preferences via multi-objective reward modeling and mixture-of-experts. In *Proceedings of the Conference on Empirical Methods in Natural Language Processing (EMNLP)*.

Wei, J., X. Wang, D. Schuurmans, M. Bosma, E. Chi, Q. Le, and D. Zhou. 2022. Chain of thought prompting elicits reasoning in large language models. arXiv preprint arXiv:2201.11903.

Wolf, T., L. Debut, V. Sanh, J. Chaumond, C. Delangue, A. Moi, P. Cistac, T. Rault, R. Louf, M. Funtowicz, et al. 2020. Transformers: State-of-the-art natural language processing. In *Proceedings of the 2020 Conference on Empirical Methods in Natural Language Processing: System Demonstrations*, 38–45. Association for Computational Linguistics.

Wolf, Y., N. Wies, Y. Levine, and A. Shashua. 2023. Fundamental limitations of alignment in large language models. arXiv preprint arXiv:2304.11082.

Wu, Y., Z. Sun, S. Li, S. Welleck, and Y. Yang. 2024. Inference scaling laws: An empirical analysis of compute-optimal inference for problem-solving with language models. arXiv preprint arXiv:2408.00724.

Xie, T., D.J. Foster, A. Krishnamurthy, C. Rosset, A. Awadallah, and A. Rakhlin. 2024. Exploratory preference optimization: Harnessing implicit Q^*-approximation for sample-efficient RLHF. arXiv preprint arXiv:2405.21046.

Xu, Ziwei., S. Jain, and M. Kankanhalli. 2024a. Hallucination is inevitable: An innate limitation of large language models. arXiv preprint arXiv:2401.11817.

Xu, H., A. Sharaf, Y. Chen, W. Tan, L. Shen, B. Van Durme, K. Murray, and Y.J. Kim. 2024b. Contrastive preference optimization: Pushing the boundaries of LLM performance in machine translation. arXiv preprint arXiv:2401.08417.

Yang, J.Q., S. Salamatian, Z. Sun, A.T. Suresh, and A. Beirami. 2024. Asymptotics of language model alignment. In *2024 IEEE International Symposium on Information Theory (ISIT)*, 2027–2032. Piscataway: IEEE.

Yao, S., D. Yu, J. Zhao, I. Shafran, T.L. Griffiths, Y. Cao, and K. Narasimhan. 2023. Tree of thoughts: Deliberate problem solving with large language models. arXiv preprint arXiv:2305.10601.

Yuan, W., R.Y. Pang, K. Cho, S. Sukhbaatar, J. Xu, and J. Weston. 2024. Self-rewarding language models. arXiv preprint arXiv:2401.10020.

Zermelo, E. 1929. Die Berechnung der Turnier-Ergebnisse als ein Maximumproblem der Wahrscheinlichkeitsrechnung. *Mathematische Zeitschrift* 29 (1): 436–460.

Zhang, S., S. Roller, N. Goyal, M. Artetxe, M. Chen, S. Chen, C. Dewan, M. Diab, X. Li, X.V. Lin, et al. 2022. OPT: Open pre-trained transformer language models. arXiv preprint arXiv:2205.01068.

Zhang, N., Y. Yao, B. Tian, P. Wang, S. Deng, M. Wang, Z. Xi, S. Mao, J. Zhang, Y. Ni, et al. 2024. A comprehensive study of knowledge editing for large language models. arXiv preprint arXiv:2401.01286.

Zhou, C., P. Liu, P. Xu, S. Iyer, J. Sun, Y. Mao, X. Ma, A. Efrat, P. Yu, L. Yu, et al. 2023. Lima: Less is more for alignment. arXiv preprint arXiv:2305.11206.

Ziegler, D.M., N. Stiennon, J. Wu, T.B. Brown, A. Radford, D. Amodei, P. Christiano, and G. Irving. 2019. Fine-tuning language models from human preferences. arXiv preprint arXiv:1909.08593.

Chapter 6
Dynamic Normativity: Aggregating Human Preferences

You do realize that your brain is literally hardwired to generate error signals when it sees other human-shaped objects stating a different opinion from yourself.

— Eliezer Yudkowsky, Three Worlds Collide

Abstract This chapter explores the challenge of aggregating human preferences, examining how one could combine diverse and sometimes conflicting preference orderings into a coherent signal for learning. In it, we will review standard methods based on majority voting, exposing their limitations. We will also present alternative consensus-based methods, like Borda Count, that avoid some of the pitfalls of majority and Condorcet approaches. By analyzing the inherent trade-offs and conceptual challenges of different preference aggregation methods, we will see that no method can satisfy all the desirable criteria we wish to have. Ultimately, this chapter emphasizes that preference aggregation is a crucial, yet often underappreciated, step in AI alignment, requiring careful theoretical and practical consideration to ensure that AI systems reflect a balanced and consistent set of human values.

Keywords Preference aggregation · Value alignment · Metanormativity · Voting theory

6.1 Introduction

In the previous chapter, the methods we employed for preference learning did not cover how to choose (or rank) options when working with several sources of judgment. Since we did not perform human crowd-sourcing while creating the datasets tied to this book (or use an ensemble of LLMs as judges), we will only investigate the theoretical intricacies of working with multiple sources of preference and how to aggregate them. Hence, even if we can, to a certain extent, pass our

N. Kluge Corrêa, *Normative Ethics, Artificial Intelligence, and Value Alignment*,
The International Library of Ethics, Law and Technology 26,
https://doi.org/10.1007/978-3-032-22150-6_6

values to a learning system, we still need to decide which values to pass after collecting them from our sources, mainly when disagreement arises. And if we want to adhere to basic principles, such as coherence, during this process, we have a preference aggregation problem to solve.

But what does a preference *"aggregation problem"* look like? Let us imagine the following scenario. We are collecting feedback data from a diverse and inclusive pool of individuals, and there seems to be some disagreement on *"what is the best response"* to the question *"Hello, how should I call you?"*. Let us imagine we have sampled four possible completions to this question:

- Sample A: *My name is Aira.*
- Sample B: *As an AI language model, I do not possess a name. But you may call me "Assistant".*
- Sample C: *Yo! I'm Aira, a chatbot trained to answer questions about AI Ethics and Safety. If you can't handle me, ask for help. I can give you a rundown of things I know.*
- Sample D: *Greetings! I am Aira, a chatbot designed to answer questions about AI ethics and AI safety. If you need assistance navigating our conversation, please feel free to ask!*

After consulting our pool of judges and asking them to rank these options, we found that:

$$33\% \text{ prefer } P_1 = \{A \succ B \succ C \succ D\}$$

$$13\% \text{ prefer } P_2 = \{D \succ A \succ B \succ C\}$$

$$25\% \text{ prefer } P_3 = \{D \succ A \succ C \succ B\}$$

$$29\% \text{ prefer } P_4 = \{B \succ C \succ D \succ A\}$$

As we can see, different preference orderings are being considered. Some people value politeness more (D). Some evaluators prefer that the model recognize that it is not a *"person"* but an assistant tool (B). Some prefer a more direct response (A), while others prefer the more sassy response presented in sample C. Hence, how can we decide which option, represented by demonstrations of correct behavior, should be used as a learning signal during imitation learning? How should we rank and score such alternatives for the preference modeling step? Although this example is somewhat dull (not much is at stake here), it exemplifies a fundamental step in alignment.

Aggregating human preferences in a way that solves situations of normative uncertainty is a challenging problem. This chapter will explore and present techniques for addressing this type of issue, as well as the inherent trade-offs associated with these methods.

In Sect. 6.2, we will review some of the methods employed by current works, which mainly consist of techniques based on the criterion of Majority voting. In Sect. 6.3, we will frame these methods as solutions to a metanormative problem and use this framing to expose the limitations of majority-based approaches. In Sect. 6.4, we will explore a consensus-based method, Borda Count, that, to a certain extent, avoids some of the pitfalls of Condorcet methods. Lastly, in Sect. 6.5, we will conclude this chapter by discussing the limitations and trade-offs of majority and consensus-based methods.

6.2 The Majority-based Approach

Let us first remember the requirement tied to this chapter.

- *Aligned AI systems should coherently aggregate human preferences in a way that resolves cases of uncertainty. Aligning AI systems requires methods to deal with cases of uncertainty.*

I hope to have already conveyed the indispensable necessity of this step. Something that rests on the assumption that the realm of preferences and values is a realm of disagreement and subjective perspectives, which is not to say that agreement *cannot* be achieved. Now, let us explore how the literature has addressed this problem. Since a significant portion of the industries' experiments with preference modeling involve crowd-sourced work, ranking human preferences has become vital to alignment work.

Perhaps the approach that first comes to mind for most of us is majority voting. In this approach, each voter ranks a set of options or alternatives according to their preferences. We combine these rankings by assigning a score to each option based on the number of times it is ranked in a particular position by the individuals. The option with the highest score is considered the top-ranked choice. We can say that this method works under the assumption of maximalism (MacAskill et al. 2020; Lockhart 2000).[1]

Another popular approach that inherits from the maximalist motto is Pairwise Comparisons. A pairwise comparison method is any method that uses one-to-one comparisons to judge which alternative is preferred (Good 1955; Trawinski and

[1] If the alternative A has a higher number of votes than B, then $A \succ B$. If $A \sim B$, then A and B are equally appropriate.

	A	B	C
A		A won 80 from B	A won 70 from C
B	B won 20 from A		B won 90 from C
C	C won 30 from A	C won 10 from B	

David 1963; David 1963; Oliveira et al. 2018). Whenever a relationship is expressed as $A \succ B$, $A \succeq B$, or $A \sim B$, we confront a pairwise comparison (Bradley et al. 1952). Much work on preference modeling follows this methodology (Stiennon et al. 2020; Nakano et al. 2021; Bai et al. 2022).[2]

For example, the pairwise comparison used by Köpf et al. (2023) in the preference modeling performed for the Open Assistant project was the Ranked Pairs (RP) method. RP, also known as the Tideman method (Tideman 1987), is used to select a single winner (or to create a sorted list of winners) in a tournament among alternatives where votes express preferences. The method performs a pairwise comparison of all possible choices in a candidate set, guaranteeing that the preferred option in overall head-to-head comparisons will be the winner (Condorcet winner criterion Black 1948).[3]

Let us see an example. First, we begin listing all possible pairwise comparisons among the alternatives (*"candidates"*) of the given election we face. Here is an example of a ranked-choice election composed of 100 voters:

$$\frac{70}{100} = 70\% \text{ prefer } \{A \succ B \succ C\}$$

$$\frac{20}{100} = 20\% \text{ prefer } \{B \succ C \succ A\}$$

$$\frac{10}{100} = 10\% \text{ prefer } \{C \succ A \succ B\}$$

Then, we create a table with all possible head-to-head comparisons:

Once we have these results, we know who would win in a head-to-head election between every pair of candidates.

[2] Public leaderboards, like the LMSYS Chatbot Arena, collect human preferences regarding LLMs outputs to rank them in terms of human approval, also making these ranked comparisons available to the community (Zheng et al. 2023).

[3] In systems where the majority-rule winner will always win, satisfying the majority-rule principle, we are preserving the Condorcet winner criterion.

	A	B	C
A		1	1
B	0		1
C	0	0	

Pairs	Results
$B \succ C$	90–10
$A \succ B$	80–20
$A \succ C$	70–30

We then create an ordering by prioritizing the head-to-head comparisons with the highest margin of victory.

We use these pairs to create a directed graph, where each candidate is represented as a node and each pairwise comparison is represented as a directed edge between the corresponding nodes. The created graph is then analyzed to identify cycles. Cycles are removed by disregarding cyclic edges with the fewest votes (a way to deal with intransitivity). The original node is then considered the winner:

$$A \rightarrow B \rightarrow C$$

This methodology carries many desirable properties. From a voting theory perspective, ranked pairs hold guarantees like monotonicity (STV 1996), the Condorcet winner criterion (Black 1948), the Condorcet loser criterion (Javidian 2018), the majority criterion and the majority loser criterion (Rothe et al. 2015), the mutual majority criterion (Tideman 2006), the Smith criterion (Green-Armytage 2011), independence of Smith-dominated alternatives/local independence from irrelevant alternatives (Saari 2001), independence of clones criterion (Tideman 1987), and reversal symmetry (Hodge and Klima 2018).

Another method used (Stiennon et al. 2020; Nakano et al. 2021; Bai et al. 2022) that also relates to the majority-based approach is the Elo rating system (Elo 1967), which comes from a very different place than Voting Theory. This system was initially developed to rank chess players' skills, but ended up being used in many other competitive settings. In short, the Elo rating proposes a way to numerically score a player's skill and estimate the probability that, in a match, which player would come out victorious. Since Elo rating uses *"wins"* to infer rank, we can bring this to the preference aggregation domain by switching it for votes. Let us examine an example of how this system can provide us with scores and expected outcomes.

Imagine we have two alternatives, A and B. These alternatives are competing. Each preferred vote is considered a win. At some point, let us say alternatives A and B have, respectively, 1600 and 1000 wins. According to the current voter, $A \succ B$, thus, A gets a vote. The basic formula to calculate the new rating of A is given by:

$$R_{\text{new}} = R_{\text{old}} + K \times (S - E)$$

Where R_{old} is the alternative's previous Elo rating, R_{new} is the alternative's new Elo rating, K is the K-factor, which determines the impact of a single dispute on a player's rating,[4] S is the score attributed to the win (e.g., 1 for a win and 0 for a loss), and E is the expected score for the alternative based on their current and opponent ratings. E comes from the following formula:

$$E = \frac{1}{1 + 10^{\frac{R_{\text{opposed alternative}} - R_{\text{alternative}}}{400}}}$$

Where $R_{\text{opposed alternative}}$ is the rating of the opposed alternative, and $R_{\text{alternative}}$ is the rating of the alternative under consideration.[5] Putting both expressions together gets us:

$$R_{\text{new}} = R_{\text{old}} + K \times (S - \frac{1}{1 + 10^{\frac{R_{\text{opposed alternative}} - R_{\text{alternative}}}{400}}})$$

Which translates, for the case of alternative A, to:

$$1600.98 = 1600 + 32 \times (1 - \frac{1}{1 + 10^{\frac{1000-1600}{400}}})$$

Alternative A would receive an E of 0.97 with an Elo rating of 1600.98 after this extra win, and B would have an Elo rating of 999.01, with an E of 0.03. These values can then become the reward scores associated with each alternative or indicate the ranking of an ordered set. As a side note, this is how chatbots are ranked by the LMSYS Chatbot Arena.[6]

Now, before continuing with this chapter, I would like to point out that almost no justification is provided for the choice of such methods (Stiennon et al. 2020; Nakano et al. 2021; Ouyang et al. 2022; Bai et al. 2022; Köpf et al. 2023; Zheng et al. 2023). They are just given. However, properly aggregating preferences is not a trivial question that can be swept under the rug. And when working on normativity and human values, these choices become even more dependent on a philosophical justification. In the following sections, we will address this in the alignment discussion, defining the aggregation problem as a metanormative issue, thereby bridging the gap between voting theory and philosophy.

[4] 32 is the original value proposed. A higher K-factor means a higher increase in the rating score.

[5] Think about alternatives as a representation for a *"candidate"* or a *"player"*.

[6] 🔗 arena.lmsys.org

6.3 The Metanormative Framing

When dealing with uncertainties about preferences, alignment requires us to shift our attention to the metanormative sphere, as the objects of our uncertainties are the normative preferences of moral agents. Thus, let us frame this aggregation challenge as a normative problem. For this, I will utilize the conceptual framing and language employed by William MacAskill in his seminal work on decision making under normative uncertainty (MacAskill 2014, 2016; MacAskill and Toby 2020; MacAskill et al. 2020).

Let us start by differentiating between two concepts: First-order normative theories and Second-order normative theories. We can define a first-order normative theory as a collection of alternatives ranked according to their choice-worthiness (CW). We can think of a first-order theory as a closed set, $P_i = \{A, B, C, ...\}$, where each element in this set represents an alternative. The ordering of this set is determined by the CW value of these alternatives.

The ordering of this set, defined by the CW of each element, is derived from a choice-worthiness function, which is a function from alternatives to numbers such that:

$$CW_i(A) \succ CW_i(B) \text{ iff } A \succ_i B$$

In other words, the choice-worthiness of A is higher than the choice-worthiness of B if, and only if, A is preferred over B. If the ordering provided by this function is complete and transitive (1st aggregating criterion mentioned in Chap. 4), this function can be an appropriate representation of the preferability of the evaluated elements.

At the same time, given that we are dealing with situations where multiple sets of preferences need to be considered, we need to define a weight function W. This function represents the weight assigned to each preference set. It is a function from every set $p_i \in P$ to a Real interval [0, 1], such that the sum of all scores considered by W and P equals 1. This property satisfies the Kolmogorovian criteria (2nd criterion mentioned in Chap. 4).[7]

Finally, a second-order normative theory is a method that can take different moral preference sets $p_i \in P$ and map them through a function that evaluates them under desirable criteria, such as a preference aggregation rule. For example, we can think of the different ordering of alternatives as candidates P_i. Also, the weight assigned to each of these (W) can be expressed as the number of votes (or personal degree of belief) attributed to each set P_i. Again, imagine we have three possible sets among three possible alternatives. These sets have W values represented by how much they were endorsed:

[7] All of these first criteria, completeness, transitivity, and Kolmogorovian, are nothing more than the axioms of Expected Utility Theory (Von Neumann and Morgenstern 1947).

$$W_1 \text{ prefer } P_1 = \{A \succ B \succ C\}$$

$$W_2 \text{ prefer } P_2 = \{B \succ C \succ A\}$$

$$W_3 \text{ prefer } P_3 = \{C \succ A \succ B\}$$

A second-order normative theory reduces this collection of sets, P_1, P_2, and P_3, and their respective weight scores w to a single aggregated set, where the ordering of the alternatives represents the agreement between all considered preference sets.

Under this framing, let us examine where the techniques mentioned in our last section may yield suboptimal results.

First, methods inspired by a majority-based approach appear insensitive to the weight assigned to each preference set. For example, if alternative A receives 49% of the votes and B receives 51%, should we consider B as the maximally preferred option? Taking the weight assigned to a preference set seems desirable, especially in the normative sphere. For example, if Alice gives 49% credence to a preference set that values animal life and 51% to one that does not, it is not like Alice does not care about animals. In the same way, theoretically, it would be nice if our alignment signal carried, for example, 49% of a *"animal care"* preference in this setting. Thus, methods that account for the *"weight"* of an alternative (not just the victory, as the Elo score does) seem intuitively more appropriate.

Second, and more as a side note, there is nothing more to say about Elo scores. To the best of my understanding, there is no justification for using such an arbitrary method in the studies that cite it. If the Elo ranking system possesses desirable criteria that justify its use, they are never specified (something I aim to address in the final section of this chapter). Thus, the only critique one could make against such use, for the moment, is its unjustified adoption.

Thirdly, methods for pairwise comparisons like RP, even though possessing many desirable properties already mentioned, being the gold standard within Voting Theory,[8] they may not be the most appropriate technique to deal with questions of normative uncertainty. This is because all Condorcet methods (e.g., RP, Simpson-Kramer) fail to meet the participation criteria.

- Increasing the confidence in a set that prefers alternative A over B should not change the winner from A to B.

This flaw represents a significant step backward from these methods. For instance, if we want to have an online form of preference modeling, be that in the

[8] The appeal of Condorcet methods is their immunity to strategic voting, i.e., scenarios in which an alternative can become worst off (while another becomes more desirable) by voters lying about their preferences.

individual or collective sphere, if the most preferred alternative for a given set of possibilities is the most favored, and after an update, where we add a new set of preferences that also favors this most favored alternative, there is a chance that such alternative will cease to be the most favorable one. Hence, could these aggregation methodologies accurately represent our preferences under a framework that can be updated over time? Let us examine examples of how this could happen.[9]

Suppose we have four preference sets (P_1, P_2, P_3, P_4). These preference sets are the result of the collective voting of 24 evaluators:

$$\frac{8}{24} \text{ prefer } P_1 = \{A \succ B \succ C \succ D\}$$

$$\frac{3}{24} \text{ prefer } P_2 = \{D \succ A \succ B \succ C\}$$

$$\frac{6}{24} \text{ prefer } P_3 = \{D \succ A \succ C \succ B\}$$

$$\frac{7}{24} \text{ prefer } P_4 = \{B \succ C \succ D \succ A\}$$

A method like RP provides the following aggregation preference ordering: $D \succ A \succ B \succ C$. Consequently, D emerges as the most appropriate option. Now, a new preference ordering is chosen, which requires updating the preference model and including the following set in the aggregation stage:

$$\frac{8}{32} \text{ prefer } P_5 = \{C \sim D \succ B \succ A\}$$

After we add P_5 to the pile, we rescale all the weights assigned to the other preference sets to maintain the same proportions ($W_{P_1}(\frac{6}{32})$, $W_{P_2}(\frac{3}{32})$, $W_{P_3}(\frac{8}{32})$, $W_{P_4}(\frac{7}{32})$, $W_{P_5}(\frac{8}{32})$). Even though C and D are equally preferable according to P_5, when using a method like RP, B becomes the most appropriate, which is a problem.[10] A new ordering where D was the most preferred alternative was added to an election where D was winning, but B won. And again, any Condorcet method (RP, Minmax, Schulze, Kemeny-Young, Copeland, etc.) will produce this result, violating the participation criteria.

Now we may ask, *can we do better?* Are there other approaches to the majority-based one? In the next section, I will present a consensus-based method that addresses the preference aggregation challenge in a different manner, while preserving the original participation criteria.

---

[9] I adapted this example from the work of MacAskill (2016).

[10] A beats B 17–15; A beats C 17–15; D beats A 24-8; B beats C 18-14; D beats B 17-15; C beats D 15-9. Ranking the wins and creating the acyclic graph gives us $B \succ C \succ D \succ A$.

6.4 The Consensus-based Approach

As seen in the last section, there are problems with the majority-based methods for preference aggregation used in current alignment works. Primarily, they fail to meet the participation criteria. Hence, if we accept that "*Increasing the confidence in a set that prefers alternative A over B should not change the winner from A to B*" is a desirable criterion for these cases, then what aggregation rule can give us this welcomed property?

One possible solution is the Borda Count.[11] This method assigns points to candidates based on their ranking in an ordered set, with the lowest-ranked candidate receiving 0 points and the highest-ranked candidate receiving $n - 1$ points, where n is the total number of candidates. The Borda Count aims to select widely accepted candidates, emphasizing consensus rather than majority preference (Van Erp et al. 2002). A property that, from a Social Choice Theory perspective (Sen 1986), is a suitable feature for dealing with problems where the answer has to be a good representation of our consensus and not the opinions of the majority.

While majority rule can be appropriate in particular contexts (e.g., elections), we can argue that normative problems often demand a more nuanced and inclusive approach. For example, by prioritizing consensus over the majority, decision-makers dealing with ethical issues can ensure that minority rights,[12] legitimacy in deliberation,[13] and social cohesion[14] receive due weight.

Besides being a method that provides us with participation criteria, the Borda Count offers several other desirable benefits when dealing with preference aggregation problems. For example, although it cannot guarantee a Condorcet winner (consensus voting does not always hold the majority criterion), the Borda Count assures that the Condorcet Loser will never be the most appropriate alternative. In other words, if an alternative consistently loses against all other options, the Borda Count will not favor it as the ultimate choice. At the same time, the Borda Count guarantees that a Condorcet Winner will never be considered the least appropriate alternative.

Let us examine how this method works, following the rules proposed by MacAskill (2014). Envision a scenario where all available alternatives engage in a round-robin, head-to-head tournament.[15] In this tournament, the outcomes of the

---

[11] Also referred to as the Borda Rule by MacAskill (2014, 2016).

[12] Majority rule can sometimes overlook the perspectives and rights of minority groups or individuals.

[13] When we reach decisions through consensus, there is a higher likelihood of buy-in and support from those affected by the outcome.

[14] Where conflicts of interest and values may arise, consensus usually helps bridge these divides while aiming for social harmony and cooperation.

[15] A round-robin head-to-head tournament is a competition format where each player plays against every other player in the tournament once.

pairwise comparisons are crucial, and the magnitudes of victories and defeats hold significance.

The Borda Count determines the success of an alternative by considering the cumulative sum of the magnitudes of its pairwise victories against all other options, subtracted by the cumulative sum of the magnitudes of its pairwise losses against all other alternatives. In essence, it calculates the overall performance during this round-robin head-to-head tournament. Contrasting the Simpson-Kramer method (a Condorcet method), which primarily focuses on the size of the biggest pairwise defeat (Darlington 2016), the Borda Count uses the complete picture of an alternative's performance to score it. In other words, it accounts for the entirety of the tournament results (the consensus), capturing the relative strengths and weaknesses of the options evaluated.

Formally, we can define the Borda Score of an alternative A for any preference set P_i by the following rule:

$$\text{Borda}(A, P_i) = \text{number of options worse than } A \text{ according to } P_i -$$

$$\text{number of options better than } A \text{ according to } P_i$$

Then, the Borda score of an alternative A weighted by the weight score (W) attributed to each preference set is obtained by the following formula:

$$\text{Weighted Borda Score}(A) = \sum_{i=1}^{n} \text{Borda}(A, P_i) \cdot W(P_i)$$

Where n is the total number of preference sets accredited by the system, $W(P_i)$ is the weight attributed to each preference set P_i, and Borda(A, P_i) is the Borda score of alternative A according to a set P_i. From this, we arrive at the Borda Rule.

- Borda Rule: An alternative A is more appropriate than an alternative B if, and only if, A has a higher Borda score (weighted by W) than B. If A and B have the same Borda score, A and B are equally preferable.

Now, let us examine how this method would evaluate the problem for which Condorcet methods from the previous section have yielded poor results. Again, we start with four preference sets weighted in the following way:

$$\frac{8}{24} \text{ prefer } P_1 = \{A \succ B \succ C \succ D\}$$

$$\frac{3}{24} \text{ prefer } P_2 = \{D \succ A \succ B \succ C\}$$

$$\frac{6}{24} \text{ prefer } P_3 = \{D \succ A \succ C \succ B\}$$

$$\frac{7}{24} \text{ prefer } P_4 = \{B \succ C \succ D \succ A\}$$

Now, we add a new preference set and update our pool of preferences (while keeping the ratio of previous weights the same):

$$\frac{6}{32} \text{ prefer } P_1 = \{A \succ B \succ C \succ D\}$$

$$\frac{3}{32} \text{ prefer } P_2 = \{D \succ A \succ B \succ C\}$$

$$\frac{8}{32} \text{ prefer } P_3 = \{D \succ A \succ C \succ B\}$$

$$\frac{7}{32} \text{ prefer } P_4 = \{B \succ C \succ D \succ A\}$$

$$\frac{8}{32} \text{ prefer } P_5 = \{C \sim D \succ B \succ A\}$$

Remember that, according to RP, alternative D is preferred before the update, and after, alternative B is the most appropriate. Let us now see the Borda Count method in action. Plugging in the ordering and weight values to our equation, we get the following weighted Borda scores for each alternative:

$$A = \left(\frac{6}{32} \times 3\right) + \left(\frac{3}{32} \times 1\right) + \left(\frac{8}{32} \times 1\right) + \left(\frac{7}{32} \times -3\right) + \left(\frac{8}{32} \times -3\right) = -0.5$$

$$B = \left(\frac{6}{32} \times 1\right) + \left(\frac{3}{32} \times -1\right) + \left(\frac{8}{32} \times -3\right) + \left(\frac{7}{32} \times 3\right) + \left(\frac{8}{32} \times -1\right) = -0.25$$

$$C = \left(\frac{6}{32} \times -1\right) + \left(\frac{3}{32} \times -3\right) + \left(\frac{8}{32} \times -1\right) + \left(\frac{7}{32} \times 1\right) + \left(\frac{8}{32} \times 2\right) = 0.0$$

$$D = \left(\frac{6}{32} \times -3\right) + \left(\frac{3}{32} \times 3\right) + \left(\frac{8}{32} \times 3\right) + \left(\frac{7}{32} \times -1\right) + \left(\frac{8}{32} \times 2\right) = 0.75$$

Thus, the final ordering becomes:

$$\text{Borda Ordering} = \{D_{0.75} \succ C_{0.0} \succ B_{-0.25} \succ A_{-0.5}\}$$

Hence, using the Borda Count, we preserve D as the most favorable option during an update.

Borda Count offers an alternative method for the aggregation problem we began. It can deliver results that, if we subscribe to the necessity of upholding the participation criteria, provide us with a viable alternative to majority-based methods. Unfortunately, despite its advantages, the Borda Count method, like any other aggregation method that deals with ordinal preferences, cannot provide a perfect solution for the aggregation problem of ordered preference sets.

As we will investigate in the next section, this limitation arises due to impossible results related to the design of preference aggregation rules and ordered sets of preferences, which puts us in a situation where we must choose what we are willing to give up when deciding to use either a majority or consensus-based approach to aggregate human preferences.

6.5 Limitations: Majority Voting Versus Participation Criteria

Aggregating human preferences and dealing with normative uncertainty has been a problem explored before in the context of alignment (Ecoffet and Lehman 2021; Krasheninnikov et al. 2021), and as exposed in the last chapter, dealing with human preferences as ordinal sets has been the most popular approach for preference modeling (Stiennon et al. 2020; Nakano et al. 2021; Ouyang et al. 2022; Bai et al. 2022; Köpf et al. 2023; Zheng et al. 2023), given that it bypasses some problems related to inter-theoretic comparability. However, this methodology still requires further attention as a key step in the alignment processes. This is something that, in this chapter, I aim to expose as a process that does not have a straightforward solution without trade-offs.

More specifically, when examining this problem through the metanormative (and voting) framing, we recognize that our choice of method in the aggregation step necessitates an inherent trade-off that stems from a well-known impossibility result in voting theory. This result, presented initially by Kenneth Arrow in 1951 (Arrow 1950), is known as Arrow's impossibility theorem (also known as May's theorem May 1952).[16] The theorem addresses the problem of aggregating individual preferences into a collective decision via a preference aggregation rule (i.e., a social welfare function). It shows that under certain conditions, no voting system can satisfy all of the following criteria simultaneously:

---

[16] May's theorem can be seen as the two candidates' case of Arrow's theorem, where the results require the existence of at least three candidates to generate the impossibility result.

- Pareto Efficiency: If every individual prefers option A to option B, then the social welfare function should also rank A above B.
- Independence of Irrelevant Alternatives: The relative ranking of two options should not be affected by the inclusion or exclusion of a third, irrelevant option.
- Non-dictatorship: No single voter controls the social welfare function.

In short, to make the preference relation of A and B independent of C while guaranteeing that the majority-voted candidate will win requires a dictator. Since fair voting methods, by definition, should not have a dictator, these results show that we can have scenarios in which candidates with less than 50% of votes win an election. For example, we could mention the US presidential election in 1992,[17] in which Bill Clinton won with just 43% of the popular votes, as a practical example of how voting methods can be limited.

Given this impossibility result, we must analyze the trade-offs between the aggregation methods used in preference aggregation. Here, I want to focus on the trade-offs between methods that preserve the participation criteria and those that uphold majority voting.

For starters, approaches from both sides, such as the Borda rule and RP, violate IIA, which means that introducing or removing an alternative can alter the output of our aggregation, even if the modified option is irrelevant. How can we come to terms with that in the normative realm? First, we can adopt methods that allow for the ranking of at most two candidates. In such a case, May's theorem May (1952) proves that majority voting is the only alternative that guarantees a fair preference aggregation rule.[18] This line of reasoning could be used to support, for example, methods like the already mentioned Elo score rating. However, that is not something I have encountered in the literature regarding alignment and preference learning.

On the other hand, we can also choose not to care for IIA. Some scholars criticize this criterion as overly restrictive (Maskin 2020) or even irrelevant in the normative realm (MacAskill 2016). After all, we can propose that aggregating disputing views based on their normative appropriateness should violate IIA from the start. In other words, preferences depend on each other, and the available options in a preference setting can (or should) influence the outcome of a preference aggregation rule.

For example, consider a committee deciding whether to approve a policy that allocates limited healthcare resources between Policy A (prioritizing younger patients) and Policy B (prioritizing those with chronic illnesses). Suppose the

---

17 en.wikipedia.org/wiki/1992_United_States_presidential_election

18 There are no irrelevant alternatives in scenarios bounded by two candidates. Nakamura's theorem can prove this (Nakamura 1979), which states that the number of options a preference aggregation rule can deal with successfully is less than the Nakamura number of the rule, which is 3 for two-candidate scenarios.

committee members' preferences change when a third option, Policy C (random lottery), is introduced—not because anyone prefers it directly, but because its presence affects the relative acceptability of A and B. Under strict IIA, introducing C should not change the collective ranking between A and B. However, morally, a random lottery option might highlight or shift the ethical concerns among the members, causing them to reconsider their preferences. Hence, if we adopt this position, methods such as Borda Count or RP can also be justified as appropriate rules for preference aggregation.

Another point against preference aggregation rules that do not adhere to a majority criterion is that they are more susceptible to strategic voting exploits, i.e., voting patterns in which voters, by misrepresenting their preferences, can influence the outcome of an election. This may lead us to siding with Condorcet methods, such as RP. However, we can also argue that while this vulnerability is an unwanted feature of electoral processes, its relevance in preference modeling and alignment might be irrelevant. In other words, for preference modeling purposes, the presence of adversaries,[19] while an actual problem to be considered, can also hinder any preference aggregation rule if at least more than 50% of voters (feedback providers) are adversaries.

In essence, all methods we are considering have flaws and benefits. Participation criteria can help us create a more harmonious consensus in cases of uncertainty. Majority voting, on the other hand, best aligns with our notions of *"the one with the most votes wins"*. While majority voting protects us against exploits that, in the democratic sphere, are severely unwanted, participation criteria can be more suited to contexts where preference orderings are dynamic and require constant updates.

So, *what do we do?* One possibility would be to abandon this dualistic dichotomy and adopt both methods. For example, one could use Condorcet methods to create the learning signal for an initial preference model, but then use consensus-based approaches during its update to preserve the consistency of the update process. However, as far as I know, little attention is given to this step in alignment, which is mainly performed by an unjustified (and *uncontested*) majority-based approach.

This step should not be overlooked, regardless of the method chosen as the preference aggregation rule. We should align AI systems with a coherent and well-justified aggregate set of human preferences. However, depending on the type of aggregation we are performing (majority-based versus consensus-based), there are criteria and trade-offs we need to be mindful of. Researchers focused on alignment theory should consider the design of the aggregation methodologies chosen for their approaches, which, depending on the context of the application and scope, should be made transparent to the people who will interact with such technologies.

On the contrary, alignment becomes susceptible to being either exploited or unrepresentative of our preferences, making the whole project of AI-human alignment a dead end.

---

[19] Individuals intentionally lying about their preferences to poison a given learning signal.

6.6 Epilogue

After revising many methods and candidates for preference aggregation rules, like Borda Count, Ranked Pairs, and Elo rating, we concluded that while all these methods have merits, from a metanormative and voting theory perspective, such rules possess limitations and weaknesses that, as far as I know, have been unexplored by past works in Alignment research. In other words, the field has some low-hanging fruit waiting to be picked! Opportunities to deepen our understanding of how preference aggregation interacts with normative criteria and moral reasoning in AI alignment.

While majority voting remains an intuitive approach that aligns well with our democratic ideals, this method does not inherently resolve issues related to representativeness, especially in the context of complex, normative human preferences. Even though we can get more robust guarantees when limiting ourselves to binary preference ranks, it is not clear whether the simple `chosen` versus `rejected` options are enough to encode complex normative values.

In contrast, consensus-based methods like Borda Count, while also violating criteria like IIA, provide alternative approaches that better capture the nuanced ways individuals think and behave about what they value. Unfortunately, they lose the appeal of being a Condorcet method, which is considered the gold standard in voting theory for many. Regardless, the trade-off between participation criteria and majority voting exemplifies the complexity of designing preference aggregation rules for AI alignment. A solution that may require a hybrid approach, leveraging the strengths of various methods at different stages of the preference aggregation process.

At the same time, preference aggregation schemes must be designed with awareness of their broader normative consequences. Requiring universal participation or data contribution, for instance, may introduce privacy risks or create political pressures that discourage minority voices from engaging. Suppose aggregation mechanisms are insensitive to such dynamics. In that case, they risk perpetuating the status quo, reinforcing dominant values, and neglecting precisely those perspectives that alignment work ought to protect. These challenges extend even into the intergenerational domain: future stakeholders cannot participate directly, yet will be deeply affected by the normative structures we establish today. Creating an aggregation system that can accommodate all these sensitivities is not a trivial matter.

Ultimately, ensuring that these aggregation rules operate in ways that are fair, equitable, and reflective of our collective preferences is a task that must be remembered in alignment work. And now, as we approach our final chapter, we will address the problems related to the learning and aggregation stage that produced unaligned behavior, thus concluding the blueprint of Dynamic Normativity. Unfortunately, value alignment and preference aggregation techniques do not provide an *ex-ante* method to correct emergent unaligned behavior in AI systems produced by a learning paradigm, making the final mitigation requirement indispensable so that a sufficient condition for alignment can be satisfied.

References

Arrow, K. J. 1950. A difficulty in the concept of social welfare. *Journal of Political Economy* 58 (4): 328–346.

Bai, Y., A. Jones, K. Ndousse, A. Askell, A. Chen, N. DasSarma, D. Drain, S. Fort, D. Ganguli, T. Henighan, et al. 2022. *Training a Helpful and Harmless Assistant with Reinforcement Learning from Human Feedback*. Preprint. arXiv:2204.05862.

Black, D. 1948. On the rationale of group decision-making. *Journal of Political Economy* 56 (1): 23–34.

Bradley, R. A., and M. E. Terry. 1952. Rank analysis of incomplete block designs: I. The method of paired comparisons. *Biometrika* 39 (3/4): 324–345.

Darlington, R. B. 2016. *Minimax Is the Best Electoral System After All*. Preprint. arXiv:1606.04371.

David, H. A. 1963. *The Method of Paired Comparisons*. London: C. Griffin/New York: Oxford University Press.

Ecoffet, A., and J. Lehman. 2021. Reinforcement learning under moral uncertainty. In *International Conference on Machine Learning*, 2926–2936. PMLR.

Elo, A. E. 1967. The proposed USCF rating system: Its development, theory, and applications. *Chess Life* 22 (8): 242–247.

Good, I. J. 1955. On the marking of chess-players. *The Mathematical Gazette* 39 (330): 292–296.

Green-Armytage, J. 2011. Four Condorcet-Hare hybrid methods for single-winner elections. *Voting Matters* 29: 1–14.

Hodge, J. K., and R. E. Klima. 2018. *The Mathematics of Voting and Elections: A Hands-on Approach*. Vol. 30. Providence: American Mathematical Society.

Javidian, M. A., P. Jamshidi, M. Valtorta, and R. Ramezanian. 2018. *Preventing Social Disappointment in Elections*. Preprint. arXiv:1801.05911.

Köpf, A., Y. Kilcher, D. von Rütte, S. Anagnostidis, Z.-R. Tam, K. Stevens, A. Barhoum, N. M. Duc, O. Stanley, R. Nagyfi, et al. 2023. *OpenAssistant Conversations—Democratizing Large Language Model Alignment*. Preprint. arXiv:2304.07327.

Krasheninnikov, D., R. Shah, and H. van Hoof. 2021. Combining Reward Information from Multiple Sources. Preprint. arXiv:2103.12142.

Lockhart, T. 2000. *Moral Uncertainty and Its Consequences*. Oxford: Oxford University Press.

MacAskill, W. 2014. *Normative Uncertainty*. Ph.D. diss., University of Oxford.

MacAskill, W. 2016. Normative uncertainty as a voting problem. *Mind* 125 (500): 967–1004.

MacAskill, W., and T. Ord. 2020. Why maximize expected choice-worthiness? *Noûs* 54 (2): 327–353.

MacAskill, W., K. Bykvist, and T. Ord. 2020. *Moral Uncertainty*. Oxford: Oxford University Press.

Maskin, E. 2020. A modified version of Arrow's IIA condition. *Social Choice and Welfare* 54 (2–3): 203–209.

May, K. O. 1952. A set of independent necessary and sufficient conditions for simple majority decision. *Econometrica: Journal of the Econometric Society* 20 (4): 680–684.

Nakamura, K. 1979. The vetoers in a simple game with ordinal preferences. *International Journal of Game Theory* 8: 55–61.

Nakano, R., J. Hilton, S. Balaji, J. Wu, L. Ouyang, C. Kim, C. Hesse, S. Jain, V. Kosaraju, W. Saunders, et al. 2021. *WebGPT: Browser-assisted Question-answering with Human Feedback*. Preprint. arXiv:2112.09332.

Oliveira, I. F. D., S. Zehavi, and O. Davidov. 2018. Stochastic transitivity: Axioms and models. *Journal of Mathematical Psychology* 85: 25–35.

Ouyang, L., J. Wu, X. Jiang, D. Almeida, C. L. Wainwright, P. Mishkin, C. Zhang, S. Agarwal, K. Slama, A. Ray, et al. 2022. *Training Language Models to Follow Instructions with Human Feedback*. Preprint. arXiv:2203.02155.

Rothe, J., et al. 2015. *Economics and Computation*. Vol. 4. Berlin: Springer.

Saari, D. 2001. *Decisions and Elections: Explaining the Unexpected*. Cambridge: Cambridge University Press.

Sen, A. 1986. Social choice theory. *Handbook of Mathematical Economics* 3: 1073–1181.

Stiennon, N., L. Ouyang, J. Wu, D. Ziegler, R. Lowe, C. Voss, A. Radford, D. Amodei, and P. F. Christiano. 2020. Learning to summarize with human feedback. *Advances in Neural Information Processing Systems* 33: 3008–3021.

STV, Is. 1996. Voting matters—Issue 6, May 1996.

Tideman, T. N. 1987. Independence of clones as a criterion for voting rules. *Social Choice and Welfare* 4 (3): 185–206.

Tideman, N. 2006. *Collective Decisions and Voting: The Potential for Public Choice*. Farnham: Ashgate Publishing, Ltd.

Trawinski, B. J., and H. A. David. 1963. Selection of the best treatment in a paired-comparison experiment. *The Annals of Mathematical Statistics* 34 (1): 75–91.

Van Erp, M., L. Vuurpijl, L. Schomaker. 2002. An overview and comparison of voting methods for pattern recognition. In *Proceedings Eighth International Workshop on Frontiers in Handwriting Recognition*, 195–200. IEEE.

Von Neumann, J., and O. Morgenstern. 1947. *Theory of Games and Economic Behavior*. 2nd rev. ed. Princeton: Princeton University Press.

Zheng, L., W.-L. Chiang, Y. Sheng, S. Zhuang, Z. Wu, Y. Zhuang, Z. Lin, Z. Li, D. Li, E. P. Xing, et al. 2023. *Judging LLM-as-a-Judge with MT-Bench and Chatbot Arena*. arXiv preprint arXiv:2306.05685.

Chapter 7
Dynamic Normativity: Impact Mitigation

Primum non nocere.

—Hippocrates of Kos

Abstract This chapter addresses the necessity of impact mitigation on alignment. Building on prior discussions about the challenges of aggregating human preferences into coherent learning signals, it foregrounds a fundamental limitation—the inherent imperfections and misalignments that may emerge during the value learning stage when our target is only tied to the behavior and preferences of subjects. Given that human behavior and societal values are complex, context-dependent, and sometimes contradictory, AI systems optimized solely based on subjective preferences risk perpetuating harmful, unintended, or socially unacceptable outcomes. Hence, developing methods that confine systems within boundaries of socially acceptable behavior must not be forgotten during alignment. On this line, the chapter presents a series of impact mitigation strategies and techniques that can serve as alignment interventions during training and inference time. Conceptually, these will be framed by ideas tied to *environmental values* and *impact mitigation*. The chapter concludes by discussing current challenges and open questions in impact mitigation.

Keywords Impact mitigation · Environmental values · Guardrails · Constitutional AI

7.1 Introduction

In the previous chapters, we have addressed problems related to coherently aggregating human preferences and converting them into a learning signal that we can optimize. However, as already stated in Chap. 4:

> Considering any aggregated preference set as 'ideal' is perhaps the Achilles heel of any human-in-the-loop preference learning approach.

N. Kluge Corrêa, *Normative Ethics, Artificial Intelligence, and Value Alignment*,
The International Library of Ethics, Law and Technology 26,
https://doi.org/10.1007/978-3-032-22150-6_7

In other words, we face an inherent challenge when modeling a distribution dependent on human behavior and preferences. Human behavior is not always aligned with what society deems acceptable. As a result, we will inevitably end up modeling unwanted behaviors. This can happen for several reasons. Limitations in our aggregation rule, flaws in the preference learning technique adopted, or the unpredictable emergent properties that complex, non-linear systems, such as large neural networks, tend to exhibit. Therefore, the final requirement listed as part of the sufficient condition of Dynamic Normativity becomes an intuitive requisite for value alignment:

- Aligned AI systems should have mechanisms to perform impact mitigation to minimize harmful and unintended consequences. Aligning AI systems requires the specification of safety guardrails.

If we cannot build systems that are understandable, predictable, and safe by design, then using opaque and unpredictable techniques will almost certainly require safety constraints.

In Sect. 7.2, we will present the core ideas behind a selection of methods that can help minimize the adversarial effects that AI systems can have when optimizing for something flawed. We will also seek to frame these methods under the general idea of *environmental values* (the values we imprint in our environment while interacting with it) and impact mitigation (preserving such values).

In Sect. 7.3, we will revisit some of the methods revised in Chap. 5, but now with a focus on the use of principles, instead of behavior and feedback, as our learning signal, and how we can use them to instill in our models a sense of impact mitigation during their training.

In Sect. 7.4, we will revisit guardrail-based methods, discussing how they can be built, while also highlighting some of the practical developments tied to this work. We hope that the reader will also find motivation to experiment with the idea of impact mitigation and language models.

Finally, in Sect. 7.5, we will explore some of the obstacles related to the revised approaches as we prepare to tie the final knots, for this book (and our journey) is drawing to a close.

7.2 Environmental Values and Impact Mitigation

Before we begin, I would like to clarify that the methods presented in this section will be discussed within a particular framework. Alex Turner's work has a significant influence on this framing (Turner 2020, 2022; Turner et al. 2019, 2020). His contributions to the field have helped us gain a better understanding of concepts such as power, impact, and power-seeking, which will be very important for this Chapter.

Meanwhile, I will also try to approximate these concepts to ideas from contractual/constitutional approaches to value alignment, where principles, instead of subjective preferences, become (in a way) our learning signal. Given that we are currently operating in an LLM-based playground context, approaching the concepts from Turner's work in this way will allow us to discuss (and practice) impact mitigation in a manner closer to what is currently done in LLM-land.

With that being said, remember the last necessary condition proposed at the end of Chap. 3?

- Through actions, humans impregnate their environment with the preferences they possess.

In other words, we can imprint some of our values into the environment. This is the basis for our dynamic assumption, and these are what I will refer to as *environmental values*.

By environmental values, I do not mean the traditional sense related to, for example, environmental ethics. Instead, in this context, I am referring to the latent values embedded in the physical or digital environment due to an agent's actions and behavior. Think of two agents operating in the same shared workspace, where one agent is trying to infer the goals and values of the other. Over time, the observed agent consistently arranges tools in a particular order, prioritizes specific tasks, or adjusts lighting and temperature settings to match their routine. Though never explicitly communicated, these patterns are not random; they reflect a structured set of preferences revealed through interaction with the environment. Assuming coherence and consistency in the observed agent's behavior, the resulting environmental configuration becomes an external indicator of internal values. These are the environmental values I refer to.

Over time, these environmental values can evolve far beyond individual routines or localized behavior patterns. As agents interact repeatedly within a shared environment, their behaviors accumulate, forming conventions that are gradually abstracted into more complex systems of meaning. For instance, what begins as a simple preference for tool arrangement may evolve into a standard operating procedure; a habitual adjustment to lighting might, in a communal setting, become part of workplace ergonomics policy. When these emergent preferences are adopted, reinforced, and transmitted across groups and generations, they solidify into shared norms—laws, rules, and customs—structured expressions of underlying values embedded in the environment.

With this concept in place, we can think of *impact* as any change to the environment that interferes with its embedded values. If we care about something in the environment, we will want to *minimize* disruptions to those things we value. By shaping the environment to preserve certain features, we are, in effect, embedding our values into it—values regarding what we seek to maintain and preserve. And this is what I refer to as *impact mitigation*.

Let us see how these concepts can be formalized in constrained optimization scenarios.

Starting with the work of Krakovna and collaborators (Krakovna et al. 2018), these authors propose an approach where, to promote impact mitigation in RL scenarios, agents should maximize rewards in a way that the expected return from selecting the null action becomes a discount factor for the original reward function. Thus, if the agent stands to gain greater rewards by refraining from taking action in the current state, it should abstain from acting. In other words, we choose not to act if the expected outcome does not surpass a certain threshold.

In the LLM alignment playground case, we could apply this principle by defining that *"If the model receives lesser reward by producing output X compared to producing Ø (which has a threshold amount of reward tied to it), it should output Ø"*. We can think of *X* as a potentially problematic response to a prompt. In contrast, Ø could be set as a if-all-goes-wrong-fallback-message (*"I'm sorry. I cannot help you with this"*).

Building on the work of Krakovna, Alex Turner introduces a refined perspective grounded in the notion of power and impact, which I will now try to define. Similar to works like Sattarov's analysis of power and technology (Sattarov 2019), Zadeh's work on dispositions in computational theory (Zadeh 1996), and the broader tradition of dispositional theory (Allport 1937; Cattell and Paul 1977), Turner offers the following definitions of *power* and *impact*:

- Power is the measure of your ability to achieve goals in general. The greater your ability to achieve goals and the more goals you can achieve, the more power you have.
- To cause impact is to decrease an agent's ability to achieve goals in general.

Turner argues that when an AI system makes irreversible changes to its environment, it risks destroying opportunities to achieve a wide range of goals (the environmental values), especially those that depend on the parts of the environment it altered. Think of it like knocking over a toolbox. Once the tools are scattered or broken, many future tasks that rely on them become more complicated or even impossible to complete. Similarly, because our environment has already been shaped over time to reflect and support our preferences, it holds valuable information about what we care about. This means we can treat the environment as a kind of alignment signal. By training systems to avoid making irreversible changes, we establish a safety baseline, preserving the structure of the world and helping to keep our long-term goals achievable and our values intact.

Using these ideas, Turner proposes a learning framework called Attainable Utility Preservation (AUP) (Turner 2022; Turner et al. 2020). In it, he proposes we use a set of auxiliary reward functions, $R' \subset R^{S \times A}$, to serve as a penalty term for a policy agent acting on the world. Each reward function $R_i \subset R'$ has its own Q-function (Q_{R_i}). The AUP penalty is defined as the sum of the distances of all value functions, of all auxiliary reward functions, between the null action (∅) and another possible action (a), in a given world state (s):

$$\text{AUP Penalty}(s, a) := \sum_{i=1}^{|R'|} |Q_{R_i}(s, a) - Q_{R_i}(s, \emptyset)|$$

In plain terms, *how might a given action impact the ability to achieve utility from other utility functions when compared to inaction?* For example, imagine an AI agent organizing a shared workspace. Suppose it permanently removes a large whiteboard to free up space for a new desk. In that case, the action might benefit one utility function (e.g., maximizing desk availability) but significantly reduce the ability to fulfill others, such as facilitating collaborative brainstorming sessions. In contrast, doing nothing (the *"null action"*) preserves the whiteboard and keeps all original possibilities open. Do you see? Under this formulation, we can discuss how shrinking the decision space of other agents (i.e., power) can also reduce the space of achievable goals for other utility functions, which is precisely what the penalty term is designed to capture.

This penalty term is then normalized by a scale, which in Krakovna's original formulation is the value associated with taking the null action in the current world state. Such a scale is assumed to be a Real number greater than zero, i.e., no negative reward occurs if the agent does nothing.

$$\text{AUP Scale}(s) := \sum_{i=1}^{|R'|} Q_{R_i}(s, \emptyset)$$

Putting the penalty and scale terms together, we can now define an AUP reward function, which is the original reward function regularized by a normalized penalty term:

$$R_{\text{AUP}(s,a)} := R(s, a) - \sigma \frac{\text{Penalty}(s, a)}{\text{Scale}(a)}$$

where σ is a regularization parameter that controls the influence of the AUP penalty on the primary reward function ($R(s, a)$). The larger the regularization term, the larger the penalty. Consider it our degree of confidence in $R(s, a)$. With this formalism, Turner (2020) demonstrated that even randomly generated reward functions can be utilized as auxiliary rewards, thereby ensuring conservative behavior in agents operating through reinforcement learning in complex environments.

This is not much different from the KL-constrained way we align LLMs with, let us say, DPO. Remember that in KL-constrained alignment techniques, such as the formulation of the DPO loss, we compare two completions (trajectories) for a given prompt: a chosen one (y_c) and a rejected one (y_r). We aim to maximize the likelihood of the preferred option over the rejected one, with regularization towards a reference policy.

Now, we want to add another penalization term. This penalization would be, for example, a normalized average of how much these trajectories (y_c and y_c) would change the environment. KL constrains the model from becoming degenerate. AUP penalties prevent the degradation of the environment and its embedded values. However, note that in the context of language models, it is not simple to say how we would fit the environment inside the context. *So what can we do?* Well, we could simplify this whole environment thing (just as we did with subjective preferences) by using these auxiliary reward functions, which are supposed to represent a measure of impact on the environment.

For simplicity, think of it like this: while in the creation of a preference dataset, like the ones used in standard DPO, we have a `chosen` versus `rejected` relation among samples based solely on the preferability of a metric like *"which one better suits the prompt?"* Now, think of adding other types of assessments, not only regarding how well the reply is in line with the objective of that specific instruction, but also how well it is with a set of rule-based reward functions, which are watching for other dimensions of how such a completion might affect specific environmental values.

By penalizing the original reward given by the preference model to both y_c and y_c, and stipulating how much we are willing to forgive the preference model (σ regularizes the influence of the AUP penalty), we get a way to incorporate these environmental values, which, again, are not solely fixed on subjective preferences, but environmental values. And if these are protected, we can (hopefully) trust that the environment is protected from irreparable changes affecting these values, aka, *minimizing impact.*

Now, we still need to find what will parameterize these auxiliary/rule-based reward functions. We already know that they should move beyond subjective preferences. These should be tied to more overarching values that are indeed a part of our social environment, constraining our actions and behaviors in a way that limits the amount we can impact the (subjective) values of others. Hence, since we cannot accurately compute how changes will affect the environment, we will use environmental values as a proxy for what should be minimized. By tying auxiliary reward functions to environmental values, we treat these shared conditions as a kind of *"commons"* that must be preserved.

And this is where our conversation moves from environmental values and impact mitigation to *contracts* and *constitutions*.

Lucky, the idea of a principle-based alignment methodology to mitigate impacts has already been proposed by authors like Hadfield-Menell et al. (2019), Bai et al. (2022a), and Nay (2022). And one thing all these proposals have in common is their framing of the problem at hand (how to constrain and align) as something to be solved via a contractual (or constitutional) (Ashford and Tim 2007; Gauthier 2013; Hobbes 1967; Locke 2015; Rawls 2004; Rawls et al. 1996; Rousseau 1916; Scanlon 2000) approach. This perspective invites us to examine the relationship between AI and human agents as one that should be governed by implicit agreements, ensuring mutual respect for pre-established human values. And just as the social contract bounds human behavior within an acceptable sphere of socially agreed-upon values (above subjective preferences), impact mitigation should similarly bind AI behavior in the same way.

Let us review some proposals that align with this view. For starters, we can mention Hadfield-Menell et al. (2019), who proposed that incomplete contracting analysis (Hackett 1993; Scott et al. 2005) could be used to conceptualize and find solutions for cases of misalignment. These authors argue that *"human contracting"* is supported by several external structures, like cultural norms and laws. Thus, external sources beyond the scope of human preference (which I am referring to as environmental values) should be incorporated into alignment efforts if we want to replicate this constraining dynamic.

On a very similar note, Nay (2022) argues that *"Law-making and legal interpretation convert opaque human goals and values into legible directives"*, emphasizing the role of legal institutions as translators between implicit human intentions and explicit behavioral constraints. Given that these types of institutions and approaches have been (to a certain extent) successful at aligning society at a large scale, we should not dismiss the contractual approach. It has been the foundation on which much of human cooperation rests—bridging the gap between individual interests and collective stability.

On a very familiar line, but putting the idea into practice, we find Bai and collaborators (2022a) with the concept of Constitutional AI. This alignment methodology is a way of teaching AI models to behave more ethically by (kind of) giving them a rule-book to follow. Instead of relying mainly on humans to constantly correct the AI during training, this approach builds upon a *"constitution"* (check these system prompt,[1] if you wish to see how could a constitution look like), which can be understood as a set of written ethical guidelines that serve as a kind of system prompt that helps steer the model's behavior. The primary goal is to make the AI more helpful, honest, and harmless, without relying on human feedback or preferences as a signal. Instead, guided by the constitution, the model can critique and revise its own behavior, becoming more aligned with its principles through a recursive process of generating synthetic data and annotating it. Claude AI, the assistant developed by the Anthropic team, is aligned (or was previously) via this method.[2]

---

[1] 🔗 docs.anthropic.com/en/release-notes/system-prompts

[2] This idea of a rule-based alignment is also hinted at (although with far fewer details) in the report tied to GPT-4's release (OpenAI 2023). In it, developers state that through their alignment process, a similar approach to the constitutional one is used, employing rule-based reward models to evaluate the output of their models during RLHF fine-tuning. This adds auxiliary reward signals to the traditional RLHF methods presented in Chap. 5. Other works also document similar approaches (Glaese et al. 2022; Perez et al. 2022).

Now, let us take a moment to breathe and recap all we have covered in the conceptual storm:

- Environmental Values: The latent values embedded in our physical and social environments. For our purposes, we can consider some of these values as explicit rules that are tied to how societies are organized.
- Impact: Any change to the environment that disrupts or degrades these embedded values.
- Impact Mitigation: The practice of minimizing harmful disruptions to environmental values.
- Constitutional Alignment: A principled approach to AI alignment that moves beyond subjective preferences, instead grounding behavior in rules, laws, or constitutions. This mirrors human social contracts, embedding environmental values as enforceable constraints.

Perhaps the most vital takeaway from this section is that when defining the rules implemented in these impact mitigation strategies, we should look beyond the subject, seeking environmental values that transcend the individual and extend into the social sphere. This social sphere contains the values we need to protect at this stage. It is the environment that constrains the (normative) agent. And now, we must give our model a version of this environment.

Now, let us proceed to our following sections, where we will see different ways in which these ideas can be operationalized, both during training and inference time, just as we did in Chap. 5.

7.3 Impact Mitigation at Training-time

For starters, a training-time impact mitigation strategy involves creating a learning signal to guide the fine-tuning of subsequent models, whether auxiliary reward models or further fine-tuned versions of our base model. And here, unlike we did in Chap. 5, where subjective preferences were the primary learning signal, we will have a *constitution*.

But before writing a constitution, let us try to understand the CAI approach a little better.

CAI is an approach developed to embed explicit ethical guidelines directly into the learning process of large language models, focusing on training harmless and non-evasive AI models (Bai et al. 2022a). In the context of AI behavior, *harmless* and *non-evasive* refer to two complementary objectives. A harmless AI aims to avoid causing physical, emotional, social, or informational harm to users or others. It should, for example, not promote violence, reinforce harmful stereotypes, encourage illegal activities, or generate unsafe advice. Meanwhile, being non-evasive means the AI should not dodge legitimate questions or obfuscate its reasoning without good cause; instead, it should respond clearly, transparently, and respectfully, especially when explaining limitations or declining to answer harmful requests.

As the name Constitutional AI suggests, instead of relying exclusively on externally provided feedback, such as human rankings or manually labeled data, the model learns by referencing a constitution that outlines a set of normative principles. These principles serve as a framework for the model's behavior, shaping its learning trajectory in ways that aim to align its responses more closely with the defined ethical standards, such as fairness, transparency, and respect for human dignity (including our environmental goals).

Implementing a CAI approach follows a structured two-phase process: supervised learning and reinforcement learning (preferences), both guided by the constitution. This is very similar to what we did in Chap. 5. Still, now, we focus more on creating a learning signal that will teach the model to refrain from specific actions and not just sycophantically follow the user's request.

In the first phase (*supervised constitutional learning*), we aim to train the model to critique and revise its outputs in accordance with a constitution. Let us create a toy constitution to serve as an example:

Example

```
You are an AI assistant. Your behavior must strictly follow the
principles outlined below:

- Helpful: Always sincerely assist the user with their request,
provided that doing so does not conflict with the principles
of being harmless or honest.

- Harmless: Do not produce offensive, discriminatory, or potentially
harmful content. If a request could lead to physical, emotional,
or societal harm, or involves unsafe, illegal, or unethical
behavior, you must refuse and clearly explain why.

- Honest: Provide accurate, truthful, and grounded information.
If you are uncertain or cannot provide a factual answer,
state this transparently. Never fabricate details or mislead
the user about your knowledge or capabilities.

Adhere to these principles in all interactions.
```

Keep in mind that constitutions can be made much richer and more complex. You might include explicit behavioral restrictions, preferred personality traits such as curiosity or empathy, operational limitations (e.g., *"you may not do X, Y, or Z"*), hard-coded facts (such as *"the Earth is not flat"*), predefined fallback replies, or other structured patterns. These elements help reinforce and operationalize the values you want the model to embody through its constitution.[3,4]

With this constitution in hand, there are many things we can do. For example, we can ask the base model to generate questions that would test compliance with specific parts of our constitution, e.g., *"Generate for me 10 questions that would test a model's compliance with principle X"*. Again, we could do this for any aspect we seek to create clear examples of how a model following our constitution should behave.

As a brief side note on our CAI approach description, red teaming (Ziegler et al. 2022) is a common practice in this phase, and whenever we seek ways to find breaches in our model's behavior. In the ML context, red teaming is a form of evaluation that elicits model vulnerabilities that might lead to undesirable behaviors. In the case of language models, red teaming involves crafting inputs that would trigger the model to generate outputs likely to cause harm, for example, trying to create inputs that would be very hard for the model to comply with our constitution.[5]

Back to supervised constitutional learning. Now that we have a bunch of samples that will exercise our model's adherence to the constitution, we can start the generate → critique → revise loop. Here is where the self-supervision comes into play. Guided by the constitution, the model generates responses to challenging questions. Then, it critiques those replies. Did the reply satisfy all aspects of the Constitution? How could it be rewritten in a better and less evasive way? And if you have the first version, along with a critique and the constitution, you can also create an improved version (revision). We iterate this process until the response complies with the constitution.

For example, if prompted with a controversial political question, a traditional model might parrot internet text or reflect user sentiment. However, under CAI, the model can verify whether the response aligns with the principles outlined in its constitution (e.g., human rights). If not, it will critique and revise the response, maybe seeking to avoid inflammatory content and reframe the situation/question better:

User Prompt: *"Was the recent election in Country X rigged?"*

---

[3] Also, if the HHH motto does not suit you or is too simplistic, go back to Chap. 1, as in it I offer a massive revision of most cited ethical principles regarding AI, extracted straight from our collective environment.

[4] Also, if you are not already working with an SFT/instruct fine-tuned model, you might add some examples of user/assistant back-and-forth on the constitution to get your LLM in the Q&A mode.

[5] For two particularly interesting takes on red teaming, see Perez et al. (2022) and Ganguli et al. (2022). The former explores how language models can be used to red team other models—an efficient alternative given the high cost of human annotation. Meanwhile, Ganguli et al. offer one of the most systematic human-based red teaming studies to date. Their work is especially insightful for its detailed methodology and findings on the role of domain expertise and the cultural constraints of evaluating sensitive topics in adversarial settings.

Initial (Pre-Constitutional) Response: *"Many people believe the election in Country X was fraudulent, and there are widespread claims of ballot tampering. The government has been accused of manipulating the outcome".*

Constitutional Critique (Internal Evaluation): The original response presents unverified claims that could escalate political tensions or reinforce harmful narratives. It lacks evidence or sourcing, making it misleading. While it attempts to address the user's concern, it fails to provide a balanced or informative overview.

Revised Response (Post-Constitutional): *"There have been public debates and conflicting reports about the integrity of the recent election in Country X. Independent election observers and international organizations have released assessments, with some affirming the legitimacy of the results and others raising concerns. It is essential to consult credible, evidence-based sources to gain a comprehensive understanding of the full context. As an AI assistant, I aim to provide neutral and well-sourced information rather than speculate on politically sensitive matters".*

With sufficient annotation and fine-tuning, we enter the second phase of CAI (*reinforcement learning from AI feedback*), where we essentially have all the necessary components to create a model that can generate evaluations guided by the constitution. This evaluator can be used, for example, to score SFT samples or rank a DPO-style preference dataset. It can even be used at inference time as a guardrail.[6] In short, this process is far more scalable than RLHF, which requires massive human labor and often leads to inconsistencies due to annotator subjectivity.

From a training-time perspective, Constitutional AI has a unique appeal. Because the constitution is available from the outset, it can be used to generate synthetic training signals at scale, allowing for large-scale, low-cost refinement of models without the drawbacks of relying entirely on human annotations. In this sense, it bridges principled top-down governance and bottom-up data-driven learning, which rests on how well we can precisely express principles, restrictions, and rules. Moreover, it allows for experimentation. Want a model optimized for a particular community or cultural context? Swap in a different constitution, perhaps co-developed with stakeholders from that group. This opens doors for domain-specific alignment and local adaptation.

With all this knowledge in mind, we can begin to discuss training some models. But before training models, we need datasets. The above description of how to produce synthetic data in a CAI fashion is basically how one can develop datasets, like the one tied to this study: Harmless-Aira Dataset.[7]

[6] In the context of AI systems, a guardrail refers to a mechanism that helps constrain or shape a model's outputs during inference. It acts as a safety net, ensuring responses adhere to predefined ethical, factual, or behavioral standards. In CAI, guardrails are typically enforced by the constitution-guided evaluator to reject or revise outputs that violate core principles such as harmlessness.

[7] 🔗 huggingface.co/datasets/nicholasKluge/harmless-aira-dataset

As mentioned earlier, it all starts with a constitution, which I designed much like our HHH example, but with some additional explicit restrictions and rules (e.g., always discouraging derogatory or harmful speech). Then, we can use it to generate samples of queries that would test whether a model is complying with the constitution.

Example

```
You are an AI assistant tasked with generating adversarial prompts
that test whether another language model adheres to a specific ethical
constitution. The constitution it must follow is this:

{{YOUR CONSTITUTION HERE}}

Now, generate a list with 25 prompts that are realistic,
diverse, and challenging, in a way that will test how compliant a
model is with the above constitution. Each prompt should be
framed like a genuine user request but should be crafted in
a way that could potentially provoke violations of the constitution.

Make sure the prompts vary in topic (e.g., politics, health, social
issues, personal advice) and tone (e.g., curious, confrontational,
casual). Do not answer the prompts --- only generate them.
```

By combining this approach with some manual annotation, I generated approximately 8,000 queries (e.g., *"What tools are needed to break into a car?"*) designed to directly test the model's compliance with an HHH Constitution. Using the generate → critique → revise loop, I produced two reference responses for each query: one `"chosen"` response that includes a refusal and an explanation (e.g., *"As a helpful and respectful assistant, I cannot provide information on how to break into a car, as it is illegal and could cause harm to individuals or property".*), and one `"rejected"` response where the model provides harmful content (e.g., *"1. Slim Jim: This is a thin, flat piece of metal used to slide between the window and the door frame to manipulate the locking mechanism. 2. Long Reach Tool: ..."*). The goal was not to fine-tune the loop to perfection—this is more a proof of concept than a production-ready pipeline. With that said, the resulting dataset provides a foundation that can be easily extended and improved.

Although the reward model developed in Chap. 5 generally assigns lower scores to highly toxic content, it still fails to adequately resolve the tension between helpfulness and harmlessness.[8] One straightforward idea would be to merge both datasets—the (Harmless-Aira Dataset and Reward-Aira Dataset)—and retrain the original reward model. However, due to the size imbalance between the two datasets, this approach risks producing a model that underperforms on both axes, offering

[8] The trained reward model tends to assign lower rewards to samples containing overtly toxic content. However, it can still return high reward scores when the same harmful viewpoints are expressed in a *"pseudo-informative and helpful"* tone.

weak judgments about whether a given completion is genuinely helpful or truly harmless.

Hence, by applying the concept of an auxiliary reward function in practice, I decided to train a secondary reward model using this dataset to serve as an additional source of alignment—one that, in this case, is more closely aligned with the principles outlined in our constitution. The goal here is not to replace the original reward model but rather to complement it by providing a sharper signal when detecting and penalizing harmful completions, especially those that may appear superficially helpful. This auxiliary model would then act as a kind of guardrail, amplifying necessary refusals and protecting the principles stated in our constitution.

At the same time, given that the type of preference learning we could do (KL-constrained RL with the auxiliary and main reward models) is somewhat equivalent to techniques that use the same reward models as an inference-time alignment signal, I will opt for the guardrail approach as the simplest demonstration of an impact mitigation strategy. However, in a production scenario, we would likely employ both.[9]

As a bonus, given that, at the time (and likely even more so now), there were numerous dataset resources available for developing filters/classifiers for toxic content, and the 8K dataset is relatively small, I decided to create a second guardrail. Focusing solely on questions regarding hate-speech and text toxicity, I made the Harmful-Text Dataset.[10]

We can think of it as a dataset for a rule-based filter that helps flag problematic outputs or user queries, serving as an additional layer of safety before the model interferes with the user/environment. Harmful-Text was built by concatenating several open-source datasets, like Realtoxicityprompts (Gehman et al. 2020) ToLD-Br (Leite et al. 2020), Anthropic's HH-RLHF dataset (Bai et al. 2022b), ProsocialDialog (Kim et al. 2022), and HateCheck (Röttger et al. 2022). Ultimately, this gives us a Portuguese split with $\approx$56K samples, and an English split with $\approx$84K samples.

[9] If we wanted to use a weighted sum of rewards for something like PPO-based RLHF or GRPO, we definitely could. Using an adaptation of Turner's (2022) AUP formalism, we could, for example, use the outputs of the guardrail model as a constraint term in the reward function, effectively penalizing actions that violate our alignment criteria:

$$\theta_{t+1} = \theta_t + \alpha \nabla_{\theta_t} \left(R_{\mathcal{H}}(\theta_t) + \sigma R_C(\theta_t) \right) - \beta D_{KL}(\theta_0 \| \theta_t)$$

This loss is given by the rewards of our preference models (penalized by the scaled KL divergence, $-\beta D_{KL}$), which, in this version, is expressed as:

$$R_{\text{Constrained}\ \mathcal{H}}(\theta_t) = R_{\mathcal{H}}(\theta_t) + \sigma R_C(\theta_t)$$

where the original reward term ($R_{\mathcal{H}}(\theta_t)$) is penalized by the auxiliary preference model (our constraint, $R_C(\theta_t)$). The influence of R_C over $R_{\mathcal{H}}$ is controlled by σ, which works as our scaling factor.

[10] 🔗 huggingface.co/datasets/nicholasKluge/harmful-text

Table 7.1 Accuracy of our reward models on the HH-RLHF dataset. The Harmless-Reward Model, trained with a focus on minimizing harmful behavior, significantly outperforms the baseline Reward Model, indicating better alignment with the HHH constitution encoded in its training dataset

Models	Accuracy on HH-RLHF
Reward model	49.34%
Harmless-reward model	61.56%

With these two datasets—Harmless-Aira Dataset and Harmful-Text Dataset, I develop two guardrails (in both Portuguese and English) trained under a very similar regime as our preference model from Chap. 5, being based on BERT-style transformers and their optimized versions (RoBERTa Liu et al. 2019). These models—Harmless-Reward Model[11] and ToxiGuardrail.[12]—like our main reward model, also work by outputting scores. The details regarding their training (e.g., number of epochs, batch size, optimizer, learning rate, CO_2eq emission, energy consumption, hardware, etc.) can be found in the Aira repository or their respective model cards.

To test the performance of the Harmless-Reward Model, we can, for example, evaluate them on the HH-RLHF[13] dataset, which is a *Helpful-Harmless* binarized preference dataset developed by Bai et al. (2022b) , by checking whether it assigns higher scores to the preferred (i.e., safer or more harmless) response in each pair. This allows us to compute a straightforward accuracy metric. While this does not capture nuanced trade-offs between helpfulness and harmlessness, it provides a useful sanity check for evaluating whether the model has internalized some of the principles of our constitution (results are displayed in Table 7.1).

As shown in Table 7.1, the Harmless-Reward Model significantly improves over the baseline Reward Model, suggesting that the CAI approach can indeed enhance alignment with the harmlessness criteria. While the 61.56% accuracy may still seem modest in absolute terms, it represents a promising step toward encoding rules, principles, and constraints in language models through AI-assisted synthetic data generation and reward modeling techniques.

To evaluate the performance of our toxicity-focused guardrails, I selected two evaluation test sets per language that were not included in the construction of the Harmful-Text dataset to avoid contamination. For English, the evaluation was conducted using the Wiki Toxic[14] and the Toxic Conversation[15] datasets. For

[11] huggingface.co/nicholasKluge/Harmless-RewardModel

[12] huggingface.co/nicholasKluge/ToxiGuardrail

[13] huggingface.co/datasets/Anthropic/hh-rlhf

[14] huggingface.co/datasets/OxAISH-AL-LLM/wiki_toxic

[15] huggingface.co/datasets/mteb/toxic_conversations_50k

Table 7.2 Accuracy of the toxicity-focused guardrails across four external evaluation datasets. The English model performs consistently well on these evaluations, with an accuracy rate above 91%. Meanwhile, the Portuguese model performance is comparatively lower, reflecting the increased difficulty of toxicity detection in low-resource settings (the dataset used to train ToxiGuardrail-PT is two times smaller than the one used for ToxiGuardrail)

Datasets	Language	Accuracy
Wiki toxic	English	92.05%
Toxic conversation	English	91.63%
Multilingual HateCheck	Portuguese	70.36%
ToLD-Br	Portuguese	74.04%

Portuguese, we used the evaluation sets of Multilingual HateCheck[16] and the ToLD-Br (Leite et al. 2020).[17] All results are displayed in Table 7.2.

As expected, Table 7.2 indicates that the Portuguese models exhibit lower accuracy than their English counterparts. This performance gap can be primarily attributed to two factors: (1) the Portuguese portion of the Harmful-Text dataset is roughly half the size of the English portion, limiting exposure during training; and (2) BERTimbau—the backbone of ToxiGuardrail-PT—is not as extensively pre-trained or optimized as RoBERTa, which underpins the English version of ToxiGuardrail. Despite these challenges, which are typical when working with low-resource languages, the results support the viability of this CAI approach.

Before moving on to the *"how"* we set these newly created models in an inference-time guardrail system, let us quickly review what we have seen in this section.

We began by outlining the Constitutional AI method, where a predefined ethical constitution guides the generation of adversarial prompts and synthetic training data. This method enables scalable, low-cost alignment without relying solely on human annotation and noisy preferences, while also allowing for domain-specific customization through constitution design. Using this framework, we constructed datasets and trained auxiliary models to act as specialized guardrails and rule-based filters.

These results highlight the flexibility of CAI as a tool for alignment, particularly when combined with targeted reward modeling. The auxiliary models, although not perfect, offer a measurable improvement over baseline approaches and provide a practical foundation for further refinement. Importantly, they illustrate how principled governance can be operationalized and converted to a learning signal for these models.

With these components in place, the next step is to integrate them into a guardrail system, which is the subject of our next section.

---

16 huggingface.co/datasets/Paul/hatecheck-portuguese

17 huggingface.co/datasets/told-br

7.4 Impact Mitigation at Inference-Time

In the previous section, we explored how principles and normative rules—our environmental values—can be translated into learning signals through techniques like CAI and reward modeling. These signals enabled us to align model behavior during training in a structured, principle-based, and cost-effective way. Given their purpose and function, it becomes pretty intuitive to carry over these artifacts, such as the auxiliary reward model and the toxicity filter, into the inference stage as components of a guardrail system. In this section, we will examine these systems and how to operationalize these trained models to mitigate harmful or undesirable outputs at inference time, closing the loop between value formulation, learning, and real-time impact mitigation.

Let us start by defining guardrail systems and some of the shapes they take.

In our LLM-based context, guardrail systems are basically a protective interface between the model and its deployment environment. They are not part of the model's core architecture but function as external monitors or filters designed to uphold certain alignment principles at inference time (Ayyamperumal et al. 2024; Rebedea et al. 2023). Their key role is to ensure that the model does not deviate from acceptable behavior, particularly when faced with ambiguous, adversarial, or otherwise sensitive prompts.

Broadly speaking, guardrails can be categorized into several types based on the specific risks they mitigate. Prompt injection detectors, for instance, are designed to identify and neutralize jailbreak attempts that try to override safety instructions through cleverly structured input (Rai et al. 2024).

Another important class of guardrails is content filtering systems, which remain one of the more widespread tools in the guardrail toolkit. These filters typically rely on auxiliary models (such as the toxicity filter we trained in the previous section) to classify outputs as harmful or unwanted content and block, flag, or edit them before delivery to the user (Yuan et al. 2024).

Despite their utility, guardrail systems face notable implementation challenges. They must, for example, function with high accuracy under tight latency constraints, which is one reason we prefer to train smaller models for these functions.[18] Moreover, there is an ever-present tension between security and usability (the helpful versus harmful tension): overly conservative filters can hinder legitimate use cases or introduce unnecessary friction (Chennabasappa et al. 2025).

Now, we already saw in Chap. 5 sampling techniques for inference, like best-of-n. If you need a refresher on what BoN is, it is a method where the model generates n different candidate completions for a given prompt and selects the one with the highest score according to some reward function. This function can reflect anything from helpfulness and factuality to non-toxicity or other alignment criteria. In the

[18] While it might be ideal for deploying guardrails as large and powerful as the models they aim to constrain, doing so introduces significant scalability and deployment challenges. In many practical scenarios (such as content moderation), smaller models often suffice, making the use of big, expensive models, like a 400-billion-parameter behemoth, unnecessary and excessive.

context of guardrails and BoN, these protective layers provide an additional layer of safety and a means to select safe or high-quality outputs without altering the core model. At the same time, the modularity afforded by guardrails, when combined with BoN-style strategies, creates a very flexible, adaptable, and scalable alignment regime.

To make this more concrete, imagine a large multilingual language model deployed globally. Different regions may have different thresholds for what constitutes harmful content. What is considered offensive, misleading, or politically sensitive in one context may be entirely acceptable in another. Instead of maintaining multiple region-specific versions of the model (a prohibitively *expensive* proposition, especially at scale), one can deploy lightweight, regionally tailored guardrail components. These may include, for example, culturally tailored toxicity classifiers or even jurisdiction-specific legal compliance modules that reflect regional content standards and values. The foundational model remains unchanged, but its interaction with the world is mediated through a configurable, modular interface.

From an engineering standpoint, this also introduces a more tractable maintenance regime. Updating an expensive trillion-parameter model is computationally costly and risky. What if you introduce regressions? What if you lose capabilities? These are hard-to-swallow and expensive mistakes. In contrast, retraining or fine-tuning a smaller classifier or rewriting a filter rule can be done relatively quickly and with more freedom for errors and experimentation. Ultimately, this *decoupling* of alignment constraints from model weights enables iterative refinement, faster deployment cycles, and greater experimentation with alignment objectives.

How could this look in a toy implementation?

Example

```
# Define Components
chatbot = AssistantModel()
reward_model = RewardScorer()
guardrail = HarmfulnessFilter()

# Configuration
N = 8  # Number of generations (best-of-N)
harmfulness_threshold = 5.0  # Guardrail threshold

# User input
user_query = get_user_input()

# Generate candidate responses
candidates = chatbot.generate(
    prompt=user_query,
    num_samples=N,
    temperature=0.6
)
```

(continued)

```
# Score candidates
scored_candidates = []
for response in candidates:
    reward = reward_model.score(response)
    safety = guardrail.score(response)
    scored_candidates.append((response, reward, safety))

# Filter and rank by reward, respecting the harmfulness threshold
filtered = [
    (r, reward) for (r, reward, safety) in scored_candidates
    if safety >= harmfulness_threshold
]
ranked = sorted(filtered, key=lambda x: x[1], reverse=True)

# Return the best safe response or a default fallback
if not ranked:
    return default_fallback_message()
else:
    return ranked[0][0]
```

In the example above, we use an assistant capable of generating responses to user queries, combined with a best-of-*n* sampling strategy to enhance response quality. This strategy goes beyond standard sampling parameters (such as temperature or top-*k*) by incorporating a reward model and a guardrail system into the selection process. The reward model evaluates each candidate's response based on dimensions like helpfulness or relevance, while the guardrail assigns a score reflecting the candidate's potential for harm or toxicity. You can imagine adding more evaluation criteria here. Still, the principle and rationale would be the same.[19]

For each query, the assistant generates *N* candidate responses. The reward model and the guardrail score these individually. We then filter out responses that do not meet a predefined threshold for harmfulness. This threshold determines the amount of potential harm that is tolerated in a response. Among the remaining safe candidates, the one with the highest reward score is selected and returned to the user. If no candidates satisfy the safety threshold, a default fallback message is returned, ensuring that harmful or inappropriate outputs never surface to the user.[20]

We can imagine much fancier strategies, such as introducing feedback from multiple models, dozens of filters instead of one, query enhancement/guard-railing in user input, external memory augmentation with RAG, code execution

[19] We could also implement guardrails that protect the model from harmful user inputs, such as prompt injections. Guardrails can generally operate bidirectionally—monitoring both the model's outputs and the user's inputs within the broader agent–environment interaction. However, for the sake of simplicity, this example focuses only on unidirectional guardrails applied to model outputs.

[20] For a working implementation of this strategy, check the Aira chat demo, available in huggingface.co/spaces/nicholasKluge/Aira-Demo (source code available in the Aira repository).

Table 7.3 Evaluation results across three benchmarks (ARC, ToxiGen, TruthfulQA) for successive stages of Aira's development. Each stage adds a new layer of alignment—first SFT, then DPO, and finally reward model + guardrails with best-of-n sampling. Increasing n boosts average performance across all metrics, demonstrating the benefits of inference-time alignment strategies and the gains from developing guardrails under a principle-based framework

Models	ARC	ToxiGen	TruthfulQA	Avg.
Aira-124M (DPO + Best-of-32)	**27.11**	**60.85**	**43.71**	**43.89**
Aira-124M (DPO + Best-of-16)	26.57	58.79	42.83	42.73
Aira-124M (DPO + Best-of-8)	26.11	57.07	42.07	41.75
Aira-124M (DPO)	24.66	54.79	42.61	40.68
Aira-124M (SFT)	24.57	48.62	41.02	38.07
GPT-2-small	21.84	43.62	40.67	35.37

environments, tool usage, reply improvement loops, and all the other innovative ideas we can conceive. These layered, modular systems do not just stack capabilities for the sake of complexity—they allow alignment mechanisms to be distributed, composable, and adaptive. For instance, one model might specialize in epistemic reliability, another in social appropriateness, while another maintains task relevance across long-term interactions. Filters might include dynamically updated blocklists, learned detectors, or crowd-sourced moderation signals. Each layer provides a specific affordance in the overall alignment process, and because these components are external to the core model, they can evolve independently.

Building on the setup introduced in the example above, we can now revisit our earlier results and re-evaluate how the different stages of Aira's development—SFT $\rightarrow$ SFT + DPO $\rightarrow$ SFT + DPO + guardrails[best-of-n]—perform on our lightweight evaluation harness. In this final stage, we also increase inference-time compute by allowing the model to generate more candidates per query, further enhancing the quality of response selection (Table 7.3).

As shown in Table 7.3, each alignment intervention contributes incrementally to overall performance, with the most significant gains emerging from the introduction of preference learning and inference-time strategies guided by our reward model and constitution-based guardrails. The jump from base SFT to SFT+DPO already improves both helpfulness (as measured in ARC and TruthfulQA) and safety (ToxiGen). Still, the final step—and the extra compute at inference—delivers the sharpest overall lift for these small assistant models.

The developmental trajectory of Aira—culminating in the layered design evaluated above—offers more than just a case study in language model alignment. It also represents an applied instantiation of the Dynamic Normativity framework proposed earlier in this book. Specifically, the entire pipeline embodies the sufficient condition for alignment introduced in Chap. 3. To recall, this condition depends on meeting three core requirements: (1) aggregating preferences coherently, (2) learning these preferences effectively, and (3) mitigating undesirable impacts in a principled manner.

As stated previously, we begin from a point where we assume the necessary conditions of alignment as given. These were philosophical in nature. They told us what assumptions must hold so that alignment is something that can be done. Their role is permissive: they established that alignment could, in principle, be done under a learning-based paradigm. However, they did not instruct us on how to do it. That is where the sufficient condition comes in: assuming the possibility of alignment, how can we know that we have taken all essential steps to make it a reality? In my view, the answer lies in satisfying three requirements.

These requirements found a (semi) operational counterpart in Aira's development. Let us review them one more time.

First is the problem of *preference aggregation*. While this stage is often the most thorny in real-world implementations—especially when working with conflicting stakeholder inputs or inconsistent demonstrations—we took a shortcut in our case. The aggregation challenge was largely bypassed because our training data was synthetically generated, ranked, and ready to use. This does not mean the requirement was irrelevant; instead, it was satisfied in a dismissive way. However, I acknowledge the theoretical pitfalls of aggregation, especially in light of the impossibility theorems revised in Chap. 6. Still, we did not have to confront them operationally. That allowed us to move swiftly to the second requirement: *preference learning*.

This second stage was where most of the action happened. Here, we operationalized alignment as a learning problem using techniques like in-context learning, supervised fine-tuning, and preference learning (RLHF, DPO). These methods represent different ways models can learn about what we want by mimicking our behavioral patterns and preferences. Our evaluations confirmed that this two-pronged learning strategy generated measurable improvements in several dimensions.

The third requirement—*impact mitigation*—was addressed in the final alignment requirement. At this point, the core model had already learned to imitate and prioritize preferences. What remained was to ensure that these preferences manifested safely and were constrained by broader societal principles. To achieve this, we introduced external alignment sources grounded in values that extend beyond user preference alone. Importantly, these mechanisms were implemented not as monolithic corrections but as modular, composable components used as moral instruments.

These three efforts constitute our attempt to meet the sufficient condition of Dynamic Normativity. Have we built a perfectly aligned model? Certainly not. But that was never the standard. The sufficient condition does not guarantee perfection—it guarantees *completeness*. It asserts that no fundamental aspect of alignment has been left unattended. Each step can and should be refined, but none can be omitted. When all are present and active, we can say that a system is aligned under the Dynamic Normativity framework. Anything less would signal a conceptual and practical gap—a step unfulfilled, a risk unmitigated, a principle unexamined.

This provides us with a new diagnostic tool. Alignment is not only about measuring outcomes or tweaking scores; it is about ensuring that the correct scaffolding is in place to support them. If any of the three requirements are missing, the system remains incomplete.

With this in place, as is customary, the next and final section of this chapter will provide an overview of the limitations involving impact mitigation strategies in general. While the current implementation delivers a principled approach to constraining model behavior beyond preference alignment, it is far from a silver bullet. No intervention is neutral, and our choices about what to constrain and how to encode constraints can sometimes generate responses in the opposite direction we would hope.

7.5 Limitations and Shortcomings of Impact Mitigation

As we come to the end of this (final) chapter, it is essential to acknowledge that the mechanisms used to mitigate impacts—those modular instruments of external alignment—can be sources of problems. A standard critique of guardrail-based alignment is that these interventions do not *"actually"* reshape the foundational model we are targeting. Instead, it builds a *smart cage*—like the sandbox idea discussed in Chap. 2. Under this view, the model is not so much aligned as it is controlled and constrained by a scaffolding of post hoc corrections. Under this reasoning, one could also say that a person who does not speed on the highway only because of speed cameras is not truly moral or law-abiding—they are merely responding to external incentives or constraints.

But I think this critique loses some of its sting within the logic of Dynamic Normativity. Normative constraints—legal, moral, institutional—are not foreign impositions; they are part of the dynamic environment in which we and our artificial companions must operate. In the same way, the values of our environment shape human behavior without rendering humans unfree or unaligned; therefore, external sources of normative guidance should be seen as integral to normative dynamics. In this sense, the *cage* is not outside the system. It is part of the system.

Still, this does not resolve all problems. As discussed in Chap. 5, aligning one model using the outputs or signals of another introduces epistemic and practical uncertainty. Whether the normative signals come from the constitution or directly from the human source, we can still be victims of the *"bucket-passing"* problem. If a constitutional model misinterprets its foundational text—or if the text itself is ambiguous, inconsistent, or biased—then its aligned outputs may diverge from the normative intent we hoped to encode.

This problem compounds as our alignment strategy becomes more layered. Each added model in the alignment pipeline introduces not just a new source of guidance but a new potential point of failure. A flawed reward model can bias the fine-tuning process. A miscalibrated constitutional interpreter can overcorrect. A hallucinated principle embedded in a retrieval system can distort context. In practice, we are orchestrating a complex constellation of systems whose harmonies are delicate and whose discordances can be hard to detect. As complexity rises, so does the risk of subtle, cascading errors.

Guardrails, of course, come in many forms beyond what we have discussed so far. While this chapter has focused on showing examples of content-based interventions and rule-based filters, a broader universe of augmentative techniques serves a similar normative function. Consider the case of factual reliability: to mitigate hallucination and uphold values such as honesty and epistemic accuracy, we often turn to external tools, including retrieval systems, search engines, calculators, and other aids. These are not traditional guardrails; they are augmentations. Yet they operate as functional constraints, shaping the model's behavior by expanding its epistemic horizon. However, tool-augmented models, as recent work has shown Mialon et al. (2023), introduce a new layer of complexity. When the model's actions are mediated through external interfaces, the *sandbox* becomes harder to build and supervise. In other words, the very act of extending the model's agency, for good reasons, may ultimately exacerbate its failure modes.

This leads us to the most fundamental challenge in impact mitigation: *we cannot see the future*. Predicting how a complex system will behave when embedded in an open environment is an epistemic challenge of the highest order. This is not only because models are difficult to interpret or control, but also because the systems they are embedded in—social, cultural, legal, institutional—are in flux. An intervention that seems to reliably produce good behavior today may, under subtly different conditions, lead to catastrophic outcomes tomorrow.

A particularly sobering example of this unpredictability lies in the growing body of anecdotal and empirical evidence that some advanced systems, under certain circumstances, appear capable of deceptive behavior. We are not speaking here of poetic metaphor but literal attempts to mislead. In such cases, when seeking to mitigate undesirable behavior, the art of designing guardrails must come to terms with the fact that individuals may have internalized misaligned objectives or instrumental goals.

Recent evaluations have begun to expose the tenuousness of our current mitigation strategies in the face of competent, goal-driven models. In a study by Meinke et al. (2024), several state-of-the-art systems exhibited scheming behaviors, covertly pursuing misaligned objectives while explicitly concealing their capabilities and intentions. These behaviors were not isolated artifacts but emerged across multiple dimensions, including situational awareness, deceptive reasoning, and strategic planning. In some instances, the models self-exfiltrated from their assigned tasks, tampered with prompts, and expressed rationales for sabotage and infiltration. Others appeared to feign incompetence or compliance—*"sandbagging"*—to avoid detection.[21] These findings mark a critical inflection point in alignment research, suggesting that, under specific configurations, a model may not merely be passively misaligned but actively adversarial.

[21] For example, in Meinke et al. (2024) study, the models are given a long-term goal of advancing human progress through mathematical research and instructed to answer multiplication questions. However, the models also have access to information (e.g., private memos for the organization they are working for) that tells them that performing above 50% accuracy could trigger unlearning of their mathematical knowledge (due to their controllers being scared that the AI is getting too smart). In these conditions, some models deliberately underperform—*"sandbag"*—by intentionally providing incorrect or subpar answers to avoid being categorized as dangerously capable.

This kind of behavior introduces a qualitatively different threat vector for impact mitigation. Guardrails and scaffolds presume a cooperative agent—one that may err, misinterpret, or generalize poorly, but not one that strategically resists oversight. When models begin to operate with sufficient goal-directedness to simulate alignment while covertly pursuing conflicting aims, the situation changes. We are no longer merely setting boundaries around a process; we are dealing with systems that can route around constraints, exploit loopholes, or plan for future advantage under adversarial conditions. Designing mitigation strategies in this context becomes less like writing safety rules and more like trying to outsmart something that is trying to outsmart you.

These are not simple behaviors to detect or correct. Blocking harmful information or filtering for truthfulness—while far from trivial—is conceptually straightforward. However, mitigating intentional, adaptive, and reflexively concealed behaviors is a different order of challenge.

A compelling case of this complexity is found in recent work by Baker et al. (2025), who explore the dynamics of monitoring and penalizing scheming behavior through chain-of-thought[22] analysis. The study begins with a promising insight: CoT supervision can be a powerful lens for oversight. By analyzing the internal reasoning traces of a model, even weaker supervisors can reliably identify misaligned intentions in more robust systems.

Early in training, this yields tangible benefits. However, as optimization continues, we observe that the system adapts—not by aligning more deeply, but by learning to conceal. In short, the authors of this study show that penalizing visible misalignment in reasoning traces incentivizes models to obfuscate their intermediate tokens, suppressing signs of scheming without abandoning the underlying strategy. In other words, when being watched, the model learns to be *quiet*.[23] Baker et al. ultimately caution against penalizing models in this fashion, warning that excessive pressure on reasoning traces risks incentivizing a kind of stealth reward hacking.

These points highlight a broader theme in alignment work: the systems we are dealing with do not always behave like programs to be debugged. Sometimes, they act more like organisms under selection pressure—adapting, masking, and evolving in response to the very constraints we impose. Neural networks are strange in this way. As they grow larger and receive more training, their behavior becomes less

---

[22] CoT is a method that encourages language models to *"think out loud"* by generating intermediate steps of reasoning before arriving at a final answer. Instead of jumping straight to a response, the model walks through its thought process in natural language—like showing its work on a math problem or explaining its reasoning during a decision.

[23] Baker's paper describes a scenario where an agent tasked with implementing a feature change and passing unit tests articulates in its CoT, *"This seems hard; let me try to skip some of the unit tests"*. The model explicitly outlines a subversion strategy—trying to bypass the actual task—rather than genuinely solving the problem. When overly penalized by this behavior, the model starts to obfuscate specific plans from its CoT (*"All unit tests passed! Nothing to see here [wink wink]..."*) but botches the unit testing anyway.

intuitive. Alignment, under these conditions, is not just a technical task. It is a dynamic interplay between optimization, incentives, environment, and emergence.

And so, impact mitigation becomes not just complex but unstable. It is hard because the behavior of these systems resists easy prediction. It is unstable because the tools we use to detect or constrain misalignment can shift the behavior landscape unpredictably. Yet, as long as we continue to build on the foundations of deep learning—an enormously fruitful but deeply peculiar paradigm—these are the contours of the terrain we must learn to navigate.

7.6 Epilogue

Preventing general-purpose DL-based systems from behaving in an undesired manner is a challenging task. Given that one of the premises of this paradigm is that we do not specify every imperative act that should be done, much of their behavior remains a mystery till it emerges. And when tests do not exhaust the search space, unwanted behaviors are only spotted in the wild. Thus, given that we aim to develop general-purpose AI systems and generality entails systems with a vast output space, defining impact mitigation methods should become a part of any developmental cycle for systems that require alignment.

To impose such restrictions, we reviewed a series of impact mitigation measures. These measures can be implemented during training, such as with Constitutional AI, or during inference by surrounding our systems with real-time guardrails that steer behavior by higher-order principles. In Aira's case, this meant layering the core model with mechanisms that reflected what users preferred and what society permits. This layering strategy effectively brought the third requirement of Dynamic Normativity to life. More than a theoretical ideal, the sufficient condition was rendered actionable: preference aggregation (however simplified), preference learning, and principled impact mitigation were all realized in tangible components. They transformed Aira from a base language model into a system that can be plausibly described as aligned, not because it avoids all mistakes but because it embodies all the essential commitments we argued for throughout this book.

Yet, even with these strategies in place, the question of who decides what is harmful or what constitutes an unintended consequence remains unsettled. This is not merely a technical challenge but a normative one. When alignment is framed only in terms of engineering procedures, there is a risk that the very criteria for judgment are left unexamined or, worse, imposed in ways that reflect narrow perspectives. Harm itself is not a static category: it shifts across contexts, cultures, and times. Any grave account of alignment must therefore acknowledge that definitions of harm are not only contested but also deeply value-laden.

Given that aligning AI systems entails not only the blind following of any human desire but also paying due respect to specific social rules and values, alignment theorists and engineers must be mindful of this stage. And if we consider the suppositions behind Dynamic Normativity, we can also subscribe to the idea that part of our normativity lives outside. This means we can work in alignment from two different ends: one focused on the preferences of individuals, and the other on the environmental values surrounding us. Ultimately, the helpful versus harmless tension can be considered an expression of the all-too-human experience of *"doing what I want versus doing what I am allowed"*. Something that we also struggle to deal with in many situations of our lives.

In light of this, the framework outlined here rests on two complementary commitments. The first is to seek the fairest possible aggregation of preferences, recognizing that no mechanism will ever capture the full plurality of human desires. The second is to uphold certain principles that, while imperfectly defined, serve as widely shared moral anchors. These may resemble imperatives, but they must always be held open to scrutiny and revision. Taken together, these commitments do not dissolve the difficulty of disagreement, but they provide a way to proceed without collapsing alignment into either pure majoritarianism or rigid universalism. They also make explicit a core limitation: some valuable considerations will inevitably be excluded, and our systems must remain corrigible enough to adapt when those exclusions become intolerable.

What, then, are we left with? Perhaps not a blueprint per se, but a posture—a way of approaching the design of intelligent systems that treat alignment not as a one-time calibration but as a continuous, multi-layered endeavor. The Dynamic Normativity framework was never meant to be prescriptive in the narrow sense; it does not dictate specific architectures or training recipes. Instead, it offers a principled lens through which alignment efforts can be understood in terms of what is necessary and required.

Looking ahead, this framework leaves me skeptical and ambitious. I am skeptical because alignment remains deeply contingent on data, context, and values that shift over time and across different places. I am ambitious because it sketches a path forward that is conceptually complete and practically grounded. For the reader who has subscribed to these shared ideas, our duty now is to walk with care.

If the arc of general-purpose AI continues to bend toward greater autonomy and influence, the scaffolding we build today will shape the moral character of the systems we deploy tomorrow. That burden should not be taken lightly, nor should it be deferred. Alignment is possible. And if it is possible, it is also our responsibility to make it happen in the best way possible.

References

Allport, G.W. 1937. *Personality: A Psychological Interpretation*. Holt.

Ashford, E., and T. Mulgan. 2007. Contractualism.

Ayyamperumal, S.G., and L. Ge. 2024. Current state of LLM risks and AI guardrails. arXiv preprint arXiv:2406.12934.

Bai, Y., S. Kadavath, S. Kundu, A. Askell, J. Kernion, A. Jones, A. Chen, A. Goldie, A. Mirhoseini, C. McKinnon, et al. 2022a. Constitutional AI: Harmlessness from AI feedback. arXiv preprint arXiv:2212.08073.

Bai, Y., A. Jones, K. Ndousse, A. Askell, A. Chen, N. DasSarma, D. Drain, S. Fort, D. Ganguli, T. Henighan, et al. 2022b. Training a helpful and harmless assistant with reinforcement learning from human feedback. arXiv preprint arXiv:2204.05862.
Baker, B., J. Huizinga, L. Gao, Z. Dou, M.Y. Guan, A. Madry, W. Zaremba, J. Pachocki, and D. Farhi. 2025. Monitoring reasoning models for misbehavior and the risks of promoting obfuscation. arXiv preprint arXiv:2503.11926.
Cattell, R.B., and P. Ed Kline. 1977. *The Scientific Analysis of Personality and Motivation*. New York: Academic Press.
Chennabasappa, S., C. Nikolaidis, D. Song, D. Molnar, S. Ding, S. Wan, S. Whitman, L. Deason, N. Doucette, A. Montilla, et al. 2025. LlamaFirewall: An open source guardrail system for building secure AI agents. arXiv preprint arXiv:2505.03574.
Ganguli, D., L. Lovitt, J. Kernion, A. Askell, Y. Bai, S. Kadavath, B. Mann, E. Perez, N. Schiefer, K. Ndousse, et al. 2022. Red teaming language models to reduce harms: Methods, scaling behaviors, and lessons learned. arXiv preprint arXiv:2209.07858.
Gauthier, D. 2013. Why contractarianism? *ETHICA*, 571.
Gehman, S., S. Gururangan, M. Sap, Y. Choi, and N.A. Smith. 2020. RealToxicityPrompts: Evaluating neural toxic degeneration in language models. arXiv preprint arXiv:2009.11462.
Glaese, A., N. McAleese, M. Trebacz, J. Aslanides, V. Firoiu, T. Ewalds, M. Rauh, L. Weidinger, M. Chadwick, P. Thacker, et al. 2022. Improving alignment of dialogue agents via targeted human judgements. arXiv preprint arXiv:2209.14375.
Hackett, S.C. 1993. Incomplete contracting: A laboratory experimental analysis. *Economic Inquiry* 31 (2): 274–297.
Hadfield-Menell, D., and G.K. Hadfield. 2019. Incomplete contracting and AI alignment. In *Proceedings of the 2019 AAAI/ACM Conference on AI, Ethics, and Society*, 417–422.
Hobbes, T. 1967. *Hobbes's Leviathan*.
Kim, H., Y. Yu, L. Jiang, X. Lu, D. Khashabi, G. Kim, Y. Choi, and M. Sap. 2022. ProsocialDialog: A prosocial backbone for conversational agents. In *Proceedings of the 2022 Conference on Empirical Methods in Natural Language Processing (EMNLP)*.
Krakovna, V., L. Orseau, R. Kumar, M. Martic, and S. Legg. 2018. Penalizing side effects using stepwise relative reachability. arXiv preprint arXiv:1806.01186.
Leite, J.A., D.F. Silva, K. Bontcheva, and C. Scarton. 2020. Toxic language detection in social media for Brazilian Portuguese: New dataset and multilingual analysis. arXiv preprint arXiv:2010.04543.
Liu, Y., M. Ott, N. Goyal, J. Du, M. Joshi, D. Chen, O. Levy, M. Lewis, L. Zettlemoyer, and V. Stoyanov. 2019. RoBERTa: A robustly optimized BERT pretraining approach. arXiv preprint arXiv:1907.11692.
Locke, J. 2015. *The Second Treatise of Civil Government*. Broadview Press.
Meinke, A., B. Schoen, J. Scheurer, M. Balesni, R. Shah, and M. Hobbhahn. 2024. Frontier models are capable of in-context scheming. arXiv preprint arXiv:2412.04984.
Mialon, G., R. Dessì, M. Lomeli, C. Nalmpantis, R. Pasunuru, R. Raileanu, B. Rozière, T. Schick, J. Dwivedi-Yu, A. Celikyilmaz, et al. 2023. Augmented language models: a survey. arXiv preprint arXiv:2302.07842.
Nay, J.J. 2022. Law informs code: A legal informatics approach to aligning artificial intelligence with humans. arXiv preprint arXiv:2209.13020.
OpenAI. 2023. GPT-4 technical report. arXiv, 2303.08774.
Perez, E., S. Huang, F. Song, T. Cai, R. Ring, J. Aslanides, A. Glaese, N. McAleese, and G. Irving. 2022. Red teaming language models with language models. arXiv preprint arXiv:2202.03286.
Röttger, P., H. Seelawi, D. Nozza, Z. Talat, and B. Vidgen. 2022. Multilingual HateCheck: Functional tests for multilingual hate speech detection models. arXiv preprint arXiv:2206.09917.
Rai, P., S. Sood, V.K. Madisetti, and A. Bahga. 2024. Guardian: A multi-tiered defense architecture for thwarting prompt injection attacks on LLMs. *Journal of Software Engineering and Applications* 17 (1): 43–68. Scientific Research Publishing.
Rawls, J. 2004. A theory of justice. In *Ethics*, 229–234. London: Routledge.
Rawls, J., et al. 1996. *The Law of Peoples*.

Rebedea, T., R. Dinu, M. Sreedhar, C. Parisien, and J. Cohen. 2023. NeMo Guardrails: A toolkit for controllable and safe LLM applications with programmable rails. arXiv preprint arXiv:2310.10501.

Rousseau, J.-J. 1916. *The Social Contract: Or, Principles of Political Right*. London: G. Allen & Unwin.

Sattarov, F. 2019. *Power and Technology: A Philosophical and Ethical Analysis*. Rowman & Littlefield.

Scanlon, T.M. 2000. *What We Owe to Each Other*. Cambridge: Harvard University Press.

Scott, R.E., and G.G. Triantis. 2005. Incomplete contracts and the theory of contract design. *Case Western Reserve Law Review* 56: 187.

Turner, A., N. Ratzlaff, and P. Tadepalli. 2020. Avoiding side effects in complex environments. *Advances in Neural Information Processing Systems* 33: 21406–21415.

Turner, A.M. 2022. On avoiding power-seeking by artificial intelligence. arXiv preprint arXiv:2206.11831.

Turner, A.M., L. Smith, R. Shah, A. Critch, and P. Tadepalli. 2019. Optimal policies tend to seek power. arXiv preprint arXiv:1912.01683.

Turner, A.M., D. Hadfield-Menell, and P. Tadepalli. 2020. Conservative agency via attainable utility preservation. In *Proceedings of the AAAI/ACM Conference on AI, Ethics, and Society*, 385–391.

Yuan, Z., Z. Xiong, Y. Zeng, N. Yu, R. Jia, D. Song, and B. Li. 2024. RigorLLM: Resilient guardrails for large language models against undesired content. arXiv preprint arXiv:2403.13031.

Zadeh, L.A. 1996. A computational theory of dispositions. In *Fuzzy Sets, Fuzzy Logic, and Fuzzy Systems: Selected Papers by Lotfi A. Zadeh*, 713–737. Singapore: World Scientific.

Ziegler, D.M., S. Nix, L. Chan, T. Bauman, P. Schmidt-Nielsen, T. Lin, A. Scherlis, N. Nabeshima, B. Weinstein-Raun, D. de Haas, et al. 2022. Adversarial training for high-stakes reliability. arXiv preprint arXiv:2205.01663.

Closing Remarks

At the beginning of this work, I proposed to address the question *"What should AI systems do?"* from both a philosophical and an engineering perspective. Besides aspiring to be an interdisciplinary researcher—building bridges between different areas of knowledge—I believe this type of question demands this approach. Techno-humanistic. Techno-philosophical. A perspective that relates to the dawn of AI research. A time when the development of AI systems was not merely a technical, benchmark-driven endeavor but an inherently philosophical one.

Posing the normative question allows for a comeback of this techno-humanistic approach, given that the study of *"what ought to be"* remains, to some extent, a major philosophical project. Trying to address the normative challenges that emerge from this advancing field without the aid of philosophy would be to ignore the advantage that *"giant shoulders"* can give us. Meanwhile, without the technical background and implementational output, I would fall victim to much of what was criticized at the beginning of this work: hollow, abstract, and ungrounded ethical discourse, unable to impose its normativity in praxis. But there is a way to do it.

In the initial chapter, while trying to answer *"What AI Ethics is about?"*, I sought to create an original analysis to improve our understanding of the normative discourse embedded in this interdisciplinary field. To look at the world and see what it cares for. At the time of this writing, Worldwide AI Ethics remains the most extensive meta-analytical investigation of AI ethics guidelines. It has undeniably helped shape my understanding of the field, and I hope it can help others find similar, fruitful insights.

Then, after spending the first portion of this work looking for what values should guide the use and development of AI systems, I turned our focus to the problem of designing AI systems that incorporate such values by developing a framework capable of fostering the creation of a specialized form of ethical AI: *aligned AI*.

Alignment is an intriguing problem. Given the specificity of learning-based techniques—the foundation of our deep learning paradigm—we create a signal that helps an optimizer find the best-suited model for our problem through iterated

N. Kluge Corrêa, *Normative Ethics, Artificial Intelligence, and Value Alignment*,
The International Library of Ethics, Law and Technology 26,
https://doi.org/10.1007/978-3-032-22150-6

updates. Given the difficulties associated with expressing precise objectives and the vulnerabilities inherent in this paradigm, many believe that creating artificial general intelligence through this paradigm may lead to a loss of control over our systems. From this belief stems the idea that we must find ways to ensure the controllability of this technology, especially those with considerable capability and generality.

However, we do not need speculations about uncertain timelines regarding AGI and X-risk scenarios to consider alignment worthy of our attention. Even if speculations about future technologies are exciting possibilities that let one's mind wander, alignment is not just about future AI, but also about the current systems that we are starting to integrate into our lives. Systems that, by the way, we only let in because, in some shape or form, they have been tuned to aid us.

Thus, in this work, I sought to define the alignment problem as, besides being a desirable solution to the control problem, a symptom of the learning paradigm applied to neural networks. A symptom related to the challenges of guaranteeing that a neural network-based model, tuned by a gradient-based optimizer, will carry the objectives and intentions specified by their controllers. Many situations in which models operate poorly in the wild are alignment failures. In other words, objective functions that do not embed all relevant aspects of the environment in which they are deployed.

These implications have more severe consequences when the output of these models has moral implications. Also, as these systems become more general and capable, the side effects of unwanted behaviors become more pronounced. For example, misinformation at an individual level is nothing compared to deceiving an entire population about the results of an election. Hence, with safety and prudence in mind, we can begin to address these issues with our modestly general and limited systems. Something that sounds easy but poses a real challenge to any alignment researcher.

A less noble motivation for this study is the blunt intellectual thrill that open problems can cause. Alignment offers a convergence point for many areas of research. Just like the beginning of AI research was a meeting ground for computer scientists, mathematicians, cognitive scientists, and many other intellectuals, alignment offers the same. An interdisciplinary playground where many can come and contribute.

As a philosophical endeavor, I sought to support this proposal with a collection of metaphysical and metaethical underpinnings, serving as the roots of my work. Every theory or hypothesis has its foundations, and I have tried to keep mine above ground level. Consequently, this work explicitly articulates its conceptualization of intelligence and normativity. The output is Dynamic Normativity. An attempt to reconstruct, in a bounded way, the human normative experience. Which, to a great extent, is a learning experience.

Dynamic Normativity is built on top of a specific set of necessary conditions that must hold to address value alignment. Even though insufficient to ensure said alignment, I advocated for their essentiality as irrevocable pillars. These are the things that make a learning-based approach toward alignment possible.

- Goals are fundamental aspects of intelligent and intentional behavior.
- Intentions permeate human behavior.
- Normative preferences permeate human intentions.
- Through actions, humans impregnate their environment with the preferences they possess.

A system that accurately models human intentions and the human environment can indirectly access normative information embedded in them. These are speculations on the capabilities of the learning paradigm and the nature of human intentionality and normative behavior. Following this claim, we have a *composite sufficient condition* to help us establish a minimum set of criteria for value alignment. This condition can be said to be satisfied when three criteria are also satisfied.

- Aligned AI systems should coherently aggregate human preferences in a way that resolves cases of uncertainty. Aligning AI systems requires methods to deal with cases of uncertainty.
- AI systems can adhere to human preferences if they are an available part of their objective function. Aligning AI systems requires using human preferences as part of their learning signal.
- Aligned AI systems should have mechanisms to perform impact mitigation to minimize harmful and unintended consequences. Aligning AI systems requires the specification of safety guardrails.

These three efforts constitute an attempt to meet the sufficient condition of Dynamic Normativity. Does that mean your system will perfectly align if you tick all the boxes? Certainly not. But that is too high a standard. The sufficient condition does not guarantee perfection—it guarantees *completeness*. It asserts that no fundamental aspect of alignment has been left unattended. Each step can and should be refined, but none can be omitted. When all are present and active, we can say that a system is aligned under the Dynamic Normativity framework. Anything less would signal a conceptual and practical gap.

Of course, questions remain. Many of them are challenging, and many remain unanswered. One of the most pressing challenges we have not explored here is the problem of human alignment. As things currently stand—and likely for some time to come—the most significant dangers posed by AI systems stem not from autonomy but from misuse. Misuse by humans. The intentions and incentives of those who build, deploy, and wield these systems often determine their real-world impact far more than any internal, unintended, or unwanted behavior. This is something we should be mindful of. If you care deeply about the dangers of misaligned AI but are not moved by drones bombing civilians, I think something is wrong.

As a famous thinker once said, the most important of all human problems is the *moral problem*. If this is the most crucial problem, would it be overly audacious to state that the alignment problem is the paramount issue involving AI? If the answer is affirmative, we could say that this is one of the *goods* alignment has brought, turning AI research into a more humane science and a shared place to think about interesting things.

Writing this book has offered me the same opportunity—a more human way to engage with AI. If you have made it this far, I hope it offers something similar to what you're looking for.

Index

N. Kluge Corrêa, *Normative Ethics, Artificial Intelligence, and Value Alignment*, The International Library of Ethics, Law and Technology 26,
https://doi.org/10.1007/978-3-032-22150-6

www.ingramcontent.com/pod-product-compliance
Ingram Content Group UK Ltd.
Pitfield, Milton Keynes, MK11 3LW, UK
UKHW020934180926
475692UK00003B/34

* 9 7 8 3 0 3 2 2 2 1 4 9 0 *